PRACTICING CARE IN RURAL CONGREGATIONS AND COMMUNITIES

PRACTICING CARE IN RURAL CONGREGATIONS AND COMMUNITIES

JEANNE HOEFT, L. SHANNON JUNG, AND JORETTA MARSHALL

Fortress Press
Minneapolis

PRACTICING CARE IN RURAL CONGREGATIONS AND COMMUNITIES

Cover image: Country Church © iStockphoto.com / Spencer Smith

Cover design: Alisha Lofgren

Library of Congress Cataloging-in-Publication Data is available

Print ISBN: 978-0-8006-9954-3

eBook ISBN: 978-1-4514-3851-2

The paper used in this publication meets the minimum requirements of American National Standard for Information Sciences — Permanence of Paper for Printed Library Materials, ANSI Z329.48-1984.

Manufactured in the U.S.A.

This book was produced using PressBooks.com, and PDF rendering was done by PrinceXML.

CONTENTS

128027

Acknowledgements

This book began as a project funded by a Louisville Institute Pastoral Leadership Grant that enabled us to benefit from the wisdom of many who have advocated for rural ministries for many years. Because of the grant we were able to meet with the Rural Church Network, the Rural Chaplains, and the Town and Country Consultation at Saint Paul School of Theology. These groups more than welcomed us; they encouraged us and willingly spent time contributing their experience and ideas to our project. Out of these meetings we identified and invited the seven rural pastors who met with us over a two-year period. We owe the core ideas in this book to this incomparable group of dedicated pastors: Brian Arnold, Johnny Arrington, Leslie King, Mark Narum, Ernesto Trevino, Steven Peake, and Cathy Whitlatch.

We also thank the many of our students at Saint Paul and Brite who come from rural churches or who are ministering with them at the moment, who have read parts of this text and been eager to offer feedback and encouragement, and who are committed to ministry in all of its complexities. In addition we have presented portions to the Town and Country Consultation, the Society for Pastoral Theology, and others, and we thank them for their commitments and interest in this work.

Several assistants along the way have helped with coordination of the project and preparation of the manuscript; we are grateful for Crystal Hughes, Stacie Stickney-Williams, Andrea Beyers Mary-Margaret Saxon, David Lott, and Nancy Barry, who gave very helpful feedback under a time crunch. Jim Niemann made a timely suggestion linking our project with Louisville and Fortress Press. At Fortress, Michael West, Will Bergkamp, Lisa Gruenisen, Marissa Wold, and Mark Christianson have been dedicated to getting the manuscript published. To our partners we are always indebted for their unending patience, support, challenge, and tolerance.

Rural congregations continue to offer hope and sustenance for individuals, families, and communities. This book is dedicated to them for their persistent and faithful presence, even in the midst of change. As we go to press with this book we want to express appreciation to them for their ministry.

Introduction

The vast majority of people in the United States of America live in metropolitan areas, but the vast majority of the land in the United States is rural. Over half of all churches in the USA are in small towns and rural areas across the country, not in cities. Almost every pastor in the country will at some time in her career serve a small town or rural church. Rural places such as the Great Plains, Rocky Mountains, Appalachia, the Mississippi Delta, and the Midwest not only make up a significant portion of the U.S., but the people who live and worship there hold a particular wisdom and face unique challenges. Rural places are different and rural places matter. What happens in rural churches significantly affects the whole body of Christ, but they are largely devalued and marginalized by the metropolitan centers of power. Rural churches have been largely overlooked in pastoral care literature. This book is an attempt to bring attention to the significance of that gap and to begin to fill it. Rural churches and communities are different from the norm, uniquely particular in context, and hold a particular wisdom from which the rest of the church might benefit.

The rural context raises questions for the practice of pastoral care in those communities. What should a pastor recommend to a person in the congregation whose grief has moved into depression when the nearest mental health center or psychotherapist is three hours away? Where do a pastor and pastor's family find support and friendships when so many of the townspeople are members of his own congregation? How does a minister help a victim of domestic violence when the sheriff in this rural county is the abuser's brother, the nearest women's shelter is 100 miles away, and the abuser sings in the choir of your church? How does a pastor challenge the environmental and safety practices of the local mining company when it provides the only jobs in town and at the same time provide care for the mine's employees who are ill or injured because of those practices?

In one small community, a developer purchased some of the farmland and announced his intention to market the land to commuters who work in the city not far away. On the one hand, the subdivision will bring much-needed revenue and life to the community; on the other hand, the town may lose its sense of community as city folks move to the country. There is fierce debate over how to respond to this potential change, and emotions are running high, ranging from excitement to fear to grief to anger. On Sunday mornings, these same people sit together in worship trying to figure out what it means to love and care for their neighbor in the midst of such conflict, in a town where everyone knows the name of every other resident. The pastor finds herself caught trying to provide care to folks who are in opposition to one another about the vision they hope for in their church and community. As a community leader, she is also being pushed to take a stand on the issue. How will this church and this community practice care for one another, the care to which Christians are called?

The situations suggested above point toward the difference it makes to be located in a small town or rural community. Pastoral care in these places is challenged by the physical isolation, lack of anonymity in the community, changing economic realities of family farming, and the expectation that small-town pastors should be active community leaders in addition to pastoral caregivers. The situations are not unique in one sense; churches in cities and metropolitan areas will struggle over similar pastoral care issues of finding resources, setting good boundaries, and caring for the sick while challenging political powers. However, while such situations arise in other areas, small towns and rural communities experience these situations in ways that are quite different from metropolitan areas, and the significance of those differences means that pastoral care requires different theoretical grounding and different practical responses in each context.

The differences also lead to unique and useful insights for pastoral care in all places. This wisdom arises in part from the need to be creative in response to physical distance from neighbor and services. It also arises from the challenge of a unique kind of closeness, social visibility, and lack of anonymity. In small towns the glaringly apparent connection between individual well-being and social systems, perhaps especially economic, means that country churches have developed certain wisdom about what it means to care for both at the same time. Rural and small-town communities have a heightened sense of community and interrelatedness; this is both a great challenge and a great gift. In living with the tension between challenge and gift, these communities have a depth of understanding about this thing called "community" that so many of us seek. They have a wisdom about the land and the relationship between care and leadership in a community of faith, and a wisdom about diversity.

ENRICHING MINISTRIES OF CARE

Loving care for the neighbor, stranger, and for self is an essential aspect of Christian ministry. Our purpose in writing this book is to enrich that ministry of care, not only for rural churches but for the ministry of the whole church. This text is designed to assist pastoral caregivers, whether ordained or lay, to draw from the particular wisdom about pastoral care that arises from rural and small-town contexts. We use the term *pastoral* not to suggest that someone needs to be ordained to provide care within the context of the church. Instead, the word *pastoral* points to the fact that we are talking about care offered within the context of a community of faith that has theological resources from which to draw. Pastoral care is unique among other forms of care by its location within this community of faith and its interest in faithfully seeking to live by the values, beliefs, and practices of that community.

This book will also promote a congregation's ability to provide pastoral care in any context. Care is context specific, yet practices and principles are often appropriate across contexts. We believe that the rural context offers wisdom born out of an appreciation for its people's unique gifts, as well as out of the limitations and peculiarities of what it means to be rural in the United States. We believe that this text will assist all pastoral caregivers in every context as we learn from the local knowledge and wisdom of communities in rural settings. This text is not written only for those who find themselves in a rural parish; it is written for seminary students, pastors, laypersons, and pastoral care specialists who want to reflect on pastoral care and who are open to the particular wisdom and challenges to be gained from rural communities. Throughout this book, we encourage you to look at your context for ministry and to think about what studying pastoral care in rural communities might suggest about how to contextualize your own care, whether rural or not. To be confronted with different context or culture often makes one more aware of one's own.

We also intend to challenge the perception of rural United States as an idealized place on the one hand and a minimized place on the other. We value what rural communities and rural churches have to offer. We also believe that the particularities of rurality have been largely unattended to by constituencies that depend on what happens in rural areas even as they render it invisible or meaningless. Many pastors, and denominations, see rural ministry as a training ground for new pastors or a transition ground for retiring pastors. More than 80 percent of the people in the United States live in cities, and most of the people in churches are city people. However, more than 80 percent of the land in the U.S. is rural land, and most of the churches in the U.S. are in small towns and rural areas. There are more congregations, and therefore more pastors, in rural regions and small towns than in metropolitan areas. An overwhelming majority of pastors will, at some point in their ministry career, serve small-town and rural churches, though they will likely have been raised and trained in cities and suburbs. What happens in rural churches and communities is crucial to the well-being of us all.

WHAT IS RURAL?

You will immediately notice that in this text we use multiple terms—*rural, small town, town and country*—to describe the context to which we refer. It is surprisingly complex to define what constitutes a "rural" community today. In part, that is because there are many types of rural communities, ranging from upscale, technology-oriented, smaller population centers to what might strike you as a ghost town because first the railroad and then the highway went in a different direction. In response to the term *rural*, many people in the U.S. conjure up an image of "pastoral" landscape, small farms set in a landscape of rolling hills and a few cows. They may include a small town where you can leave your doors unlocked and share communitywide picnics. When pressed a bit, they may also begin to include the not-so-pastoral image of mining towns, but rarely will they also move to include the ski resorts of the Rockies or the Native American reservations of the West and Southwest. Part of this book's intent is to unsettle preconceived notions, positive and negative, about what "rural" is. We want to expand the imagery and break down stereotypes because we believe that the category "rural" is a worthwhile category for study. We believe there is enough commonality that runs through "rural" that it is useful and meaningful to think about "rural" congregations and communities, even though there is a lot of variety and difference across kinds of rural places.

Though we understand the limits of any typology in that boundary-setting is always a construction of, more than a reflection of, a reality, this section sets out some of the means by which we define "rural," the types of places that can be included in that definition, and the lenses through which this book approaches the discussion of "rural" congregations and communities.

Most researchers and statisticians use one of the U.S. federal government definitions of rural, but even those are not consistent. John Cromartie and Shawn Bucholtz point out that government definitions can be based on "administrative, land-use or economic concepts."[1] In all cases, setting the line between urban and rural or metropolitan and nonmetropolitan begins with defining urban and then designating what is left as rural. Rural is that which is not the norm; the place "other" than where most people live and work. Administrative boundaries, like county lines, are drawn by municipal and jurisdictional bodies. Land-use bases involve looking at population size and density; for instance, for many years rural meant any town or county with fewer than 2500 people in residence. When ties to a common economic base are taken into account, a small town, by population, that borders a city or is close enough that most workers commute to the city is not defined as rural but rather as part of a metropolitan area. Recently the government added a new category to the mix, "micropolitan," which uses the economic base along with a population restriction that refers to what the popular culture might refer to as a "small city," one with a population between 10,000 and 50,000.

Why does this kind of boundary-setting matter? First, thinking about the decision-making principles and practices for setting definitions of what constitutes rural and nonrural reveals some of the paths for thinking about difference and similarity between places and thus why place matters. Second, these boundaries become crucial when decisions are made about resource dispersion and what kind of public assistance is made available. A small town tied economically to a larger city center may have access to health care in a way that another town of the same population size may not. This book uses a variety of terms to refer to places under the umbrella of "rural," but in general we are not referring to micro- or metropolitan areas. Using a diversity of terms helps to reveal the need for a wide contextual lens where one place is not the same as the other.

It has been said, "If you've seen one rural place, you've seen *one* rural place." Setting lines of demarcation based on administrative, land-use, or economic ties is but one aspect of defining what we mean by rural. Several rural researchers propose typologies for thinking about different kinds of rural communities. These breakdowns into types of rural are generally trying to engage the different economic and cultural realities in each type. Some rural communities are built on the natural beauty of the area, like the ski resorts of Colorado. Some are large open-space farm communities, like the small towns of Iowa. Some towns and the people who live there are barely surviving, like those in the Appalachian hill country. Some are in transition as metro- and micropolitan expansion reaches further into the countryside. Below we will highlight some of these different kinds of rural communities that will be given more contextual depth in the following chapters of the book.

On the surface, some rural communities actually do look like the farm landscapes many imagine. These are land areas of large open spaces, sparsely populated with economies based on agriculture, timber, or mining. One group of rural researchers, the Carsey Institute, identifies these communities, primarily located in the Great Plains in the center of the country, as "declining, resource dependent."[2] What once might have been solid middle-class self-employed educated families working the land are now declining populations as food-production methods change and the land becomes depleted. While some of these small towns are now attracting immigrant workers with low-skill, low-paying jobs in places like meatpacking plants, in general the residents are an aging homogeneous group. Church, school, social involvement, and trusted neighbors characterize the foundation of, but declining reality, in these regions.

Yet many seek out this picture of rural life, minus the land-based work, as some of these formerly "resource dependent" areas are attracting "exurbans," those who work in metro- or micropolitan areas but want to live "in the country." Often those in this group are hoping to find the safe, clean, honest, and trustworthy community that has fed our imagination of rural for at least a century. Yet they also bring "urban values" and may find it difficult to find a place in a community that generations of a family have called home before them. Others seek out the scenic or outdoor recreation areas of the country, such as the Rocky Mountains. These "amenity"[3] based areas attract economically well-off active retirees and young adults and are growing at a fast pace. They may rely on a strong tourism-based economy that also creates a population of low-wage service workers. The exurban and the amenity-based communities are growing with people who in some way want to "get back to nature," whether it is through the scenic beauty of lakes and mountains, outdoor activities, or acreage and a vegetable garden.

Surprising to many who think of poverty as an urban core problem, most of the places entrenched in poverty are in nonmetropolitan areas. The vast majority of these "persistently" poor areas are in the South; many are the remains of former Appalachian mining towns and are substantially African American. The people live without adequate infrastructure, minimal education, and little job opportunity. Families may live in these areas for generations, while in the changing farm communities of the Midwest young adults leave out of a sense of possibility, opportunity, and resources. The young of chronically poor rural communities often see little hope for a different future, whether in the hills of their grandparents or in the cities they see on television.

THINKING ABOUT PLACES

Different rural communities described above only begin to give a sense of the rich diversity in rural USA. Each kind of place carries its own sets of gifts and challenges. As we think about these places, identifying kinds of questions or possible frameworks for analysis can guide us toward interpretive breadth and depth. What kinds of things are we looking for and seeking to understand as we approach a contextualized pastoral care in rural areas?

Rural sociologists Cornelia Flora and Jan Flora propose that we ask about the community's resources or capital.[4] Community capital is any resource that a community has that can be invested to create new resources. They identify natural, cultural, human, social, political, financial, and built capitals. In farming communities the land, natural capital, is transformed into financial capital. In scenic places, the consumption of natural capital is transformed into social capital and built capital as the wealthy seek out these places for recreation and construction. Some towns may not have much financial capital to invest, but they may have the human capital of labor force ready and willing to work in even low-paying jobs. They may have the cultural capital of a commitment to hard work and civic involvement. Church leaders can use this approach to name the strengths of a community and congregation that can then be strategically capitalized upon.

Paul Cloke, a British rural studies scholar, describes three frameworks for conceptualizing "rural."[5] The first is a "functional" framework that basically follows the pattern of the typologies presented above, depending on land use, population, and spatial boundaries.[6] The second and third frames move beyond function to examine the workings of power and the construction of meaning. Understanding a place includes more than researching demographic and economic trends, it also involves investigating the culture of a place. What norms, practices, institutions, and worldviews are operating in the community? Where are they held in common and where are the conflicts between them? Cloke's "political-economic" frame invites us to think about rural communities as they are produced by political-economic forces beyond the spatial boundaries of rural/city. We might ask how what happens in rural areas is shaped by or in response to what happens in the rest of the country and to what extent political power from outside coerces certain effects in rural communities. Changing demands for food and fuel, driven by the demands of free-market economies that depend on the large population areas of the country, may radically change the realities of food production in rural areas. Conflicts over water rights and environmental preservation reflect political power struggles as well. Who owns and/or controls the water? Of course, the reverse move must also be considered: How does, or can, rural wield power in the larger political economy?

Rurality is also a socially constructed reality that requires another means of interrogation, Cloke's third frame. What do we *mean* by rural? What happens when instead of "rural," we say "country" or "town" or "village" or "wilderness"? Looking at rural from this lens asks us to consider the meanings that become attached to rural life. These meanings come from both within and outside the rural community. When someone is described as being "from the country," it means more than physical location; it implies certain qualities and characteristics, positive and negative depending on who is saying it to whom. Romanticized farm life and the unsophisticated "redneck" are two images constructed out of certain mores and practices that may function to keep power in place through processes like commodification and discrimination. These meanings are not "chosen" per se but are continually present in self and other representation, experience, practices, and decisions. These meanings come to frame how we see self and other, rural and urban, and they may be interrogated by the church and others based on how they function for good or ill.

With globalization and increased access to technology, other questions that must be asked are: How is "rural" being urbanized and how is "urban" being ruralized? In this book we argue that there are in fact differences between rural and urban, metro and nonmetro, and yet we are not claiming that rural and urban should be constructed as dichotomies or that they do not intertwine. Postulating "rural" requires us to think about particular dynamics of "hybridity" and multiplicity that are at play in any community. Cloke's definition is particularly helpful here: "Rurality can thus be envisaged as a complex interweaving of power relations, social conventions, discursive practices, and institutional forces which are constantly combining and recombining."[7] The church's practices of care will be enriched by considering all these aspects as they impact persons' lives in any context.

CONTEXTUAL PASTORAL CARE

To care for one another is to actively respond to and engage each other in life's journey in ways that lead to increased love and justice in the world. The theological assumptions that ground our understanding of care begin with the claim that God creates us in a deeply interconnected web of relationship in which we are all dependent on one another. In and through this relational existence we come to know God as love and come to understand the Christian call to "love one another." This love is not a warm feeling, although it may include that; it is active and participatory engagement in the whole of life of other persons and of the global society. It involves individual healing and social justice making. Human flourishing demands attention to persons and societies; what happens in the world shapes and impacts persons and what happens to individuals affects the whole world. As Larry Graham reminds us, care for persons also requires care for the world.[8] In a deeply relational existence, a person cannot be known outside his or her context, and healing requires change in the person *and* in the world.

This text develops in consonance with an emerging contextual approach to pastoral care. In 1993, John Patton described a "communal contextual" approach to care that stressed the importance of the whole community as both practitioners and beneficiaries of care.[9] This paradigm for care emphasizes human interrelatedness and mutual responsibility that is at the core of what it means to be human created in the image of God. As will become evident throughout this book, rural communities, in part because of their lack of multiple specialists, are especially attuned to relying on one another for care, rather than the pastor or other professional alone. It is also apparent that in small towns, churches and pastors are expected to care for the whole community, not just their own church community. In some ways, town and country churches can exemplify the best of "communal" pastoral care, an example that could be instructive for others who would like to engage in this form of pastoral care.

When the community is the heart and soul of care, contextual analysis becomes an increasingly significant resource for care. In more recent years, many have stressed the importance of taking context into account in order to provide meaningful pastoral care. What do we mean by "context"? Context is all that which surrounds any particular person, church, or community, or any particular problem. Much like "culture," context is the whole web of meanings, practices, and institutions that shape, hold, and perhaps create, the particular. Pastoral theologian Emmanuel Lartey defines culture as a "distinctive way of life" for a particular group of persons, including "the ideas, values and meanings embodied in situations and practices, in forms of social relationship, in systems of belief, in mores and customs, in the way objects are used and physical life is organized."[10] This should not be taken to mean that culture or context is monolithic or static. Culture is always changing, adapting, and responding to new events and new people. To speak of rural context or culture is not to suggest that there is *one* rural; there are many rurals. There is also something we can identify as a rural way of life, something that seems to be recognizable across rural differences. In the following chapters, we will encounter many diverse forms of rural life. Our intent is not to suggest that there is one kind of rural: we stated above our intention to break through some of those reductionist stereotypes. When we talk about rural in a general way, we encourage you to also think about the particularities or differences between one rural and another. Lartey reminds us that "every human person is in certain respects 1) like all others, 2) like some others, and 3) like no other."[11]

In many respects, the path toward this text reflects our commitments to contextual pastoral theology and care, and it echoes the kinds of commitments we heard from the many town and country ministers we consulted along the way. We are three different people, with differing perspectives, but a shared commitment to the well-being and wisdom of marginalized peoples. We believe that care for the sick, the stranger, and the outcast requires standing in solidarity with and advocacy for those who are often excluded from leadership and decision-making power. While we do not claim to have perfectly succeeded in overcoming the hegemonic powers at work in our own contexts and in our lives, we have tried to offer at least a partial step in that direction.

OUR OWN CONTEXTS

In light of our commitments to contextuality, it seems appropriate to say something of the contexts in which we, the three authors, are located, especially as that relates to our rurality, or lack thereof. We are a trio of academicians teaching in denominational seminaries who are also ordained clergy in our respective denominations, and have served as pastors of local churches.

JEANNE HOEFT

I am a city person. I was born in a large Midwestern city and have lived in several of the largest metropolitan areas in the United States; however, my parents were raised in small Minnesota towns. I grew up with two contrasting images of rural that in some way reflect the stereotypes of the idealized and denigrated rural that permeate U.S. culture. On the one hand, my mother often declared that as a young person she couldn't wait to get out of the country and into the city. Rural could be a place of too much closeness and lack of sophistication. On the other hand, I experienced my mother's family farm as one of the more stable, peaceful places in my life. I also enjoyed the visits to my paternal grandparents' small town where everyone knew who I was and I was allowed to walk freely to the park or market.

In my first appointment as a pastor in a small southern city, the members of the church were from families of the rural areas around the city. I quickly realized that they spoke a language and lived out of a worldview that I did not really understand. I began making excursions with them to areas where they were experts in the land and community, to a culture that was new to me and that I needed to understand. I asked a lot of questions and they were good teachers, confounding many of my preconceptions about "country" people. When I began teaching pastoral care, I found that most of the students were from the rural Midwest surrounding the seminary and would be going back to serve churches in those areas. It was not long before I discovered my own lack of knowledge of their context, the lack of attention to rural in pastoral care literature, and the difference that a rural context makes. My students began to teach me about what it means to do pastoral care in town and country churches where, among other things, they have limited access to services, multivalent relationships with church members, and shape the calendar as much by the seasons of planting and harvesting as by the liturgical season. I needed a textbook that spoke to their context more directly.

****

SHANNON JUNG

I must have been predestined to be a Professor of Town and Country Ministries at Saint Paul. Growing up in rural Louisiana at an open country church, I went to the Belgian Congo when my parents were called to be dental and educational missionaries. My graduate work was done in Christian ethics in Nashville at Vanderbilt, and I was ordained in 1973. I have preached in countless smaller-membership congregations and always felt a particular rapport with them.

Twice, when I was teaching college, I served as a part-time (but full!) pastor of rural congregations, one in Bluff City, Tennessee, and also at Dilworth, Minnesota. For some years, I directed a Center for Theology and Land at the University of Dubuque and Wartburg seminaries, and that gave me an opportunity to do some writing on rural ministry and the best practices that exemplary rural congregations taught me.

Since 2005, I have taught courses in leadership and mission in town and country ministry at Saint Paul School of Theology, Kansas City. My doctoral work in ethics has proven to be very compatible with teaching how to read rural contexts, and also to considering the impact of economic and environmental issues in rural communities. I am very interested in and writing on the ethics and spirituality of eating, a rural specialty. My social location raises questions about how leadership and pastoral care are related for rural congregations and communities.

****

JORETTA MARSHALL

I am a professor at Brite Divinity School in Fort Worth, Texas. I grew up in a small Midwestern farming community of 150 people, and my father's family farm was located on the edge of the neighboring town, about two miles away. We spent lots of time at the farm, and my uncles continued to live on that farm and the surrounding farms until the family farm was sold during the crisis of the 1980s. The church we attended was the only one in that community and was the social context for much of my early formation. My understanding of ministry and church has been shaped and nurtured in that context. Although I have lived in urban and suburban settings for the last twenty-five years, I carry a deep and abiding love for rural life. At the same time, I am aware of the changing dynamics of rural communities and am fearful of the idealization or romanticization of what rural has come to represent. Adequately training pastoral caregivers who value rural communities and those connected to them is central to my call as a pastor and teacher.

This book is written by three different people trying to speak with integrity from our individual perspectives and yet also speaking to commonly held values and theological understandings, especially the value of the rural church. You will no doubt notice differences in our voices, in our emphases, and in our slightly differing theological perspectives. We hope this will enrich the text and offer you a layered, thought-provoking reading of the challenges and gifts of rural communities.

****

LISTENING TO RURAL CHURCHES

We could call the process by which our work on this text proceeded as relational or "conversational." As we began this project, our commitments to contextual pastoral theology and to the participation of multiple voices from the local context itself directed us first to places where people of the church were already focusing on the gifts and challenges of rural ministry. As teachers and scholars we bring that perspective to the question of meaningful pastoral care in rural communities, and while that is important, it is not the only view or necessarily the most important. Trying to be mindful of the way power works through defining what counts as important, we talked to those currently involved with rural ministry. In each case, we sought to listen to the ideas and concerns of the town and country church and to ask about what they saw as the wisdom and needs of rural communities as they sought to practice a ministry of care. After a brief description of our consultants in the project, we will outline the themes that arose from those conversations and that provide the framework for this text.

In the first phase, we consulted with larger groups who were already gathering around the issue of rural ministry. At the Town and Country Consultation at Saint Paul School of Theology, we talked with pastors and denominational leaders who meet annually to learn from one another. We met with the Rural Chaplains Association, a primarily United Methodist group of rural pastors, lay and ordained, as they explored the intersection of rural ministry in the U.S. and Mexico. The Rural Church Network is an ecumenical group of denominational agency leaders and scholars who invited us into conversation about the future needs of rural churches and communities. In the second phase of the journey toward this text, we identified seven town and country pastors, lay and ordained, who are committed to the value of rural ministry, represent some of the diversity of small-town and rural USA, and are known as effective creative leaders. These individuals served as our conversation partners, keeping us grounded in the contextual concrete. The group, men and women, from Lutheran (ELCA), United Methodist, Presbyterian, and Baptist churches included:

- An ordained pastor of a Cooperative Parish of four churches in a small Ohio town where the largest growing industry is tourism but in which poverty is nevertheless persistent.
- A local lay pastor, serving a church in a northern Colorado town (pop. 2500) whose residents depend on ranching, agriculture, and tourism for their livelihood. This small town sits in the Rocky Mountain high plains about fifty miles away from even a Walmart.
- An ordained pastor of a church in a small Kansas town of about 6000, about an hour away from a metropolitan area. Earlier in its history the town was a railroad town, but now many residents work at the state hospital located there or commute to the nearby city.
- An ordained pastor of a four-point parish in North Dakota, not far from the Canadian border. One of the churches is located in the county seat (pop. 1300), while the others are in rural communities of less than a hundred residents where many farm people and others are benefiting from a recent oil boom.
- A part-time bi-vocational pastor of a mining town (pop. 1200) in the Appalachian Mountains. The church was once known as a black church but now has a racially mixed congregation that emphasizes hospitality to the "lost and outcast" in a town that continues to struggle economically.
- A pastor who was raised and trained for ministry in Mexico and currently is a missionary for the National Hispanic Plan of the United Methodist church. He also serves as pastor of a primarily Spanish-speaking church in the Southwest near the Mexican border.
- A former missionary to Argentina and pastor of a two-point charge in Iowa and chaplain to the meat plant in the area. The plant has brought an increasing Hispanic/Latino population into this land of family farms.

EMERGENT THEMES

In our conversations with the persons and groups named above, we identified four themes that inform and expand the thesis of this text that rural churches are unique and hold a wisdom from which the rest of the church might benefit. The themes below give more substance to the specific ways in which rural is different, unique, challenged, and gifted. In many cases, the themes represent areas that are both gift and challenge. It is in the tension between gift and challenge that the rural wisdom about care, discovered or reinforced as we prepared for this text, seems to emerge. While the particulars of these themes become manifest in different ways in different communities, we did hear them emerge in some way across difference. We will give a brief introduction to these themes here, but they will be developed further in the following chapters.

1. **Care is shaped by place.** As contextuality has increasingly emphasized social location, gender, race, ethnicity, class, sexual orientation, and so on, context is becoming a central category of analysis. What smaller communities tell us is that physical location, or place, also matters to identity, worldview, and way of life. Rural or small town is in large part a matter of geographical location, and the people of these communities have a heightened sense of *where* they live as much as *how* they live. Two of the ways that geography forms rural communities are location in relationship to other towns and cities, and the way in which either location or the land itself determines the usually singular economic basis. Accessibility to services such as health care is directly tied to distance from cities and towns. Land-based economies of mining, farming, timbering, oil production, and tourism in rural communities are more or less the single basis for economic thriving of a community, such that any changes in that base are not easily absorbed. There may still be an appreciation of the land and nature present to a greater degree than in urban or suburban places.

2. **Care engages community.** There is a sense of interdependence in rural communities that pushes care beyond a particular congregational membership to being offered by and for the whole community. There is an embedded understanding that pastoral care belongs to the ministry of the church and not to the appointed or ordained leader of a congregation. The local community embodies care in ways that are unique and particular in meeting the challenges of living. This communal care is fostered in part by geographical location, lack of anonymity, and, for many, a long history with their neighbors. In small towns it is not just the pastor who is responsible for care, but there is a sense of mutual responsibility that assumes the whole church will be involved in caring for any of those in need in the community.

Community is a difficult concept in this context. It is used to describe a group of people who live and worship in close proximity, but it is also used prescriptively to describe an ideal toward which this group of people seeks to be related to each other. Rural and small towns do have a particular wisdom about community in both senses, and about the challenges of living up to the ideal, which leads to the next theme.

3. Pastoral care and public leadership intersect. The interconnection of sociocultural issues and individual or family needs is perhaps more apparent in small towns and rural areas than elsewhere. Pastors and church leaders have a unique role beyond the particular congregation as public theologians and community leaders who engage in a practice of care for the community as a whole. Their voice and presence are noticed in a world where anonymity is almost impossible. Their public theology shows up at school board meetings, in the local diner, or at the funeral home in ways that make their voice more expansive than many pastoral leaders experience in suburban or urban settings. The local pastoral leader often becomes a dominant voice or representative within the community at large. Pastors can have a distinctive role in convening the community for discussion and action. They can interpret what is happening in the wider area and serve as culture producers[12] and spiritual and/or moral directors. The pastoral leader may be the one who names the responsibility of the community to care for the past and the future or the one who presses for dialogue in the midst of diversity. Visibility, multileveled relationships, and lack of proximate colleagues also pose unique challenges and provide wisdom about the place of pastors in the community from which pastors in other settings can benefit.

4. Care responds to the multiple diversities in community. Rural communities have insight into issues of diversity in ways that are unique and distinct. The challenge of insider/outsider is ever apparent in rural communities in that they are much less homogeneous than many in urban or suburban contexts perceive. Difference is experienced through diverse racial and ethnic populations; class diversity that is experienced close to home, in the same pew or just down the street; and theological diversity that can either divide a community or create a rich space for celebrating the multidimensionality of God. In addition there is often a tension between newcomers and old-timers that sometimes creates an insider/outsider community. The presence of the "other" is often felt as a challenge to that ideal of community held by many who live in small towns. With the growth of new populations in rural areas, their own future will depend on finding a way to live in harmony and mutual productivity. Old-timers may need to learn not only to like and appreciate new residents but also to include them and learn from them as fully contributing citizens. How these communities wander the journey of inclusiveness is instructive to the church and to other communities.

FLOW OF THE BOOK

In Part I, Chapters 1 through 4 move through the four themes identified above in more depth, providing a pastoral theological lens for thinking about concrete issues of care. These themes are meant to be understood as unique to rural communities and small towns but also as bits of practical wisdom for the whole church, metropolitan and nonmetropolitan alike. Chapter 1 argues that healing and transformative care is shaped by place. Place—the land and the meanings associated with it—shapes identity, can foster a sense of connection to God, and calls us to consider the basic human need for *home*, for belonging somewhere. Community in rural contexts highlights the strengths and limitations of closeness, and Chapter 2 discusses the need for healing and transformative care to engage the whole community. Local churches, including their formal and informal leadership and the congregation as a whole, are agents of care for the church and the larger community. Pastoral care is more than the ministry of the pastor; it includes the day-to-day practices of ordinary care engaged in by the whole church. Pastors also act as carers for the community, not only the congregation; healing and transformative care includes making theology public, bringing a theological voice to the larger community.

In Chapter 3, we suggest that rural contexts demonstrate that pastoral care and leadership intersect. Healing and transformation require care and leadership, both within the congregation and in the community, and without both we miss the deep intersection of the personal and the political, individual and social, in people's lives. Leadership organizes and mobilizes congregations and communities toward change, but it must include a perspective of love and care for all. Leadership, in the interest of care, will be relational, collaborative, and patient. This is noticeable especially in times of rapid change, such as with the influx of newcomers into small towns. Diversity is always present. If the church is to move toward healing and transformation, care must be taken to move toward inclusion and respect for difference, the focus for Chapter 4. Caring with others asks us to watch our own generalizations and to give significant attention to issues of power and privilege that can fracture communication and community.

Part II is meant to demonstrate how these guiding themes can shape pastoral care in particular situations of poverty, violence, and illness. While the scenarios presented in these chapters are located in small towns, these situations are certainly not unique to rural communities and small towns. It is our hope that pastors and congregations gain insight into the uniqueness of pastoral care in rural places but also find new ways to care in all kinds of places. Care in all kinds of places could benefit from understanding healing and transformation for a just and loving world as being shaped by place, engaging community, intersecting with leadership, and attending to diversity.

Notes

1. John Cromartie and Shawn Bucholtz, "Defining the 'Rural' in Rural America," ed. U.S. Department of Agriculture, Amber Waves (Economic Research Service, 2008).

2. Lawrence C. Hamilton, Leslie R. Hamilton, Cynthia M. Duncan, Chris R. Colocousis, "Place Matters: Challenges and Opportunities in Four Rural Americas," Carsey Institute, University of New Hampshire (2008).

3. This is a term used both by Cornelia Butler Flora and Jan L. Flora, *Rural Communities: Legacy and Change*, 3rd ed. (Boulder, CO: Westview, 2008); also by Hamilton et al., "Place Matters."

4. Cornelia Butler Flora and Jan L. Flora, *Rural Communities: Legacy and Change*, 4th ed. (Boulder, CO: Westview, 2012).

5. Paul Cloke, "Conceptualizing Rurality," in *Handbook of Rural Studies*, ed. Paul Cloke, Terry Marsden, and Patrick Mooney (Thousand Oaks, CA: Sage, 2007), 20–21.

6. Ibid., 20.

7. Ibid., 24.

8. Larry Graham, *Care of Persons, Care of Worlds: A Psychosystems Approach to Pastoral Care and Counseling* (Nashville: Abingdon, 1992).

9. John Patton, *Pastoral Care in Context: An Introduction to Pastoral Care*, 1st ed. (Louisville: Westminster/John Knox, 1993).

10. Emmanuel Lartey, *In Living Color: An Intercultural Approach to Pastoral Care and Counseling* (London: Jessica Kingsley, 2003), 31

11. Ibid., 34.

12. Jackson W. Carroll and Becky R. McMillan, *God's Potters: Pastoral Leadership and the Shaping of Congregations* (Pulpit & Pew) (Grand Rapids, MI: Eerdmans, 2006).

PART I

The Wisdom and Challenge of Rural Care

1

Care Shaped by Place

Janice and Tom Anderson were sitting at the table with other friends at the church picnic. These people had known each other at least a good part of their lives. Most went to high school together; a few went off to college but returned afterward to the town they grew up in. They knew each other's parents, siblings, and cousins, and the related stories. Tonight the group is sharing stories about the fate of their young adult children and the fate of their own lives given the directions their young adult children seemed to be headed.

Tom was particularly agitated with their son's announcement that he was not planning to come back "home" after graduation. Over the school break Michael announced to the family that he did not want to come home and work the family farm. Instead he planned to get a master's degree in business and try to get a job with a big firm somewhere.

Tom was recounting to his friends the hard work that he and his father and his father's father had put into this land and about the sacrifices they had made to make it even possible for Michael to go to college. He recounted the story of his great-grandfather staking out his land and how important the land is to the future of the family. He recalled the struggles his family and many others in town faced during the farm crisis of the 1980s. They were some of the few that were able to hold on. He would hate to see the land fall out of the family's hands. All the while Tom was talking, the others at the table were nodding affirmatively, reliving the familiar story that they and their families shared with Tom and Janice.

*****

Care is happening at this table, and it is happening in the context of Christian friendship. Their care for one another is shaped by the love and concern grown out of a shared history, a building of trust, a sense of interdependence and participation in a community of faith, whether they can articulate it or not. When Steven, the pastor, joins the table he participates in this circle of care, but as the pastor he will also bring something different to the table. He brings the authority and training of the pastoral office, and he may also bring, by virtue of the office combined with trusting relationship and vital faith, the possibility of building on the care that is already taking place in a way that facilitates more healing and transformation. Others may well make the same move, but our focus is on how the pastor can be intentional about seeing this conversation as an opportunity to not only support Tom and Janice and their friends, but to encourage healing change within each of them and their family and to broaden that care to include the community in a way that moves toward God's hope for the world.

Specifically this chapter looks at how healing and transformative care can be shaped by place. The care that is happening in the event described above is being shaped by place—the table, the church, the town, the land—whether anyone realizes it or not. This bit of practical wisdom, that place matters, is something that rural and small-town people remind us to attend to. People in rural communities are often particularly attuned to place, to what it means to be located there and not somewhere else, to what it means to develop in relationship to a place. There is a heightened awareness of where they are and why they are there, whether or not their attachment is positive. In part, this awareness is a result of not being located at the center of power, in metropolitan areas. As discussed in the introduction, this book's major claim is that place matters in the sense that it matters *where* care is being practiced as much as *how* and *with whom*.

This chapter looks at how place, and the meanings people attach to it, shapes persons and what that means for care in the context of Christian faith. A discussion of "place" as something that includes more than the coordinates on a map leads to thinking about the particular kind of place in the scene above, a Midwestern farming community. Next, this chapter looks at how persons construct identities in relation to place and considers what it means to be God's creatures in terms of our need for "home" and personal relationships with the earth. Finally, the chapter suggests possibilities for practicing care shaped by place with specific reference to the situation that opens the chapter. How could the conversation at the picnic table actually be a step toward more healing and justice for the families, congregation, and community represented there?

PLACE IN RURAL CONTEXTS

Healing care in Chimaltenango, Guatemala is different from care in New York City, which is different from care in Stanley, North Dakota. Transformative care, even when practiced by the same people, is done differently when it takes place in a church building, a hospital, or a soup kitchen. It looks different, sounds different, smells different, and feels different. This seems obvious when stated so simply, but in what ways does the "where" of care matter? How can the people of the church influence more intentionally the impact of place on care in ways that foster the richer life that Jesus imagined for us all? Why does moving from one place to another make such a difference, while moving between another two places hardly seems different at all? How does a conversation at a picnic table in a Midwestern farming community present an opportunity for a particular kind of care?

The most common understanding of place is that it is space turned into something with meaning. Persons make a home "my place" by bringing in things that they like or have significance. When open space is given a name it becomes a place. One geographer, Yi-Fu Tuan, says that if space is "that which allows movement, then place is pause."[1] Place marks investment of time, energy, resources, and self. Place makes the abstract of space something that matters, something one will act to protect, and something one will grieve if lost.

There are several layers to place-making. Place involves first, a physical location that can be marked on a map, identified by the latitudinal and longitudinal coordinates. Built places might move from one coordinate to another but they are nevertheless located at each moment in a specific location. Maps represent human interpretations of the land and political boundary-making; thus places always develop in the web of human social relationships. Places develop in power struggles over naming, owning, and control of resources, both human and natural. Within any place there is a constant interaction of multiple interpretations of what it means to be in that place and what kind of place it is. Geographer Tim Cresswell reminds us to think about the way power is functioning in these interpretations.[2] To refer to place is to participate in power that is exercised through cultural norms, discourse, institutions, and practices. An analysis of power dynamics will ask the question: Who benefits from this interpretation of reality? Who benefits from doing things this way? An analysis of the workings of power will also ask: What is being left out? What are alternative ways to think about something? What is not being said? Who is excluded from the picture or story being told as it is? The narratives of place told by people in rural communities are told from particular vantage points that are also shaped by larger cultural discourses.

Stories about place are always told at multiple levels all at once. British geographer Keith Halfacree suggests a threefold approach to thinking about the many aspects of a place.[3] First is the "formal representation" of that place in the dominant discourse. How are rural places and small towns referred to by those in power? How are they portrayed in media, literature, and political rhetoric? Second are the references residents make to themselves and their living places. What does it mean to the residents to live where they do? How do they both internalize and resist the way they are represented by others? People develop relationships with places, emotional attachments that form their sense of who they are. Cultures develop when people share a common area. Places become imbued with meaning and a kind of subjectivity. Think about how often someone says something like "this place speaks to me" or "this place is just begging for . . . ," and many people speak as if places call them to be, as in "this is where I belong." Cresswell describes place as a "field of care."[4] In other words, places define what matters, where energy and resources are invested. To speak about place is to speak about a complex interrelatedness between earth, built structures, and human relationships.

A third aspect of a place is the actual day-to-day lives of the people living there. How is the place structured and what do people actually do there? How are the narratives of meaning intersecting with the workings of economic, political, and individual agency to shape the work and relational life of people living in the community?

A contextual approach to care will see Janice, Tom, and Michael's situation as one manifestation of the currents of power, practice, and meaning in the culture at large, and not simply as one family's interpersonal struggles. For instance, we will find that young adults leaving small towns and rural areas in the Heartland is a major issue for the region, not just this family. The tensions related to the out-migration are strongly influenced by the economic and political changes in agriculture in this country. To care for this family will mean giving attention to both the particular relational dynamics between these family members and to the interconnections between this family and their particular place. One aspect of this place is what it represents in the cultural imagination of the United States and what is at stake for the country in keeping that image alive.

THE FAMILY FARM AS ICON

Care for the Andersons and others in this town requires that the pastoral caregiver understand the layers of meaning that "Midwestern farming community" holds in the broader culture. Acres of rolling fields, the barn and farmhouse, a few cows, the garden, a swing hanging from a tree limb, and a hardworking, honest, and trustworthy farmer (of European descent) with his wife and children. The small-town center with a post office, store, café, school, church, doctor's office where everyone knows each other and cares for one another—this is the image that most of us in the United States conjure up when we hear "Midwestern farming community." It is the picture in children's storybooks and in U.S. American paintings, like *American Gothic*. For those in the U.S. tied to European immigrants of the eighteenth and nineteenth centuries, this picture represents the core of who we are as a nation and what we are about as a people. Though very few people in the United States still earn a livelihood via farming, this image is a powerful symbol of one aspect of our history, and like all symbols it reveals and obscures much. It reveals, for instance, our values of hard work, self-sufficiency, neighborhood ties, and the importance of land. It obscures the politics of land acquisition, the economics of low-wage laborers, the struggle over farming policies, and inequalities based on gender, race, ethnicity, and other social identities. It obscures the reality that while perhaps many long for what the symbol represents, very few want to actually live that life. In many ways, as a culture we are tied more to the symbol than we are committed to the real people of rural agricultural communities and their small towns.

People have a high respect for rural life, but they do not want to live in the remote areas of the Great Plains, or the Heartland, as it is often called. Perhaps what we want is the symbol, the dream, the ideal, but not the reality. In 2001 the Kellogg Foundation interviewed thousands of people in urban, suburban, and rural settings about their perceptions of rural America. People in all three settings held an interesting set of dichotomous perceptions:

> [R]ural life represents traditional American values, but is behind the times; rural life is more relaxed and slower than city life, but harder and more grueling; rural life is friendly, but intolerant of outsiders and difference; and rural life is richer in *community* life, but epitomized by *individuals* struggling independently to make ends meet. Rural America offers a particular quality of life including serenity and aesthetic surroundings, and yet it is plagued by lack of opportunities, including access to cultural activities.[5]

In two items rural persons rated themselves significantly higher than their urban and suburban counterparts rated them. Rural people rated their level of sophistication and their level of tolerance much higher than others rated them. Rural folks also were more likely to see themselves as having stronger families than urban/suburban residents. Each population reported that rural life is needed to "preserve that which defines America," and the "family farm epitomizes the best of American life."[6]

The Kellogg report found that most U.S. Americans think that rural life is agriculturally based, set in beautiful landscapes of pastures, livestock, and crop rows, whose residents value religion, self-reliance, and community. While this is not an accurate picture of rural America as a whole (less than 10 percent of rural residents make their living via farming) it comes closest to reality in the rural Heartland. Certainly a pastor coming into a Midwestern farming community will want to be aware of the assumptions about what that life actually entails and check her own emotional responses to this iconic image. The pastor might also want to keep in mind the depth of this image ingrained into the community itself. To what extent do they see themselves as fitting this image and/or feel pressure to maintain this way of life for the sake of the whole country? How do they live with the dichotomies identified in the Kellogg report? Sometimes the strong need to maintain an image results in minimizing or excluding from consciousness some aspects of actual life on the farm or in the rural Midwest that do not quite fit the image. Most people from urban and suburban areas have little to no knowledge of the business of agriculture or the day-to-day life on the farm. A pastor will want to wonder about how members of the community acknowledge the discrepancies between what they do and what people think they do. Transformation toward healing and justice requires attention to the excluded or denied aspects of the pictures we create and the stories we tell.

In order to offer meaningful pastoral care, a newcomer pastor to a farming community like the one the Andersons live in will want to gain some knowledge about farming and agriculture in general and in particular about farming in that area. A pastor who has experience with farm life will want to make sure not to generalize too much from that experience. Knowledge and experience are good starting places for care but always with the caveat that each person, and each community, while in some ways like all others or some others, is also like no others. So what do we know about Midwestern farming communities and agriculture that can provide a base for thinking about day-to-day life in that setting? What kinds of theological understandings might guide our interpretations of life on the farm?

LIFE ON THE FARM

Considering the realities of the history of agriculture and how central agriculture has been in the rural landscape will help the pastor understand the congregation in agricultural communities. Memories and values will vary by generation. The land has played different roles in their sense of self as persons and as community. This may contrast sharply within generations and with the majority culture. The fact that people in the majority culture have, for the most part, forgotten that persons are "landed," always located on some piece of land that could be identified with lines of latitude and longitude, does not negate the impact of land. Indeed, the history of land and of those who work it may be as influential in human history as any other single dynamic. There was a time when this would not have been disputed because every family had some connection to land—if not the land of their origin as immigrants, then the land of the family's history in the United States, the land of the storefront, the land of national parks and camping, and our individual land of residence. Most people could remember their parents' or grandparents' connections to land. Decades ago people were more aware than now that their future and the land's were interconnected. Rural peoples remember this, even if they do not still live it. Until the third quarter of the twentieth century, the overwhelming majority of the human race lived by growing food and herding animals.[7]

The first European settlers who landed on the eastern shores of North America learned much from the indigenous peoples about living on the land. They formed agriculturally based colonies that for several decades supplied raw materials to Europe for value-added manufacturing. Some products returned as finished goods for the colonies. In the nineteenth century the family-owned and -operated farms, ranches, and local businesses became the norm in most regions of the country as an eager population settled the land between the coasts. The Homestead Act of 1862 enticed many to move westward to stake (and work) a claim. Technology dramatically and constantly changed nearly every aspect of the way food and fiber, products and services, were made and transported. The Industrial Revolution was the first wave marking this continuous change. However, for the most part, the structure of agricultural and small-business sectors of the expanding rural economy remained very much centered in family units and oriented to the land until well into the post–World War II years of the 1950s. Farmers, ranchers, bankers, dentists, doctors, and business people all had a stake in their local community. Shopping locally, volunteering for community services, being part of the local church or civic club, and patriotism were ways in which the rural community became a "great place to raise your kids." Those who were born during the Great Depression and World War II, the elders of the congregation, may remember a golden era of agriculture. While farm prices fluctuated in the 50s and 60s, several factors came together in the 1970s to increase the income and optimism of U.S. farmers.

Farm magazines were predicting that the 1980s would prove to be the "Golden Age of American Agriculture." They could hardly have been more wrong. The prices of products declined, some say engineered by encouragement of overproduction. Declining prices led to a decline in the value of land; the decline in the value of land led to bankers' unwillingness to continue to lend the large sums of money they had encouraged only two or three years before; farmers found that they could not pay those loans; farm foreclosures soared in number; there was an exodus of people from the farms to the city or anywhere else they could find jobs, though many preferred to stay on the land even in much-reduced living conditions. Thus began the farm crisis of the 80s whose impact continues and has caused an upheaval in American life, and perhaps resulted in a different understanding of land ever since. It is estimated that some 600,000 farmers went out of business in the 80s, and that rippled through seed companies, farm machinery firms, grocery stores, gas stations, voluntary associations, and school systems. This left virtually no rural congregation or community unscathed.

The concentration and centralization of land ownership and federal subsidies tied to size of holdings and of production disadvantaged the smaller farmer. So long as land values continued to rise, bankers were willing—indeed eager—to loan money to farmers so that they could expand. Farmers were interested in increasing their income. All was well, as land values continued to rise until 1980–1984, when all of a sudden they plummeted. Farmers could no longer borrow the capital to support the acres and machinery they had projected. Many could not pay their debts, and only those who were well capitalized or had no debt survived. Many farms had to be liquidated or auctioned off.

This also left in question such foundations of the American belief system as the value of sacrifice and hard work, the importance of the "family farm" system of agriculture, the economic security of one's children, the role of government and the economic system, and even the "American Dream" itself. It raised significant questions in smaller membership and rural churches about what this meant theologically; was it God who was punishing them? In response to these crises, the church mobilized hotlines, conducted seminars, hired staff, and cooperated with the Extension Service to mitigate the impact of the economic crunch. Such organizations as the Rural Chaplains or the Rural Church Network or the United Methodist Rural Fellowship and the National Catholic Rural Life Conference were created to address these concerns and to cushion the impact of foreclosures.

The well-being of the community no longer depended on local, owner-operator production. Much land went out of local control and operations became increasingly large-scale businesses run from elsewhere. Being subject to firm policy regulations, banks and federal agencies did not or could not take into account community well-being or leadership. If the farmer who was the Scoutmaster or church council president defaulted on his or her loan, they were often lost to the community. The pool of leadership and of voluntary associations shrank. Town and country stores and businesses became franchises whose owners do not live locally. People's level of trust in and participation in government declined significantly (and this among the people who were and remain the most patriotic in the country). It has seemed to many rural peoples that the policies of their government have worked against their well-being and have assisted large corporations in gaining control over them.

Today farming has an entirely different look than it did years ago. The 2007 U.S. Census of Agriculture, the latest available at this moment, reports an overall increase in the number of farms, but a closer look reveals the results of the changes we have been describing. Between 2002 and 2007 there has been a large increase in the smallest-size farms. These are farms that are called "hobby" or "gentleman's" farms; in short, it is hard to imagine supporting a family or making a living from them. Either the people who are farming them are in retirement and producing only enough for tax purposes or they are working other jobs. They could be called "lifestyle farms"; their residents are not too dissimilar from suburbanites. There is a net loss of medium-sized farms, the owner-operator farms that are actually making a living from farming. The long-term increase in the largest farms (2000 acres or more) continues. The group with over a half-million dollars in annual sales has increased significantly. In summary, 2.5 percent of farms have 59.1 percent of farm sales. For the contemporary generation, farming has become a business much like other corporations.

There are far fewer family farms (owner-operated, with sufficient income to constitute a livelihood) than there were three decades ago. The prices paid to those who farm, or mine, or fish increase far less rapidly than the cost of production. These land- (and sea-) based rural industries are more and more entrusted to hired labor who are paid by the hour or by the bushel. This is very different from the way the older generation understands agriculture and the land. They have come under the economic and policy control of centers of power that do business in Minneapolis, Chicago, New York, and Los Angeles.

It is still true that farmers or hired workers are on the front lines of taking care of the land, and that the way farming is practiced increases or decreases topsoil loss, pesticide and fertilizer usage, freshwater conservation, wildlife management, and the sustainability of the land. When farmers owned the land themselves, their future was tied to keeping the land healthy and sustainable. That nexus disappears when someone else owns the land or controls one's agriculture practices. The consequence of uncoupling the nexus between ownership and labor is that the regeneration and long-term health of the land is not protected. The methods that farmers use to produce food have a major impact on our health and the health of the earth community. In many ways, they are our eco-representatives; their practices have a disproportionate impact on the air we breathe, the nutrition we consume, and the water we drink. Economics and power (ownership) enter into the care we take of the land, and of the way we identify with it.[8]

There are any number of other land issues that rural peoples are particularly aware of. These play into pastoral care issues and the quality of community and congregational life. One is simply: Who owns, and who works, the land? Do they care about the quality of food grown there, of the life lived there? Who controls the use of land? Another is the quality of the natural world in the neighborhood: the quality of water, the arability of the soil, the extent of erosion and runoff. Another is the movement of peoples into and out of the land: migrant workers, resident immigrants, youth, and so on. What is the quality of life around that place? How does the local government view the land; is natural capital an issue for them? What is the sense of public land? Is land accessible to poor people?

Certainly those who live in the midst of the land have a stake in its well-being. But then so do all those who depend on land for healthy food, for clean air, for good water; so do those who care about the distribution of a sufficient quality of life for all on the land; so do all those who care about their health and the long-term sustainability of a sufficiency for all and a shared happiness. How then is the church, which has been at the center of community, to respond to changing realities while recognizing the mix of various meanings of place? What does it mean to practice care in this complex reality? What are the most viable and transformational ways to do ministry in this context?

The Andersons and other families in their community live in the midst of these and other tensions and changes in agriculture, sometimes experienced as a choice between survival and corporate takeover. The fact that the Andersons were of the few that actually were able to maintain their farm through the farm crisis of the 1980s may mean that this farm represents even more to them.

STAYING OR LEAVING?

The place in which Janice, Tom, Michael live poses particular developmental crises for the people who live there, especially the youth. Even though the Midwestern farming community holds such a prominent status in the U.S. American mythology, as a result of the changes described above, most of those actual communities are slowly dying. Some have suggested that by the end of the twenty-first century most of these small towns will have disappeared. The farming communities of the Great Plains/Midwest generally fall into the category of "declining resource dependent" described in the Introduction. While rural areas adjacent to metro areas are growing via urban sprawl and scenic areas are growing due to the in-migration of the wealthy and retirees, rural agricultural areas in the Plains and the Mississippi Delta are losing population. Deaths and migration to small cities or metro areas are not being offset by births and newcomers. "Will I stay or will I leave?" may be one of the central developmental questions for young adults raised in the Heartland's small towns. In the Kellogg report cited above, almost 50 percent of current rural residents said that they had thought about leaving the area.

The reasons for the dearth of young adults seem to center around two issues—jobs and lifestyle. For the educated middle class there is little opportunity for economic success or meaningful high-skill or professional employment in small towns. Changes in agriculture may have made the family farm a less appealing occupation. The low-wage unskilled work has virtually no opportunity to earn a higher wage if she or he stays in the small agricultural town. In order to thrive, a community needs a diverse labor market and range of jobs. In addition to jobs and economic security, persons want a certain quality of life in the place they live. They want not only access to but a range of options for good schools, good health care, libraries, and recreation. These are shrinking rather than expanding in most rural areas in the middle of the country.

Two sociologists, Patrick Carr and Maria Kefalas, concerned about the declining populations in the Heartland, studied young adults' decision making about whether to stay or leave.[9] They identified four groups: stayers who seemed to be "destined" to stay, marry, work in low-wage or low-skilled jobs, and raise children in the community close to extended family and childhood friends; seekers who cannot wait to get out and experience the world; returners who go away and come back either because they fail to make it "out there" or because they want to go "home" to the small-town ambience, perhaps to raise a family; and achievers who, Carr and Kefalas argue, are raised to leave. Achievers are the bright successful children, like Michael, who from the beginning are on the college prep plan. In fact, even as towns mourn the decline of their towns, they are often proudest of those who grow up and leave to take high-paying positions or do something "significant" with their lives in a city.

Most people, because they live in metropolitan areas, are only vaguely aware of the demise of this iconic American community. When told of the problem, many respond with certainty that something should be done to save these towns but have only a vague idea of why they feel this way or how the task might be accomplished. Even the residents themselves cannot clearly articulate why and how their town, their community, should be saved. Anyone entering the scene portrayed at the outset of this chapter without awareness of the background and centrality of this issue for a whole population in this country would miss a key aspect of the tension in the Anderson family. Michael is actually following a very common path for young adults in towns like his. His decision, while in some respects is his own, also reflects the economic, political, and cultural power struggles within a region and between that region and the globalized world. In the U.S., many families will encounter tensions as young adults go about establishing their own identity, but families in the rural farmland of the Great Plains experience that tension in a particular way that can remind us that identity is constructed in relationship to place and to the land, as well as to people.

PLACE AND IDENTITY

Identity is the answer to the question of "who": Who am I? Who are you? Who is he or she? The question, "Who are you?" is basic to human interaction and connection, and therefore to any act of care. One of the core commitments of meaningful pastoral care is the desire on the part of the caregiver to understand the other while simultaneously acknowledging the impossibility of the task. Caring requires the kind of listening and attending that begins with the simple desire to enter into relationship that honors a primary need of all human beings—to know and be known by other human beings. Before the desire to change must come the desire to connect, and that connection requires efforts at understanding the world from the other's perspective. To care for Tom, Janice, and Michael will involve first trying to understand the meaning that Michael's announcement holds for each of them, which requires also gaining some understanding of how each identifies self and the other two. Episodes of struggle or disorientation, like the one this family is experiencing, even if they are only momentary, are often struggles to incorporate new experience into identity, and are often the times that evoke a pastoral care response.

Identities are not wholly given to us, nor are they wholly of our own choosing. No one carries with them throughout life one stable, unified, or essential identity. Identity is established in an ongoing dynamic interface of the social and the individual, of the personal and the political. With the passing of time and the accumulation of experience, identities are always a work-in-progress, an ongoing negotiation between what I make of myself and what others make of me. We carry multiple identities that shift and change depending on context. There are some aspects of identity established and nurtured early in childhood that remain resistant or slow to change, giving the appearance of stability and providing enough continuity with the past that we are recognizable to our self and others.

Identities are constructed in relation to place, including the homes, towns, cities, and communities we live in and the land on which those places are located. Social psychologist Stephanie Taylor studied the intersection of identity and place narratives in conversations with women, asking them to talk about the places they have lived. She found that though in postmodern society mobility seems to reign, there is still strong evidence that identity is constructed in relation to place and constrained by normative narratives about who people are and how we should behave. We tell the story of who we are in narrative fashion, in terms of "sequence and consequence"[10] (what happened when and why it happened), but the narratives are not wholly our own invention, they follow familiar patterns and incorporate cultural norms, whether in congruence with or resistance to. Taylor suggests, for instance, that the "born and bred" narrative is alive and well in postmodern identity constructions. According to the norm of "born and bred," a person is "from" somewhere, a place where there is long, generational connection, a place called "home," a place with which a person experiences a common identity. Most postmodern place narratives do not identify such a place as a specific and stable location, but in Taylor's conversations almost everyone referred to the ideal that one would have such a place in their lives. Rural communities with land-based economies may have a strong born-and-bred normative narrative since, while people can move and some work can be done anywhere, farming, mining, and logging, for example, are tied to land—which does not move except inch by inch over centuries. However, a postmodern normative narrative is emerging, one that Taylor calls the "opportunity and choice" narrative, which suggests that each person is free to choose who and where they want to be. Yet Taylor also found that the women she talked with sought to "choose" a kind of "idealized individuated home"[11] that referred back to the ideal of a place that is one's home, a place that "is" me.

Michael's identity is being formed by the mix of story lines—the stay or leave question for small-town young adults, the generational "born and bred" on the family farm, and the postmodern wealth of opportunity and individual choice. Care for Michael by pastor, family, and friends will involve listening carefully for these multiple story lines and for the unique way that Michael is negotiating them in his own development, and to remember that this is one moment in time in a long-term work in progress.

Each of us comes to understand ourselves as persons formed by, at least in part, the places in which we reside. Meaning-making happens in circular fashion; we give meaning to the place but the place also gives meaning and identity to us. As Tom recites the stories of the farmland on which his family has lived and worked for generations, it is clear that his sense of who he is is tied to that place. Part of who he is has grown out of that land. Janice and Michael have also been molded by life in that place, but their story will not be the same as Tom's. Part of what a caring pastor will want to do is listen for the story of how each of them, and the larger community, understands his or her self in relation to the place in which they have grown.

People tend to define themselves and others partially in relation to the places they live, and the way we identify the place we live is always tied to the way we identify ourselves. The prevailing meanings assigned by the larger culture to a place always influence the personal identity narratives. This happens both when the prevailing meaning is positive, as in the iconic American farm, and when it is negative, as in the image of degradation and destruction linked to historic mining towns. In his study of the people who continue to live in former mining towns, David Robertson found an interesting twist to their self-portrayal in relationship to the place they live. The larger narrative of failure was interpreted at the local level as tenacity for survival and a community built on the commonality of hardship and struggle. This was the way the people described themselves, the town, and even the land. Robertson found that for these people the mine and mining were central figures in their identities, even after the mines have closed. Many described mining as "in their blood" and themselves as "tough" and "rugged" as the rock they mined. The land itself, because of their closeness to it, seems to have given both the town and its people their identity.

We have not found a similar close study of the intersection of identity and place in farming communities of the Heartland, but some have suggested that there is an "agrarian" sense of self and the world that arises out of living in this place. People from small towns and rural areas seem to describe themselves more in terms of place than suburban or urban folks.[12] Those who describe themselves as "country" reflect an "agrarian ideology," according to David Hummon, which means they value the "simple life" of self-sufficiency and closeness to nature. They see themselves as easygoing, tolerant, quiet, and resilient, not unlike the plains and rolling hills that characterize the land upon which they live and work. Marty Strange, arguing for the preservation of family farms, suggests that there are a set of "agrarian values" that define the heart of family farmers: self-reliance, frugality, ingenuity, stewardship, humility, and commitment to family, neighbor, and community.[13] He also points out that the "bigger is better" norm that is creeping into farming conflicts with these values. If that is so, then we might wonder how people like Tom and Janice are incorporating this tension into their sense of who they are in the midst of these multiple, and sometime competing, possibilities for their identity projects.

As farmer parents and as children of farmer parents, Janice and Tom come from a legacy that ties security and success for current and succeeding generations to land. Hope for a better future is in the land, the farm.[14] As they age, Tom and Janice's attachment to the farm may become more apparent, especially if they face having to leave the farm because they are no longer able to keep it up and there is no family successor to take over. For some older adults, especially those who have lived in one place for most or all of their lives, their sense of self is so deeply tied to the place that one without the other is unimaginable.[15] We might expect grief over losses realized and anticipated, as well as a sense of uncertainty about who they will be in the future.[16]

However, Janice and Tom will not have the same experience of the farm and farming life. Janice and Tom will ascribe different meanings to both the past and the future possibilities. Farm women, like Janice, often have quite different experiences of farm life from their husbands and tend to feel more ambivalence about encouraging their children to remain on the farm. During the crisis of the 1980s, many wives of farmers became the primary breadwinners in the family by taking nonfarming jobs while their husbands worked to keep the farm afloat. Women often question the sacrifices of time and health involved in farming. They recognize, often more quickly than men, the toll that farm life can take on loved ones and family. As in other social arenas, women's work on family farms can easily go unrecognized and undervalued.

As the pastor enters the conversation about the future of the farms, the farm families, and the farm community, she or he will want to listen for the way each person frames the narrative of the past, the present, and the future in terms of their life in this place, remembering that stories about the place are also narratives about themselves. Care will involve helping persons see how their narratives share common threads and discussions about the values those threads represent. Empowerment to affect the future positively, in line with articulated values and a sense of who one is, will involve new insights into the master narratives of the culture. While some of the cultural norms that frame identity and place will be deep and resistant to change, we are not completely determined by them; there is always a range of possibilities for identity construction. Reconciling relationships often involves acknowledging the way in which we are made by the people with whom we share our lives. In this case, for example, Michael and his father, Tom, may want to talk about what "home" means to them, or what they have learned from each other and the land about being "hard-working" and "self-sacrificing." An astute pastor will be able to foster these conversations in ways that invite listening with a desire to understand the other, rather than change the other. The listening itself will be a step toward meaningful change. Additionally, a pastoral caregiver will assist Janice, Tom, Michael, and the whole community in remembering that this is not only about relationship to self, others, and land but about the relationship to God as well. There is always a spiritual aspect to identity, and the church is the context in which we should be able to explore who we are in relation to God. Pastoral care will involve placing the narratives of the culture and these individuals in conversation with the narratives of the Christian tradition.

PLACE IN A THEOLOGICAL FRAME

What theological and spiritual questions are raised by the situation described in this chapter so far? What resources exist in the Christian faith to address these questions? Place is a central category in Christian faith, though not always articulated as such. A quick recollection of biblical story brings to mind the centrality of "the promised land" in the Hebrew Bible or the "journey to Jerusalem" in the New Testament. Divine/human encounter takes place in a place, and the place matters. God is not limited to one place or another, but God is always experienced in a place. This place might be a church or a forest, but the place matters and it is not simply incidental to the experience. The place itself influences the character of the encounter. In some circumstances the place becomes a symbol of God's presence and activity in the world such that the place serves as a reminder and mediator of God's grace. People return time and time again to some places, like churches or mountaintops, because they expect an encounter with God in that particular place. This is not to say that some places are sacred in and of themselves but that places become sacred in the dynamic relationship of God, creature (including human), and place.[17] If we are seeking to make God's love and justice more apparent in the world, we must attend to the places we and others inhabit, doing what we can to make them more likely to facilitate spiritual and material experiences of God's grace.

This chapter has suggested that people from small towns and rural areas have something to teach us about place in relation to Christian care, in terms of both its gifts and its challenges. Within the larger questions of a theology of place, two particular areas emerge out of our discussion here: the relational interconnections between God, land, and humanity and the human need for "home." The Andersons and their friends, and the people of other land-based communities, such as mining and logging, know something about the land that most others do not. Their knowledge is crucial for our theological understanding and spiritual/material well-being. Like no others, farmers have intimate knowledge of the processes and elements of the earth. They know too of the struggle to live dependent on the land and the economic and political forces of capitalism. Sharon Butala, a writer from rural Canada, suggests that it is life lived close to nature and the land that marks rural life, and the yearning that farmers have to "save the farm" is in fact a yearning born out of deep knowledge that "in lives lived out on the land and in nature, we preserve the essence of what it is to be human."[18] We agree with her that we cannot afford to lose the practical wisdom that has been passed down through generations of farmers, and add that this wisdom of the earth is also a practical wisdom of God. Butala puts it this way: "In a larger sense the physical closeness to Nature is a closeness of the unseen forces that rule the universe; in the landscape there is always the unrealized awareness of the edge of existence, of the mystery of being."[19]

Christians proclaim God as creator and source of all life. God brought and continues to bring the earth and its creatures into being. As contemporary theologians and scientists have made clear, we live in a deeply interrelated dynamic organic web. God's spirit moves through this web, creating us in, for, and of relationship with the earth and all its creatures. We are deeply dependent on one another. First, we live because the earth lives. As many have said, the earth is our "home." We are created in partnership with the earth. We are nurtured and sustained by the earth, and the earth needs our care in order to be a creative and nurturing home for us and otherkind. Many theologians have turned their attention to land and ecotheology. One of those, Sallie McFague, points out that our sin in relation to the earth is that we "refuse to accept our place" in the larger scheme of things.[20] We refuse to see our own dependence and the limitation of our power to control. The land and the earth's processes continually make those two things abundantly clear.

If we want to make a difference in the quality of Earth Community, the most helpful thing we could do, according to Michael Pollan and others,[21] would also increase our sensitivity to land. One suggestion is that we all grow a bit of the food we eat. This is a fairly simple thing to do, but in fact it would persuade us of our ultimate dependency on the natural world of which we are a part. One March day a group of us planted spinach, radishes, shallots, and bibb lettuce. The day was blustery with a threat of snow, and the rest of the next three weeks didn't look much nicer. We worried. Would the plants emerge? What would encourage them to break the soil? Not much. During that three weeks, we became very persuaded of the limits of our efforts and the miracle of the soil and seeds. When the plants emerged, it was a miracle. We were reminded of what farmers know: we are all dependent on soil and God.

There are any number of other land issues that rural peoples are particularly aware of. One is simply: Who owns, and who works, the land? Do they care about the quality of food grown there, of life lived there? Who controls the use of land? Another is the quality of the natural world in the neighborhood: the quality of water, the arability of the soil, the extent of erosion and runoff. Another is the movement of peoples into and out of the land: migrant workers, resident immigrants, youth, and so on. What is the quality of life around that place? How does the local government view the land? Is natural capital an issue for them? What is the sense of public land? Is land accessible to poor people?

Certainly those who live in the midst of the land have a stake in its well-being. But then, so do all those who depend on land for healthy food, for clean air, for good water. So do those who care about the distribution of a sufficient quality of life for all on the land. So do all those who care about health and the land's long-term sustainability. Agrarian communities remind the church to think theologically about the earth, and it is important for the church to work with agrarian peoples to articulate a theological understanding of the land. Church leaders, then, must work with congregations to put our theological commitments into action.[22]

Another aspect of the interrelationship between God, earth, and humankind is the healing power of nature. It is not only our physical health that is at stake here, but our spiritual and emotional health as well. Many suggest that we have an intrinsic need for closeness to nature. Overdeveloped urbanization may have left this need largely unfulfilled for many in this country. Health geographers and environmental psychologists have consistently found that just being outside can improve mood, reduce stress, raise self-esteem, and increase creativity.[23] Many spiritual traditions, especially those of indigenous peoples, stress the importance of nature and nature's ability to connect us to God. Well-known pastoral counselor and teacher Howard Clinebell developed a model of pastoral counseling based in ecotherapy and ecoeducation and an "earth-grounded" understanding of the human person. In this model, individual well-being is enhanced in three ways: "by becoming more fully, intentionally and regularly nurtured by nature, by becoming more aware of the larger meanings of their place in nature and the universe (ecological spirituality), and by becoming more involved in nurturing nature by active earth-caring"[24]

It might seem odd that we suggest that rural farmers may be people to turn to for wisdom about ecospirituality and the healing power of God through nature. Farmers themselves might think that this is not something they know anything about, or care to know about. We often see farmers, or miners, or loggers as those who most exploit the earth. Yet family farmers are a source of wisdom because of the struggle they have with the land, between the need to make a living and feed the people, and a deep respect for the land itself. Few ecotheologians draw on the experience of farmers to develop a theology of land. Those who present a reading of nature as all quiet, peace, and harmony do not remember the havoc and destruction of blizzard or tornado. Nature is much more complex, as spirituality should be, than the lake and forest in the landscape painting suggests. Indigenous spiritual traditions seem to grasp this ambiguity in the ways of the earth, and the ways of God, more readily than we. God, through the processes, brings both the snowstorm and the miracle of the first bloom of spring. Rural pastors need to be able to help those who work close to the land develop a theological language for the work they do and to see their closeness to the land as an opportunity for spiritual growth.

A caring minister might want to engage in conversation with Tom, Janice, and others in the community about how they experience God in relation to the land. Do they think of themselves as keepers of the earth's resources? How does their farming nourish their relationship with God? How have changes in farming over the years fostered or diminished their connection to the earth, to God? In what ways is farming God's work? Can the work that Michael is planning to do also be seen as God's work? In what way can being raised close to the land support Michael in his new direction? Many times even religious communities do not engage in this kind of theological language for their own circumstances, but doing so can enrich the sense of God's presence and activity in their lives.

The second area for theological reflection that springs from our discussion of place is the human need for a place called "home." Struggles over population changes, losses in rural farming communities, and gains in scenic recreation communities raise questions for the church about the meaning of "home" and the need of people for a place to belong. Many geographers, philosophers, and theologians suggest that people need to have a sense of rootedness, but rootedness is disrupted by the mobility of the postmodern world. The meaning of home and attachment to place might have changed given new virtual realities, but we are nevertheless embodied, emplaced human beings who are always located somewhere. We seek locations that make us feel that we are connected; that we belong; that we matter. When we have a sense of being at home, in the right place at the right time, we have a glimpse of *shalom*, where God's peace, justice, and love reign. Unfortunately the places where people live are not always homes, as in when they are places of abuse or inadequate protection from disease; but Christians are called to created a world where house and home are one.

In a moving account of return to her roots in the Kentucky hills, bell hooks describes the necessity and ambiguity of that place called "home." When she left the rural South, she found material well-being but always felt out-of-place, like a black country girl in the city. In many ways the home of her childhood was a place of oppression and violence, but at the same time the hills of Kentucky and the agrarian life were a place of safety and nurture. hooks suggests that "without the space to grow food, to commune with nature, or to mediate the starkness of poverty with the splendor of nature, black people experienced profound depression."[25] Home in nature was a site of resistance. She claims that "black folks" need to be called back to their agrarian past, in order to remember and experience their home in the realm of God.

Christian tradition points to home as a place on earth and in heaven, in the now and in the yet-unrealized future. It is something we hope for and in hoping make real. To be home is to be at one with God, resting in the awareness of God's ever-present love. hooks describes this longing for home.

> All my life I have searched for a place of belonging, a place that would become home. Growing up in a small Kentucky town, I knew in early childhood what home was, what it felt like. Home was the safe place, the place where one could count on not being hurt. It was the place where wounds were attended to. Home was the place where the me of me mattered. Home was the place I longed for it was not where I lived . . .
>
> "Nature was the intimate companion of girlhood. When life inside the concrete house was painful, unbearable, there was always the outside. There was always a place for me in nature.[26]

The church must ask: How do we foster homes for all people? How do we foster a sense of belonging not just for some, but for all? We must attend to those who feel out of place in the places where we feel most at home. Perhaps it is our dependence on and connection to the earth that can be a beginning for developing this kind of belonging. In and through the land we can learn of our deep interconnection to God and all creation and find that we do indeed "belong," in the sense that we have a unique and valuable place in the universe. In and through the land, we can learn what it means to be both dependent and yet individual, to be both secure and yet conscious of the possibility that storm and chaos may erupt at any time. To have a home, or to feel at home, does not require a particular place or particular family constellation; it does require a sense of safety, respect, physical and spiritual well-being, and being known by others. The longing for home that many feel is in some sense a longing for God.

This longing for home, for God, is present in all of us, even those of us who have a sense of being at home in the world. The realm of God is never fully realized and persons are never fully all that they can be—thus the longing that keeps us seeking and growing. If Tom and Janice have experienced their town as home, and if in general it feels that they do belong where they are, they might also be encouraged to remember the moments when it has not felt so welcoming or when they have felt out-of-place in their own hometown. These kinds of memories can help them see alternatives that Michael may be pursuing. Perhaps even Michael still calls this town "home," and knowing that he has such a place gives him the confidence to move into unknown places.

There are two other ways that thinking of making a place home as a spiritual practice and the longing for home as a longing also for God can impact a community like this Midwest farming community. Tom and Janice and others in the congregation might want to begin attending to those young adults who do stay. How is the community providing a good home for them? Additionally, they might want to think about those who live in the community but feel out of place, as if they do not belong—those for whom the community is a place to live, but not a home. How might Tom and Janice and others in the church turn their attention to changing that reality? Some people may have lived their whole lives in that town and still not feel that they belong there. One way to respond to the crisis of changing economic realities and population decline might be to seek the kin-dom[27] of God by letting the earth wisdom of the community be the base for a new kind of home-making.

PRACTICING CARE

Care in the situation described at the beginning of this chapter will include care for each individual in the Anderson family, for the family as a whole, and for the whole community. Because of the importance of place, the realities of farming and declining population, the personal, political, and spiritual significance of the land, we can see that care in this situation requires movements of care toward personal well-being for the people involved and movements of social transformation toward the well-being of this whole community. As the pastor sits down at the picnic table to join in the discussion, the first awareness must be *where* this conversation is happening; in other words, let the spirit of God through the land be acknowledged. The fact that the concern raised by the families gathered here is directly related to the place in which the conversation is occurring suggests that the location, the surroundings themselves, have a role in the story and in the care. At some point in the conversation Steven, the pastor, may want to turn the attention of the group to the actual ground beneath their feet, the landscape, and the built spaces around them. These places carry symbolic meaning and connections to the wisdom and healing power of God; but Steven will need to help the group open up the narratives attached to these places, asking about what is not said, what is excluded, making sure that the story is not one-sided, for example, reciting only the idealized or romanticized story without the struggle and ambiguity. Could the changes in their families and town be seen as a continuation rather than a rejection of a tradition?

Also crucial to care in this situation is to place the personal story of Michael, for instance, in the context of the larger economic situation that allows everyone to see the way external powers are shaping, constraining, and opening up choices for these young adults. In an over-individualized culture such as the United States, there is a tendency to see family or personal struggles as residing primarily in the character of the persons involved, which then focuses the response on the change needed within those persons. As this chapter has pointed out, the struggle to "stay or leave" is a developmental challenge that arises out of the current state of agricultural economy driven largely by powers external to local small towns. Pastor Steven may need to be the voice of conscientization, which can expand the focus to include social struggles.

All levels, persons, families, and community are experiencing change and loss. One of the healing tasks will be to grieve those losses and to do so without overly romanticizing the past. Another task ahead will be to empower the persons, families, and community to see themselves as agents of hope and transformation. This requires a realistic assessment of where power lies, how power is operating, and in what ways the people at this table have the capacity for effecting change in a direction that they believe will move toward God's vision for life on earth. The pastor can facilitate this assessment and assist in creating a narrative of hope for the future of these families and this community. One place to start reconstructing a story of the future may be to think with them about what God has revealed to them about creativity and change in the face of loss and decline as they and their ancestors have farmed the land. What season is it for this place? What kind of home for future generations can and should this place be? Actively participating in creating a future for the community can be a path to reconciliation within families. As the families at the picnic table begin to acknowledge their own identity struggles, their grief, their fears, and their hopes for the future, they can move into actively creating a future of healing and transformation.

Notes

1. In Tim Cresswell, *Place: A Short Introduction*, Short Introductions to Geography (Malden, MA: Blackwell, 2004), 8.

2. Cresswell, *Place*.

3. Keith Halfacree, "Rural Space: Constructing a Three-Fold Architecture," in *Handbook of Rural Studies*, ed. Paul Cloke, Terry Marsden, and Patrick Mooney (Thousand Oaks, CA: Sage, 2007).

4. Ibid.

5. Sheryl A. Kujawa-Holbrook, *A House of Prayer for All Peoples: Congregations Building Multiracial Community* (Bethesda, MD: Alban Institute, 2002).

6. Ibid.

7. Larry Rasmussen, *Earth Community, Earth Ethics* (Maryknoll, NY: Orbis, 1996), 2.

8. For a substantiation of these claims, see Shannon Jung, *Hunger & Happiness: Feeding the Hungry, Nourishing Our Souls* (Minneapolis: Augsburg Books, 2009).

9. Patrick J. Carr and Maria Kefalas, *Hollowing Out the Middle: The Rural Brain Drain and What It Means for America* (Boston: Beacon, 2009).

10. Stephanie Taylor, *Narratives of Identity and Place* (New York: Routledge, 2010).

11. Ibid., 131.

12. David Mark Hummon, *Commonplaces: Community Ideology and Identity in American Culture*, SUNY Series in the Sociology of Culture (Albany: State University of New York Press, 1990).

13. Marty Strange, *Family Farming: A New Economic Vision*, new ed. (Lincoln: University of Nebraska Press/San Francisco: Institute for Food and Development Policy, 2008), 239.

14. See Cornelia Butler Flora and Jan L. Flora, *Rural Communities: Legacy and Change*, 3rd ed. (Boulder, CO: Westview, 2008).

15. James J. Ponzetti Jr., "Growing Old in Rural Communities: A Visual Methodology for Studying Place Attachment," in *Journal of Rural Community Psychology* (2003).

16. Carolyn Norris-Baker and Rick J. Scheidt, "On Community as Home: Places That Endure in Rural Kansas," in *Home and Identity in Late Life International Perspectives*, ed. Graham D. Rowles and Habib Chaudhury (New York: Springer, 2005).

17. For discussions about "place" as sacred, see John Inge, *A Christian Theology of Place: Explorations in Practical, Pastoral, and Empirical Theology* (Aldershot, UK/Burlington, VT: Ashgate, 2003); Belden C. Lane, *Landscapes of the Sacred: Geography and Narrative in American Spirituality*, expanded ed. (Baltimore: Johns Hopkins University Press, 2002); Sallie McFague, *The Body of God: An Ecological Theology* (Minneapolis, MN: Fortress Press, 1993).

18. Sharon Butala, "The Myth of the Family Farm," in *Farm Communities at the Crossroads: Challenge and Resistance*, ed. Harry P. Diaz et al. (Regina, Saskatchewan: Canadian Plains Research Center, 2003), 72.

19. Ibid., 73.

20. McFague, *The Body of God*, 112.

21. Ibid.

22. For more along these lines, see L. Shannon Jung, *Food for Life: The Spirituality and Ethics of Eating* (Minneapolis: Fortress Press, 2004); *Sharing Food: Christian Practices for Enjoyment* (Minneapolis: Fortress Press, 2006); *Hunger and Happiness: Feeding the Hungry, Nourishing Our Souls* (Minneapolis: Augsburg Books, 2009).

23. Craig Chalquist, "Ecotherapy Research and a Psychology of Homecoming," in *Ecotherapy: Healing with Nature in Mind*, ed. Linda Buzzell and Craig Chalquist (Berkeley, CA: Sierra Club Books, 2009).

24. Howard John Clinebell, *Ecotherapy: Healing Ourselves, Healing the Earth: A Guide to Ecologically Grounded Personality Theory, Spirituality, Therapy, and Education* (Minneapolis: Fortress Press, 1996), 63.

25. bell hooks, *Belonging: A Culture of Place* (New York: Routledge, 2008), 38.

26. Ibid., 215

27. Kin-dom is an alternative to the term "kingdom" that stresses the interconnection of all life rather than the hierarchical relationship of ruler and subject. In the kin-dom of God we know ourselves as "kin" to one another.

2

Care Engaging Community

Justin is a seventeen-year-old high school student whose family moved from an urban area into a rural community in the Rocky Mountains when he was in sixth grade. Alongside those who have lived in this area for generations, the community attracts many retired professionals and young adults who move here because of its surrounding beauty and an abundance of recreational opportunities. With an economy structured around tourism, those who have lived here for generations or those who have moved here as a retirement option can often afford to live within the city limits. Yet, there are many who service the hotels, restaurants, and other businesses that live on the edges of the village or in neighboring communities because of the increasing cost of housing.[1] Emily, Justin's mother, grew up here, and Jerry, his father, hoped he could build a carpentry business in the area. The family moved here because of their concern about the friends with whom Justin was spending time in the city, and they were struggling with financial burdens. Ultimately, Emily and Jerry thought the mountain community with its outdoor activities would be a better place for Justin to grow up. Three years after arriving, Justin's parents divorced. Emily works as a receptionist in a local hotel owned by family friends. Jerry continues to work on building his business, but has been contemplating a move back to the city as soon as Justin graduates from high school.

None of Justin's immediate family attends a local church, although Emily's family is connected to the United Methodist Church that Emily's mother attended before her death three years ago. The pastor of that church, Rev. McKenzie, knows Justin and his mother because of that connection and is aware of Justin's potential for a college football scholarship. Justin, however, is eager to stay in the area after graduation because he has developed many friends here and he hopes to work for one of the outfitters that guides tourists and hunters. The longstanding coach of the high school football team, Bill, also goes to the United Methodist Church, and Rev. McKenzie knows many of the families and the names of the youth because of their connections to various school events and to church. At the end of the football season during Justin's last year, some of the football players and their friends plan a celebration party. A couple of young adults and former football players bring alcohol to the party.

On the way home, Justin's car hydroplanes and goes off the road. He is killed instantly when his car goes off a steep embankment. Early reports indicate the presence of beer bottles in the car and there is a suspicion that Justin was legally drunk at the time of the accident. The football team is in shock, and Bill is angry because no one is taking responsibility for the presence of the alcohol. He feels this accident not only looks bad for the team and the school, but he also carries some guilt for not "giving enough direction" to his team players. Some parents are calling Coach Bill, wondering whether their kids are involved with drugs. Others call because of their deep grief, and they are concerned about how their kids will process the accident. Many of the parents expect the coach to "do something," and he calls Pastor McKenzie for help. In addition, the school principal calls upon the clergy of the churches in town to ask for help at the school as they discuss the accident with other students. There are few formal counseling resources in the community and the school has not had an incident like this in several years. They trust that the pastors will know how to handle the situation.

In the meantime, Justin's family has a funeral to plan. The grief is complicated by the divorce between his mother and father, both of whom have refused to talk to one another in the last few years. Last year Justin moved in with his father and now Emily blames Jerry for letting Justin go to the party. Coach Bill recommends to them that his pastor and church would be glad to help them in planning the service. The funeral home calls Pastor McKenzie to lead the memorial service. Because of the number of people who want to attend the service, they request that it be held in the school gymnasium.

*****

On the one hand, there is nothing unique about this tragedy; it happens every year in communities of all sizes and contexts. On the other hand, there is something peculiar about rural areas and the particular nature of the town where this case occurs. As we have been suggesting throughout this text, the dynamics of rural contexts call for particular understandings of pastoral care. In addition, and perhaps more significantly, the unique nature of rural contexts can teach us something about pastoral care.

Healing and transformative care in rural contexts immediately engages understandings of "community." The goal of this chapter is to examine three aspects related to the nuances of community in rural contexts and to see how these ideas expand notions of care. First, rural contexts highlight the strengths and limitations of community, particularly in the way that individuals, families, and pastoral leaders perceive closeness between them. In addition, these communities wrestle with issues common to families and youth in urban and suburban culture, but they take on a distinctive quality in rural life. Second, rural communities embody a theological commitment to care as it is offered by the formal and informal leadership of a congregation. As local churches become agents of ordinary care for the larger community, they engage the public theology of a church through its prophetic voice, presence, and ministry. Third, concrete practices of care that are healing and transformative address not only the needs of individuals and families, but also of communities.

COMMUNITY IN A RURAL CONTEXT

Community is a term that represents multiple realities to individuals and collectives. On the one hand, as is noted in the previous chapter, people often use the language of community when they identify with a place. For example, people say they reside in a community called Aspen, Colorado, thereby indicating that they live in an amenity-rich part of the Rocky Mountains and one that is different from other less-amenity-rich parts of the Rocky Mountains or the farming and ranching country of the plains. The specificity of place gives texture and concreteness to the lifestyle of a town surrounded by natural beauty, rich in opportunities for hunting, fishing, and skiing, and economically dependent on retirees and couples with second homes, as well as tourism.

Yet, the word *community* is also used to refer to more than a place, as it conjures up images of *how* people relate to one another. Often the characteristics ascribed to community include such things as feeling connected or bound to one another. Churches refer to themselves as "communities of faith," indicating that their spiritual emphasis brings them together, that they know one another at some level deeper than simply in passing, and that they care about one another over time and space. Theologically, the term *community* often refers to qualities in gathering places of worship that reflect fellowship, a sense of belonging, and mutual trust. Two aspects of community begin to shape the lives of people in the case of Justin and his family, in particular: 1) a real sense of closeness and knowing one another, accompanied by the very real absence of anonymity and privacy, and 2) an idealization of community that has an impact on families and youth, with resulting disappointment when hopes are not easily met. A cursory look at each of these elements is helpful in exploring the concept of community in rural contexts.

CLOSENESS AND RELATIONSHIPS

As noted above, accidents and tragedies such as the one described in this case occur in urban and suburban areas as well as in less-populated areas. However, in less populated areas the degree of impact of an accident upon those who live in the area is greater and broader, creating a relational connection that embodies both strengths and limitations. Although this accident may lead the evening news in an urban area, a relatively small percentage of the total population in that viewing area is directly affected by the tragedy. In a small town, particularly one where the football team is a major source of pride and the school is an institution around which a significant part of the community ethos is built, an accident like this has a deeper impact on a larger percentage of the population. News of such an accident travels not by television broadcast, but from person to person, over the Internet or the phone, and at the local convenience store. The perimeter of the town is not marked by the "city limits" but extends to multiple smaller communities and rural households that converge to create a school district large enough to have students, a football team, and a marching band. These small communities are often connected not only by extended families, but by churches and congregations that relate to one another in order to sustain themselves in a smaller and limited population center. People come together at moments when a tragedy occurs because they literally "know" one another and are aware that thriving in small places means caring about the extraordinary moments in people's lives.

One can be certain that almost everyone in the town knows someone involved in this case, whether it is a teacher or youth in the school, a young adult who was at the party, a member of the emergency crew who responded to the accident, or a friend of a friend whose family knows Justin's. Institutions such as the school and the church have a more central place in the embedded rituals of rural areas and become part of the core around which the ethos of community is developed. Not only are teachers more visible and recognizable, they and other leaders within the school system are often known by name or by connections through friends and neighbors. The school system becomes one of the primary institutions for community gathering. For example, football games become a place for many folks across socioeconomic and geographic distances to gather on Friday nights. The smaller number of students in a local school results in a larger percentage of youth who are given the opportunity to participate in sports or marching band. In reality, a larger percentage of the youth are needed in order to make extracurricular activities sustainable at all. The centrality of the school system is reinforced by how easy it is for the community to access and know the teachers, administrators, school board members, or others who work in the school system. Long-term teachers and coaches know other siblings of their current students and are more likely to have taught a generation or more from the same families. The school system becomes a place of community connectedness, and the rituals of concerts, sports events, graduations, and more become moments for the community to gather in significant ways.[2]

A closer and deeper connection is realized as people know one another and their families across time and space in a way that is distinct from urban or suburban areas. Because Emily grew up in this community and still has relatives who live here, there are some who have known her or her family over time and who assume an investment in her life. She is not simply another mother who lost a son in a tragic accident; she is also the daughter of Betty and Joe who used to run the local grocery store in town that was owned by Joe's family for over thirty years. The store no longer exists, as is the case with many other locally owned businesses, and now a gas station/convenience store takes its place in order to serve the tourism industry. As a football player, Justin is known by almost everyone because he is a good player on the only football team in town. The coach and the players, along with the cheerleaders and marching band members, are connected to many people in the community including families of former students, teachers throughout the school system, and others who live in the area. The divorce between Emily and Jerry is "public," simply because information is easily accessible and quickly transmitted to a larger percentage of the whole. Hence, one of the first characteristics to recognize about community in these contexts is that events have a higher impact upon a larger percentage of the population given the smaller numbers of people and their interconnectedness. People feel more bound to one another, as one person's pain is closer in proximity to the whole. This is a strength that brings relational richness to rural communities.

While the breadth and depth of connectedness is almost self-evident and needs to be considered as a strength and sign of community, such relatedness also brings limitations like a lack of anonymity and a temptation to make assumptions about what people "know" about one another. People in rural areas often assume that they know more about a family or an individual than may actually be the case. For example, having grown up in the more anonymous realities of suburban culture, Jerry feels like "everyone knows his business," or at least thinks they do. Many people still consider him to be an "outsider." His loss creates a greater disruption, as he is aware of the accident being "the talk of the town." The lack of anonymity is exacerbated by his own inadequate financial resources in a community whose transient population is attracting more upper-income residents who are pushing the price of living higher and making it more difficult for Jerry to thrive. People assume much about Jerry's reality, and it is difficult for him to privately carry his grief.

This lack of privacy and anonymity has an impact not only on the individuals and families who live in rural communities, but it is also a dynamic Rev. McKenzie experiences. The pastoral leader lives in between expectations of others that she will be "part of a community" while also remaining a "visitor and guest" in that community. Pastoral leaders are always outsiders in rural settings, and this carries strength as well as an accompanying cautionary note. The strength of this tension rests in the fact that because Rev. McKenzie does not fully belong to the ethos and history of that community, there is an opportunity to see new things in a community or to challenge old stories. Such an outsider status offers pastors a certain distance that is required in leadership and pastoral care. The pastor, while deeply moved and touched by the loss of life and the grief of the whole community, is able to bring a perspective and offer comfort in part because she is not so deeply immersed in the community. The profession of being a pastor requires that leaders continue to offer care in the midst of their own incredible grief, anger, and sorrow.

The struggles and tensions of being part of a community and yet an outsider are also embodied in assumptions that people make about the pastor or in the expectations they have about knowing the pastoral leader in more intimate and deeper ways. Congregation members may expect the pastor to convey more knowledge about a family or history than might seem appropriate or helpful. In addition, living in a rural context for some brings on a heightened sense of isolation and aloneness. Rev. McKenzie may identify people in the parish with whom there is a closer connection or a growing sense of mutual appreciation and friendship. These can be particularly significant relationships in the context of rural ministry and are reminders of the thorny issues of what are often referred to as "boundaries." Distinctive to the rural parishes is the way in which pastoral leaders and congregational members bump up against such things as complex dual relationships, a lack of privacy, and an assumed sense of knowing one another, or the realities of relational connections that often lack clarity.

Dual relationships, or the awareness that people carry at least two roles in the same relationship, are common and part of ordinary life. It is not unusual to know someone in two different kinds of settings: a pastoral supervisor might also be a good friend; a dentist might be related to a member in the congregation; or a child's teacher is also a member of the community of faith. These are quite normal realities in communities. What makes pastoral leadership in rural communities a bit more complex is that the number and intensity of dual relationships can be quite astounding. If there are only a few police officers in the community and there are only one or two churches in the community, the likelihood that a pastor will know one of the first responders to Justin's accident is quite high. In addition, people are often related to one another and carry histories and realities that are not easily identified or readily transparent. While this is true in urban and suburban contexts as well, in rural contexts the intensity of those relationships because of simply a smaller population base requires an increased diligence and attentiveness on the part of a pastoral leader.

Pastoral leaders become increasingly vulnerable to the negative messages received from their parishioners, to the isolation of location and the lack of friends who understand them, or to the yearnings of some parishioners who would like to be more connected. Because of the context, it is more difficult to find networks of support outside of one's congregation. At the same time, pastoral leaders come to know the members of their congregations in ways that create deeper connections. Realizing the importance of connection in rural communities does not equate to being "best friends" with parishioners; it does, however, encourage pastors to walk with care as they build meaningful relationships that sustain the church. Becoming close friends with some in the congregation but not others sends the message that some are more likeable or important than others. In addition, being close friends with members of the congregation can make it difficult to say a challenging word or to encourage a change in traditions that might be in the best interest of the community, but not something that a "friend" would like. While it is essential that pastoral caregivers are friendly to those with whom they minister, it is equally important that they continue to find friends in places beyond their congregation such as interdenominational colleagues, friends from seminaries, or others. Pastoral leaders are called to be their pastors, not their best friends. Caring leadership requires that increasing attention be paid to how people communicate with one another and to how interconnected the webs of relationships are in the church.

The importance of being healthy and paying attention to the ways in which people relate to one another in the context of churches in rural communities cannot be overstated. Pastoral care requires healthy habits about leadership, as well as an ongoing opportunity to critically self-reflect about the ways in which pastoral relationships with others create various dynamics that work at the boundaries of intersecting lives.[3] Becoming the pastor of a local congregation in a rural community requires that one honor and care about the ways in which people are connected to one another. At the same time, a pastoral leader must also be aware of the vulnerabilities and complexities of living in such places where closeness and knowing one another are central values and where everyone appears to know everything about everyone else.

For pastoral leaders who reside in rural locations, a sense of being bound together, a sense of closeness and knowing one another, are common. For many, this sense of connection is what initially draws them to this place. Families and youth who are part of rural communities encounter multiple issues and, in part, also wrestle with this sense of closeness and the disappointment that the idealized vision of what they hope to find does not match their experience.

YOUTH AND FAMILIES

People carry multiple expectations about the relationships they hope to have with one another in rural communities. Some who left the community as young adults return—like Justin's mother—hoping to find the connections she experienced growing up. She remembers that the whole community watched over her, reporting to her parents when she crossed the line or offering praise when she did something exceptional. Others retire to a rural area in hopes that the community will provide a feeling of "closeness" while still maintaining some of the pleasures (a good coffee shop and an up-to-date hospital) and the anonymity that they loved about life in their previous locations. Still others come looking for jobs or trying to build businesses here based on the changing economy of tourism and related opportunities, hoping that they will establish friendships that will support their new places in life. In this particular town, outfitting companies hire young adults from the community as well as from elsewhere in order to provide the recreational opportunities for which tourists come to visit the region. These young adults often feel less connected to the community, yet they appreciate the fact that people know one another in ways that are distinct. Community as it is experienced in the relational connectedness of persons—both real and perceived—comes with blessings as well as limitations in rural contexts.

Families that look to a rural community in order to find a peaceful and meaningful place to raise their children, such as Justin's parents, are often disappointed in the realities that they meet, especially for youth, young adults, and families. Individuals and couples with children deal with the same celebrations and problems in life as those who live in nonrural areas. They marry, divorce, remain single or are widowed, have children who leave home or who remain in the area, have children who don't live long enough, have youth who struggle with sexual identity and orientation, worry about what will happen to the next generation, and celebrate life in rituals marked by birth and death. Families in rural areas consist of the same kinds of diverse compositions as those in urban or suburban areas as they are marked by financial pressures brought on by poverty and wealth, hectic lifestyles, changing economies, and more. Not unique to rural areas are the changes in family structures and life represented in smaller families or diverse family structures, but rural areas change at a lower rate of speed. For example, the divorce rate and single-headed households in rural America are growing, as in the culture at large, but at a lower rate than is found in urban and suburban families.[4]

A weakening of the kinship network among intergenerational families in the rural context is apparent in many areas. In towns and villages once centered on agrarian living, a decline is evident among generations that have farmed the same land over time and who choose to remain in the business of agriculture.[5] As more young adults move toward cities, urban centers, or towns that surround the urban context in order to find employment, the economies in rural communities shift and the stresses and strains on family networks grow. Even in the case of Emily, Justin's mother, one sees a kinship system that is more fragmented than in earlier times in the life of the community. Emily is more connected than Jerry and yet less connected than she might have been had she stayed in the area after graduating from high school. Because others in her extended family also left the community upon graduation and did not return, there are fewer family members in the town than she might have experienced in an earlier period in rural America or in some other parts of the county.

Children, youth, and families face particular challenges in rural areas in terms of education. School systems feel the pressure of increased demands on preparing their children and youth for the world in which they live. However, with less financial revenue from taxes, it is often difficult for rural communities to enhance their offerings or build institutional infrastructures that match urban or suburban worlds. Young adults who are identified as "achievers" are moving from small towns to find education and jobs in metropolitan areas.[6] Those who stay are less empowered with the resources needed to face the challenges of rural living.

In parallel ways, a study from the Carsey Institute notes that "a smaller share of nonmetro young people are pursuing higher education." This, in combination with young adults who move away from rural communities, leaves a population in rural communities that "is less engaged in schooling, more engaged in work, and has lower educational attainment."[7] The loss of jobs in rural areas combined with less education often results in a lower economic standard of living and more families living on the edge. As youth move through late teen years and into young adulthood in rural areas, those who want to seek more education often end up leaving the community. Those who stay have fewer economic opportunities, establish families or become parents earlier than young adults in the metropolitan areas, and join workforces with lower wages.

Unique about amenity-rich towns is that there is an influx of young adults looking for work, but those persons do not necessarily stay in the community or contribute to the institutional and social fabric of the community in long-term ways.[8]

In many parts of the rural United States, the out-migration of young adults is countered with a growing aging population, smaller family compositions, and greater racial-ethnic diversity. In amenity-rich towns, older newcomers arrive to retire, but do not necessarily stay long. They often come without children or come to join children who live there in order to find a way of life that they have dreamed about over the years. In areas of the country where poverty is more persistent, older populations live on the edge of financial collapse.[9]

Youth in rural areas are particularly at risk for such things as alcohol use, teen pregnancy, depression, and suicide. While many families struggle with these issues, those who seek a move to the country in order to find the ideal context to raise their children are often unprepared for what they find. Families arrive in rural communities expecting lower rates of drug use and less violence, which is true in some respects. However, youth in rural areas remain vulnerable to realities that are present in the culture at large.

Justin's use of alcohol is not uncommon among youth in rural, suburban, and urban environments. What is unique, however, is that the use of alcohol among teens in nonmetropolitan areas is higher than among their counterparts in metropolitan areas. A disturbing reality is that not only do more youth and young adults in rural areas drink, but they are more likely to "engage in binge drinking, heavy drinking and driving under the influence (DUI) than urban children."[10] The access to vehicles in rural communities is higher, the use of alcohol is higher, and the statistics of alcohol abuse are higher for children, youth, and young adults in rural areas.

The growth of methamphetamine and OxyContin use among rural youth increased exponentially in rural areas in the last decade, although it appears to currently be on the decline. According to the 2007 Muskie School of Public Service report, "[Y]oung adults (ages 18-25) in the smallest rural areas use meth at a rate that is nearly twice the rate of young urban adults (2.9% vs. 1.5%)." The report makes the point that "[t]he smallest rural communities have the least resources to prevent and to treat these substance problems."[11] While there is less use of "hard drugs" and the use of methamphetamine appears to be slowing in rural areas, the availability of alcohol and methamphetamine, alongside fewer resources available in rural areas to treat addictions, results in higher levels of problems related to usage and addiction.

Youth depression and suicide appear at rates higher among rural teens than elsewhere. Although the statistics for the general population of youth appear to be going down for suicide, this is not the case in rural areas, and in particular, in western and mountain states that have "consistently higher suicide rates than the rest of the country, and all of the states with the highest suicide rates have many counties that would meet most definitions of 'rural' . . ."[12] The lack of institutional supports and structures to respond to the needs of teens, the remoteness of rural living, and the loss of economic options for young adults contribute to an increase in depression and suicide among teens in rural contexts.

All of these factors exist concurrently with a growing desire by families to "return to the land" or to move into rural areas create new and lively tensions in rural communities. And, as many of the reports on youth have discovered, the resources for smaller towns and villages are fewer than one finds in the metropolitan areas. The idyllic setting of rural America seems to signal to families a false sense that they and their children will be safer in the country. Those who come from more urban environments expect their schools to live up to the standards of the ones they have left. They hope for no violence or crime in the school system. Yet, what they find are often schools with fewer resources (in part due to the lower number of people paying taxes on property and other things and, hence, less revenue for school systems) to address issues as they arise. In the case study, this translates into fewer professional staff in the area trained in trauma and counseling. While it is somewhat true that there is less violence, gangs, and hard drug culture in rural America, it is also true that youth are at risk in ways that are hard to imagine.

This accounting of the struggles of youth and families in rural areas may leave churches and those who lead them in a state of despair. Yet, it is precisely at these points that communities of care must extend their models beyond the individualized offer of support alone to broader understandings of the role of the church in ordinary care.

COMMUNITY IN A THEOLOGICAL FRAME

Healing and transformative care requires that congregations recognize their role in creating stronger networks for ordinary care. The church—those who represent it at formal and informal levels—extends care to the broader rural community in a way that is unique. Because relational connection is an important strength of rural areas, pastoral care is often embodied informally and naturally. The pastoral leader and the members of congregations offer support in ways that reinforce the social norm of being a good neighbor. Such care offered by ordinary women and men of faith becomes a significant resource when thinking about what is needed for Justin's family or for others who may feel trauma from the experience of having death so close. Whether the church plans for a community meal after the funeral or delivers food to Justin's mother and father, the natural rhythm of church members caring for one another suggests that they will become everyday companions in the journey of sorrow and grief. This norm parallels the history of relatedness evident in rural agricultural communities where farmers depended on one another to get in their crops or take care of their chores even though they did not necessarily agree with or even like one another.[13] Embedded in the meaning of community is the sense that mutual needs and support systems overshadow differences of opinion or other kinds of adversity. Reaching out to one another or to the pastor of the church often occurs prior to people turning to any professional system of care that might be available.

This reliance upon ordinary care does not mean that no one turns to professional counselors in times of struggle and trial in rural areas. However, a lack of formal resources for counseling or mental health care in rural areas invites more opportunities for pastoral leaders and congregations to become part of a natural network of care.[14] In the scenario above, there is no crisis response team or cadre of professional counselors to whom the school or others in the community can turn. The isolation and separation from trained mental health professionals means that pastoral leaders and the few other mental health professionals in the community become part of the backbone of a professional community of care. And, even though Rev. McKenzie may not have advanced training in trauma, the school district hopes the church and its leadership will provide resources for care.

In rural areas, care is less dependent on highly trained professionals who specialize in psychology or psychiatry, and more clearly connected to everyday people who show up to offer support in the midst of whatever is happening in the moment. A lack of trust of outsiders and professionals, combined with the lack of structures and infrastructures that support care, results in fewer people accessing professional counselors in rural areas.[15] And, even where the networks for counseling exist, they are not always available to everyone because of financial reasons. Those who have insurance or who can afford to go to professionals sometimes do, while those who are day laborers or service workers rarely have insurance and cannot afford to seek out professional care. They rely more on the lay community of care that is present in neighbors, friends, and pastors. Similarly, although Rev. McKenzie is aware that one of the retired persons who joined the church recently is a psychiatrist who practiced in an urban context, the insider and outsider status makes it more difficult for that person as a professional to offer the kind of daily and spontaneous care that sustains communities. Pastoral leaders and local church members contribute to the network of care on a daily basis. Pastoral care becomes a ministry of the whole church and does not belong to ordained leaders or professional counselors in the rural context.

The community—whether members of the church or not—turns to Pastor McKenzie and the local community of faith as they work through their grief and prepare for the funeral. Fewer churches in a location suggests that those institutions carry greater weight, as they become places for folks to gather to observe the rituals of community, such as baptisms, weddings, or funerals. From Native Americans to European settlers to contemporary persons who migrate to rural communities, institutions that promote religious and spiritual connections have always been part of the culture. In the landscape of the contemporary rural United States, religion continues to carry greater weight than might be true in urban or suburban contexts.[16] As is common everywhere, not everyone in rural contexts attends church, and religious institutions seem to have diminished in importance in the rural contexts much like they have in more urban and suburban places. However, as Leland Glenna suggests, the church in rural areas seems to be losing its power less quickly than it does in the city. Glenna notes that while the church may be losing its place among the great social institutions in many areas, "it tends to linger longer in rural than urban areas."[17] Hence, it is safe to assume that one of the significant social connectors in the small community where our case is situated is indeed the church. The fact that the school system turns to local clergy persons, or that the coach turns to his pastor for help, is not unusual, but it does reinforce the reality that power is granted to the church in times of chaos and heartbreak in ways that are different from urban or suburban settings. The qualities of community are built around the institutional fabric in ways that are unique, particularly as one considers the role of institutions such as the school and church.[18]

Churches operate as part of the social network and fabric of shared life in a town. The fewer churches, the more possible it is that the place where people experience one another and build a sense of commonness is through the local community of faith. Rural sociologists Cornelia Butler Flora and Jan Flora remind us that "human interaction is the foundation of all communities."[19] In reflecting on the relationships that emerge in rural contexts, they suggest that social connections and relationships, "characterized by norms of reciprocity and mutual trust," are important in rural communities. They go on to note that two types of "social capital"—that of bonding and bridging—provide the base for relationships and human interaction in community. Bonding "consists of connections among homogeneous individuals and groups. . . ."[20] Persons who have strong bonding often know one another over time and in various settings.

Bridging social capital "connects diverse groups within the community to each other and to groups outside the community."[21] It is likely that the community expects the church to be not only a place that cares for its members, but one that bridges across the divides of a community. Congregations become places where persons come together, especially in the face of tragedy, across various ages, socioeconomic classes, racial–ethnic traditions, and other representations of diversities. The capacity of a church to bridge the divergences within a community relates directly to the effectiveness of that congregation's public pastoral presence. In the case we are looking at in this chapter, it is possible to see how the church becomes another place where both bonding and bridging occur as it hosts the grief of a family and a community. The church and its members embody care in ways that not only transmit information about the family and their needs, but literally organize the community for purposes of mourning and loss.

As the pastor prepares for the funeral, Rev. McKenzie is not simply offering a memorial service for Justin and his family and friends, but for a community. The pastor's presence and the congregation's active involvement create both bonding and bridging experiences. Herbert Anderson and Edward Foley remind us that pastoral care, in part, is the process of listening to the narratives of people's lives and bringing them into conversation with the stories and rituals of faith.[22] In such activities of care, the church becomes a place where the public stories about this accident are told and retold, alongside the various narratives of faith that intersect with this story. The way in which different narratives are honored signals to the community whether there is acceptance for a diversity of perspectives and experiences.

Rev. McKenzie's words and the ritual of the funeral service become public expressions of hope offered not only to Justin's family and friends, but to the whole community. The pastor's interpretation of the stories will be heard by a higher percentage of the population than would be true in any other context. Pastoral care takes on additional public dimensions as the values and commitments of the faith become part of the retelling of the accident and the funeral. The scripture, words, and songs from the service will be heard not only by those in attendance at the funeral, but may also appear in the newspaper or on the local radio station. In addition, there is often a public retelling of the funeral itself as people remember various moments and refer to them in the days ahead. The concrete acts of care extended by the congregation during and after the funeral become public witnesses of the pastoral commitments of this congregation. The way in which they prepare for persons to come to the funeral, to greet one another over a lunch prepared by members of the church, or deliver meals to the family provide public acts of pastoral care. Embodying values and commitments of faith, the congregation and its leadership become part of the fabric and texture around which experiences of community are built.

Ordinary pastoral care represents the way in which the church, its members and leaders as well as its physical building, becomes a public space for the community in which it is located. As noted earlier, institutions such as the church have a more visible place within the public structures of rural culture. Although everyone may not know the current pastor of a church, they often know where it is located, and they have had occasions to visit the building for a wedding or funeral of someone they know. In the illustration of our case study, Justin's family is not "formally" connected to the church, but if Emily is asked what church she is connected to or what pastor she wants to officiate at the funeral, her experience with her mother's church makes her feel connected to this community. The pastoral leader, the members of the church, and the building itself provide a structure and place for the public mourning of this teen, even when the funeral is held in the school gymnasium. People expect the pastor and the church to be present and to take leadership in the moment. The idea of a community church highlights the fact that those within the village or town may understand the church to be "theirs" in some very tangible way. The church not only ministers to the community in its grief, it also is called upon to speak to the significant issues of the community.

PRACTICING CARE

Healing and transformative care occurs as churches and congregations in rural areas address issues important to the community or as they bring people together to talk and strategize about responding to concerns. As churches and congregations become leaders in public conversations on behalf of a town, village, or community, pastoral care benefits not simply those who attend the church, but the community as a whole.

In the case we have been examining in this chapter, pastoral care is needed not simply in order to provide comfort to those affected by a tragic death, but to participate in and lead public conversations about the issues that surround the event. It would be a mistake to assume that the only pastoral care activity of the church and its members is that of caring for those who experience hurt, anger, or trauma from the accident that kills Justin. If pastoral care is limited to individualized moments of offering hope and solace, leaders miss other significant ways in which pastoral care naturally extends into the public sphere. Even before Pastor McKenzie and the church are invited formally to participate in leading the community's grief, the church and its members have been involved in examining—or ignoring—the challenges that youth are facing in their community. This accident is symbolic of many of the deeper struggles that youth and their families, and the members of the community, face on a daily basis. Justin's death raises the occasion for a community to deliberate about the use and abuse of alcohol as well as to reflect on interventions they might like to make as a community. The way in which the church participates in or leads conversations about these issues indicates to the community whether the congregation cares about more than just the funeral.

Some argue that the church ought not to be involved in the "public" sphere of the community, largely suggesting that the primary purpose of the church is to serve its membership and, on occasion, to stretch to care for the spiritual and emotional needs of others such as Justin's family and friends. This, however, seems misguided in the context of rural communities in particular. Here, more than in urban and suburban contexts, the presence and voice of the pastoral leadership and the congregation carry an implicit, if not explicit, authority and power. It is important in rural contexts to be aware of power and the dynamics that are present in a community in order to make certain that a congregation is not negatively drawing upon, or denying, its place in the community.[23]

Many ethicists and theologians argue that the church has a unique place in community discourse, particularly in light of the damage caused by injustices and tragedies. In the recent decade or more, the role of public theology has been a topic for conversation among theologians, educators, and those within the pastoral care field.[24] Theologian and scholar Linell Cady suggests that theology can contribute to conversations that relate to the public spheres of everyone's lives. Cady identifies three components needed in order for conversations to take concrete shape and be helpful. Public theology must bring an open form of argumentation to the conversation and be open to debate, it must focus on timely issues, and its style of communication must be accessible to everyone.[25] The rubrics of good pastoral care can be understood to be essential as leaders seek to bring theological claims into conversation with issues present in the community. This does not mean that the church has an answer for the community, or that it uses its theological commitments to claim a corner on the truth; rather it means that those things important to pastors from a theological perspective are also usually important to the community.

Because of the central role that churches play in the institutional life of a community, it is important that the church walk carefully into these conversations in the public realm. The church's role is not to threaten or be overly confident about what is right. Instead, the church is to seek out ways to nurture the very best for the community as a whole. Gloria Albrecht, in *The Character of Our Communities*, suggests that if the church is to embody its claims, "we must literally place ourselves in the midst of concrete justice struggles and live in such a way that we participate in the building up of just communities of nonviolence."[26] Such communities are able to embrace and be transformed by diversity at the same time that they seek ways to resist oppression for others. It is possible to draw upon these two elements of community by pointing to churches that understand that pastoral care is more than a privatized act of hospitality or grace. In a similar way, ethicist Eleanor Haney reminds her readers that transformation in communities occurs as churches take steps to resist injustice and nurture qualities of community shaped by mutual care and support.[27] Indeed, the church's role is to assist the community in seeking justice.

Defining justice, however, is difficult in many communities, including those in rural areas. There are multiple definitions and perspectives to consider as communities begin to address issues that they share in common, whether they are the use of alcohol among their teens or the disadvantage of the young adults who remain in the community without access to higher education or better jobs. It would be impossible, for example, to write a text on rural pastoral care without examining a number of issues about which much has been written from multiple perspectives. And, admittedly, it is impossible to present only one answer to any of the issues facing persons in rural areas. Agreement among rural leaders about how issues ought to be resolved cannot be expected at any greater extent than in urban contexts. What is distinct in the rural United States, however, is that the church can invite people into conversation in ways that nurture the best of community.

There is little doubt that tensions exist in rural areas between the individual and the wants, needs, or desires of the larger community. For example, Justin's mother and father moved to the community hoping that they would find a better situation for their son. Emily remembers the smallness of the community in her growing-up years and how her best friends hung around the grocery store when they got out of school. It is hard for her to catch up with the community, as it has changed over the last several years, and she is particularly surprised by the presence of alcohol and the rumors of methamphetamine among teens. They hope for more money to be spent in the school system as it engages intervention and support models. Families like Justin's are looking for excellent public schools with a low tax base where their kids can excel in both sports and music. At the same time, those who have moved into the community after retirement want good health-care facilities and hope that any extra dollars go into securing physicians for the area. Those who have remained in the community over time are hopeful that the new folks coming in will bring financial resources with them, but not make more demands on the community's already-overtaxed financial base. They know there is not money for better roads, an improved school system, and a new hospital. All of these desires are equally important, yet there is not enough money to respond to everything.

The tensions in the broader community parallel those in churches and places of worship. Debates about who makes decisions, the direction of ministry, worship services, and the use of financial resources are not uncommon. One would hope that churches would allow justice to appear in stronger ways, but as Albrecht notes, the move from "rugged individualism" to "community" as an ethos in the culture does not necessarily guarantee that the marginalized will experience the kind of care that liberates.[28] One can imagine, for example, that even the notion that the funeral in our case study might be held in the school gymnasium rather than the church might raise concerns for some. Or, the fact that Justin's family members are not really "members" of the church might be of importance to others. Churches are not isolated from the tensions and struggles that emerge in rural communities.

Community is an essential aspect of healing and transformational care in three ways. First, rural contexts highlight the strengths and limitations of closeness, not only for individuals but for families and for pastoral leaders. Second, through their formal and informal leadership, local churches and the building that serves them become agents of ordinary care for the larger community. Third, pastoral care engages the church's prophetic voice, presence, and ministry through its embodiment of public theology.

The question becomes, then, what is it that congregations and communities of faith can do in light of the issues that are pressing on them? We would like to suggest three things. First, good pastoral care requires deep listening and the ability to ask questions that invite people to continue to discern what is important to them. Such listening does not assume that one knows the answer before a question is asked. Likewise, pastoral care requires a commitment to the hearing of multiple perspectives rather than just one dominant voice or idea. The art of listening fully enables many voices to be heard, including those whose voices are usually quiet or less present in community conversation. Listening asks what justice might look like for those on the margins of the community as well as for those who appear to have the most power.

There is a temptation in the church, as in other well-intended groups, to jump toward advocacy of a particular position without listening carefully to the voices of others, including those who are marginalized or who have less power. It is important to wonder, for example, what might be learned by listening not only to the voices of parents who are anxious about their youth, but also to the youth themselves who are caught in cycles of alcohol use that have been passed on to them by previous generations. How might hearing from all persons help a community discern what might be "good" for the community? Pastoral theologian Sharon Thornton suggests that an "emancipatory practice" of "radical mutuality" might offer some direction. Such practice begins with a high level of respect and includes listening as one of the first acts.[29]

Second, it is important to build places of conversation that are not reactive, but that seek out common ways to approach the issues at hand. Daniel Kemmis, in *Community and the Politics of Place*, urges those who are in rural communities to regain their sense of the "public" or common ground through the art of public discourse and cooperation. Building upon his experience in Montana's political sphere, Kemmis notes that what made those on the frontier survive was not simply rugged individualism or a giving in to the kind of bureaucracy that places too many restrictions on people. Instead, what he urges is a move toward cooperation as people seek "common ground" built around shared values important in the development of community.[30]

What Kemmis and others suggest is that the future of rural contexts depends upon an awareness of these tensions and an ability to invite people into the future by conversation about what is good for the "public." In a similar way, Flora and Flora suggest that towns and villages that can tolerate and move through conflict have a higher chance of politics becoming less a matter of personal rancor, thereby allowing persons to tend to the process of community conversation. Their hope is that communities flourish more as they work on discourse that involves more people along diverse paths.[31]

Third, in order for communities of care to become partners of care, they must participate in the development of interventions that lead to transformation for the individuals, families, and institutions within their communities. Many of the issues that arise within rural communities are complex and complicated. They are not easily answered. At the same time, there are potentially positive interventions in the life of every community. The church and its leadership become partners in community as they seek new and creative ways to understand themselves as agents of care.

Shaped by the unique characteristics of rural community, care becomes concrete and explicit in both personal and public dimensions. Church leaders and congregations respond not only to crises, but to the normal ebbs and flows of life in recognition that rural contexts embody a relational connectedness that brings both strengths and limitations, a lack of formal resources for care that requires a stronger network of ordinary care, a stronger center of power in institutions such as the school and the church, and a diversity that is unique.

In addition, while it is clear that there are contextual differences between various kinds of rural communities, present in all of them are the pressures and tensions experienced by youth, young adults, families, and an aging population. Many of these tensions will continue to be present in this text as we talk about economics, violence, health-care systems, and more.

Care in rural communities reminds us that the private expressions of pastoral care are deeply connected to the more public acts of community care. Rural congregations have much to teach us as we continue to reflect on the public nature of life together and on the way in which the church might lead conversations within community.

Notes

1. The Rocky Mountain areas include amenity-rich or high-amenity rural areas. There is a difference between rural areas that experience greater economic benefit from their amenity-based culture (the Rocky Mountain area, for example) and those that are rich in resources but have higher rates of poverty (parts of Appalachia, for example) or the heartland of the Midwest that was once largely agrarian. In amenity-rich contexts, there is less chronic poverty as older persons move into the area for retirement or establish second homes. Population has increased in amenity-rich areas, unlike the decline in rural populations of the Midwest or chronic poverty areas. In addition, there is less racial-ethnic diversity than is the norm in the United States, although a growing number of Latina/Latino persons find work in these areas. For more information, see Cornelia Butler Flora and Jan L. Flora, *Rural Communities: Legacy and Change*, 2nd ed. (Boulder, CO: Westview, 2004, 1–20); Lawrence C. Hamilton, Leslie R. Hamilton, Cynthia M. Duncan, Chris R. Colocousis, "Place Matters: Challenges and Opportunities in Four Rural Americas" Carsey Institute, University of New Hampshire (2008). See also the chapters in this text on diversity and poverty.

2. Flora and Flora note the importance of "social capital" in rural communities. The church and the school, along with those who are part of these systems in a town, negotiate the social capital in ways that are unique to rural life. See Cornelia Butler Flora and Jan L. Flora, "Social Capital," in *Challenges for Rural America in the Twenty-First Century*, ed. David L. Brown and Louis E. Swanson (University Park: Pennsylvania State University Press, 2003), 214–27. In addition, the Carsey Institute notes that "joining" occurs at higher rates in the Midwest than in other rural contexts. See Hamilton et al., "Place Matters," 17.

3. See Karen A. McClintock, *Preventing Sexual Abuse in Congregations: A Resources for Leaders* (Bethesda, MD: Alban Institute, 2004); Kibbie Simmons Ruth and Karen A. McClintock, *Healthy Disclosure: Solving Communication Quandaries in Congregations* (Bethesda, MD: Alban Institute, 2007).

4. See Katherine MacTavish and Sonya Salamon, "What Do Rural Families Look Like Today?" in *Challenges for Rural America in the Twenty-First Century*, ed. Brown and Swanson, 75–76.

5. MacTavish and Salamon, "What Do Rural Families Look Like Today?," in *Challenges for Rural America in the Twenty-First Century*, ed. Brown and Swanson, 74, 82.

6. See Chapter 2 on "place."

7. Anastasia Snyder, Diane McLaughlin, and Alisha Coleman-Jensen, "The New, Longer Road to Adulthood: Schooling, Work, and Idleness among Rural Youth," Carsey Institute, University of New Hampshire (2009).

8. See Patrick C. Jobes, *Moving Nearer to Heaven: The Illusions and Disillusions of Migrants to Scenic Rural Places* (Westport, CT: Praeger, 2000), 4. See chapters on diversity and poverty.

9. See Nina Glasgow, "Older Rural Families," in *Challenges for Rural America in the Twenty-First Century*, ed. Brown and Swanson, 86–96.

10. See Muskie School of Public Service Research and Policy Brief, "Substance Abuse Among Rural Youth: A Little Meth and a Lot of Booze," June 2007. See also *Results from the 2010 National Survey on Drug Use and Health: Summary of National Findings*, NSDUH Series H-41, HHS Publication No. (SMA) 11-4658 (Rockville, MD: Substance Abuse and Mental Health Services Administration, 2011).

11. Muskie School of Public Service Research and Policy Brief, "Substance Abuse Among Rural Youth."

12. Suicide Prevention Resource Center, "Preventing Youth Suicide in Rural America: Recommendations to States," April 2008, 4.

13. Daniel Kemmis tells the powerful story of a community that comes together in spite of deep differences during a barn-raising in Montana. As he notes, ". . . life was harsh enough that they had no choice. Avoiding people you did not like was not an option. Everyone was needed by everyone else in one capacity or another." Daniel Kemmis, *Community and the Politics of Place* (Norman: University of Oklahoma Press, 1990), 71.

14. Pastoral care has focused both on the kind of lay care that is embodied in communities of faith and the specialization of pastoral care and counseling. The latter has developed most extensively in urban and suburban contexts or in larger congregations, few of which are in rural contexts. However, the strength of community remains a persistent theme in pastoral care literature. See, for example, Margaret Zipse Kornfeld, *Cultivating Wholeness: A Guide to Care and Counseling in Faith Communities* (New York: Continuum, 1998), 15–44.

15. For example, research suggests that while trust in neighbors and a willingness to help one another is high, trust in government is considerably lower. See Hamilton et al., *Place Matters*, 17.

16. Religious connection varies in rural regions, just as it does in metropolitan areas. According to a study by the Carsey Institute, Midwesterners and those in chronic poverty areas are more likely to attend church. Areas with amenities (both rich and in declining areas) have a higher percentage of people who attend only a few times or not at all. See Hamilton et al., "Place Matters," 18.

17. Leland Glenna, "Religion," in *Challenges for Rural America in the Twenty-First Century*, ed. Brown and Swanson, 265.

18. See ibid., 262–72.

19. Flora and Flora, "Social Capital," in *Challenges for Rural America in the Twenty-First Century*, ed. Brown and Swanson, 214.

20. Ibid., 217.

21. Ibid.

22. Herbert Anderson and Edward Foley, *Mighty Stories, Dangerous Rituals: Weaving Together the Human and the Divine* (San Francisco: Jossey-Bass, 1998).

23. The analysis of power in rural communities continues to be of interest to scholars in many areas. See, for example, the work of Ruth Panelli, "Rural Society," *Handbook of Rural Studies*, ed. Paul Cloke, Terry Marsden, and Patrick H. Mooney (London: Sage, 2006), 63–90.

24. There is deep debate among theologians and ethicists about precisely how the church ought to be engaged in public life. Mark Toulouse articulates some of the different ways in which scholars have wrestled with the intersection between the "public" and Christian faith. See Mark G. Toulouse, *God in Public: Four Ways American Christianity and Public Life Relate* (Louisville: Westminster/John Knox, 2006). Other works of interest include John B. Cobb Jr., *Postmodernism and Public Policy: Reframing Religion, Culture, Education, Sexuality, Class, Race, Politics, and the Economy* (Albany: State University of New York Press, 2002), and Martin Marty, *Education, Religion, and the Common Good: Advancing a Distinctly American Conversation about Religion's Role in Our Shared Life* (San Francisco: Jossey-Bass, 2000).

25. Linell E. Cady, "A Model for a Public Theology," *Harvard Theological Review* 80, no. 2 (April 1987): 193–212.

26. Gloria Albrecht, *The Character of Our Communities: Toward an Ethic of Liberation for the Church* (Nashville: Abingdon, 1995), 139.

27. Eleanor Haney, *The Great Commandment: A Theology of Resistance and Transformation* (Cleveland: Pilgrim, 1998).

28. Albrecht, *The Character of Our Communities*, 139.

29. See Sharon Thornton, "Honoring Rising Voices: Pastoral Theology as Emancipatory Practice," *Journal of Pastoral Theology* (Spring 2001): 64–80.

30. Kemmis, *Community and the Politics of Place*. Although Kemmis's agenda might be interpreted as a particularly political one, it is also clear that he is suggesting something about the nature of community that is essential to the future of rural cultures and contexts.

31. Flora and Flora, "Social Capital," in *Challenges for Rural America in the Twenty-First Century*, ed. Brown and Swanson, 224.

3

Care Intersecting with Leadership

Pastor Ray Williams has been called to a two-point charge in southeast Georgia. He wonders initially what in the world God (or the congregation's search team or the bishop or the call committee) might have had in mind assigning him to a place that is so unlike his home in Atlanta. The church members welcome him, and there is a reception on Saturday night at which he is told, "It has been a while since we had a pastor. We are so pleased that you are here."

The Sunday worship service seems to go pretty well. Pastor Ray has learned not to deviate too much from the traditional order of worship for the first few months. People say nice things to him on the way out of the church and he spends the rest of the day unpacking. When he gets up on Monday morning, however, he wonders, "Where do I start?" He calls one of the senior members of the church, and asks if he could come over and talk to her.

"Well, Pastor Ray, what can I tell you? We pretty much count on the pastor to lead worship and to visit the sick and shut-ins and take care of things as they come up. We don't have a lot of energy for new things, but most of the folks like each other and like the church. We're not too fancy or fussy."

Pastor Ray wonders if this attitude is one that is shared widely. The church seems to expect for him to be engaged in the minimal and important activities of pastoral care, but not much else, and they seem to regard him as a hired professional. Like many local churches, it would appear that the congregation understands care to be the role of the pastor, and leadership seems disconnected from that care. Alternatively put, leadership and care are seen as somehow dichotomous or even opposed to one another.

Pastor Ray overhears a conversation in church that concerns the building of a hog feedlot in some proximity to the church. He figures that he could ask this senior member about it. He is told, "Oh, pastor, you don't need to worry about that. Some of the people in the church are opposed to the idea because of the smell and also the possible pollution of the water supply; others see it as an economic opportunity that could provide some new jobs. But that's really not something you want to get involved in."

*****

This case represents many smaller-membership churches that seem to be sagging a bit. There is a "good enough" attitude, which may be fairly demoralizing for newer (not just younger) pastors who have a different vision of what the church is.

No doubt, Pastor Ray came to this congregation eager to be the ideal clergy leader that he has imagined. He, like most of us, tends to operate on the basis of what he thinks is right and gets discouraged when his expectations of how the church ought to be, run into imperfect reality. Pastors in any congregation know the puzzle of how to lead a congregation into a model Christian community (which it might have looked like on their initial visit!). And then, on top of that, to consider how the whole congregation, oneself included, could minister to and with the community outside the church walls. These considerations can certainly feel overwhelming. This case may be somewhat typical of recent seminary grads who come to a church and realize there is a real process involved in negotiating a leadership style that fits the parish and the parish leadership. This is of course also the case with experienced pastors. How can the pastor and lay leaders encourage a broader view of what is entailed in discipleship and mission in their community? Clearly the issue of the hog feedlot is one that has the potential to divide the community and the congregation. The task of healing in this case seems also to involve the task of transformation. The leadership of the congregation and of the community seems very connected to pastoral care. How might Pastor Ray's care include aspects of congregational and community leadership? The dimension of the pastor or church's being the public theologian comes into view here.

Indeed, Pastor Ray's reaction that all this can be overwhelming is one that is widely shared. The issues are very personal. It is not just how pastors in general lead congregations in general, but how can *I* lead *this* particular congregation or congregations? Pastoral care is a matter of addressing particular people's need for healing, and also the community's need for a public theologian to help impact community life. The context of that person's ministry will shape the style and effectiveness of his or her ministry. This chapter is designed to give pastoral leaders some benchmarks as they set out or find themselves in the middle of leading rural congregations. What do the pastor's and the congregation's spiritual and public roles entail in this case?

Leadership in a Rural Context

There are certain theological parameters that define the mission of all churches. How those parameters are played out in the *particular context* or place of ministry in the congregation is an essential issue for the pastor and leadership of a rural church. The style appropriate to a large church in the city is different from that exercised in a two-point charge in a town and country location. It will probably surprise pastors of town and country congregations just how much is known about their lives and how little anonymity is possible in a small town. This can be a blessing (people know you are sick and bring "hot dishes") but also a curse. How is one to keep secret anything at all? At any rate, contexts are different and it is worth considering some of the particularities of rural pastorates. We will take up elements of the rural context in this section of the chapter. The first element of context is size.

1. **Size of congregations/community impacts church structure and governance.** Roy Oswald suggests that ecclesial officials not assign just-out-of-seminary, eager pastors to small churches for the sake of both the pastors' morale and because these churches have learned to follow the lead of the "first family" of the church rather than that of the pastor. For good reason. There is a Catch-22 situation here: because the young pastor encounters resistance when she begins to act like the leader, the situation degenerates and the pastor becomes discouraged and soon moves on. The congregation learns that it cannot count on the mobile pastor and needs to count on and depend on "first families" who are resident.[1] The best options for leadership all include dealing creatively and lovingly with this local family.

The revolving-door mentality of many first parishes has resulted in a very short two- or three-year period before the pastor relocates. The people in the congregation know this and are reluctant to commit to transient relationships or to poison long-term ones. Not understanding the context (place), the pastor asks to be reassigned. When she is reassigned, there is a sense in the congregation that "we weren't good enough" for her and that this mobile professional didn't like us as we were. It tends to reinforce the inferiority complex of the church and may lead them to blame the judicatory. The possibility of future commitment on the part of the congregation is lessened. The pastor often leaves demoralized (and may or may not shake the dust off her sandals) .

Of course, many bishops and other church officials have resisted Oswald's advice, and some of those energetic pastors have found ways to lead seemingly sleepy congregations into being caring centers of faith. Returning to our case, Pastor Ray appears not immune to the revolving-door syndrome. He is somewhat perplexed, perhaps having made some assumptions about the nature of this parish or about their willingness to accept and implement his ideas for them.

2. Being adopted as a leader is the way one begins to exercise leadership. The pastor might do better if he were to "join the church" and exercise leadership from within. He will find that being adopted as a trusted pastor is the necessary path to leadership.

Pastor Ray had come to a standstill early in his ministry. Perhaps that is to the good. He begins to think about the question of what his best approach to ministry in this southeast Georgia town might be. And he has wisely "gone to the balcony"[2]—taken time to reflect on the situation creatively—to think about his own spiritual life and also the mission of a congregation. His focus is turning to this particular congregation now. How can he work with the congregation to provide caring leadership in the church and community? And what about this hog feedlot issue?

Pastor Ray is confronted with the task of diagnosis.[3] He needs to analyze (with the help of others) just what ministry is in this context, and what God is up to in this community. That is what "going to the balcony" might provide—a way forward that keeps some of his best options open. In some ways seminary graduates have been "urbanized" so that an informal rural context where the web of customs and norms is not visible to the naked eye invites the graduate to make assumptions that are more appropriate to the urban context. And those assumptions may be inappropriate in a smaller town or community. Thus any new pastor or recently reassigned pastor needs to know the territory. James Hopewell suggests that each congregation has its own unique web of meanings, and thus studying the congregation and community is the first order of business. This is especially true in rural and smaller-membership congregations because much of graduate training in the U.S. carries urban values. There is interplay between the ascribed roles of pastor and the achieved status of being accepted and trusted. The interplay often revolves around the questions on the part of the laity: "Are we okay?" "Can you like us as we are?"

3. Learning the context means exploring certain things. What are the sorts of things that Pastor Williams would want to know? What is the history of this congregation? What is its relationship to the community? What are the assets in the context of the church, its history and people? What is the relationship of this church to this community? What are the assets of this congregation—physical assets, spiritual assets, skills of its people, interests, organizations that interact with or partner with this church, with this embodied faith? How might those assets be affirmed and raised up? How does the congregation deal with disagreements or conflicts? Who is the pastor in this context?

As he begins the process of learning what this congregation's "thick web of meanings" and customs are, Pastor Ray begins to see patterns in various descriptions of the rural context.[4] There is enough similarity in town and country contexts that we are confident that we can locate some generalizations across the species. For example, people in town and country contexts still tend to operate relationally. In terms of leadership, then, this is vital:

There is no substitute for getting to know the people and context of one's particular congregation and community if one is to provide caring leadership. (This may involve something as prosaic as daily walks to the post office, the café, or visiting everyone in the congregation with a trusted elder.)

If a pastor and lay leaders want to develop a caring leadership, they need to understand their context, to know *where* they are. At the risk of being reiterative, let us repeat: one needs to do a diagnosis of one's context; one style of leadership does not fit all. That is the bedrock need that this book addresses.[5]

Pastor Ray would do well to think of himself as a cultural anthropologist for the first six months of his ministry. In that way, he would put himself in a situation where he assumed that he knew nothing about the place where he has landed. He could enlist the members of the congregation to teach him about this context (and also the hog feedlot issue!). He could also develop relationships and have conversations with those who are not members of "his" congregation.

One way to do such a diagnosis is to consider the four characteristics that have structured these first five chapters: place, community, styles of leadership, and diversity. Those will shape section 3 of this chapter, which looks at the action implications for ministry.

Therefore, how Pastor Ray goes about doing a diagnosis of this place should pay respect to the people's relational understanding of themselves—their work, marriages, kin, alliances, customs, mindset, and so on. To be sure, looking at statistical tables and zip code analyses of the demographics of the town or countryside are useful tools, but the real learning comes from people's sharing who they are and what they do for a living, how their first cousin came to be jailed, and what the economic situation in the community is, and who are the ignored or looked-down-upon groups.

4. There is an agrarian mindset at work in the rural context. Most town and country communities are a mix of people, some of whom were born there and have an essentially traditional or agrarian mindset, which values relationships above role functions. Others and the pastor exhibit a functional rather than a relational bent, and have a cosmopolitan mindset, which tends to be more functional and task-oriented. Neither is wrong, and indeed both have strengths. But woe to the leaders who do not understand that people with these mindsets approach issues in different ways and that their representatives may serve on the same church board. So, when tragedy strikes in the form of a fire or flood, the agrarian tendency is to turn to resources in the community first; only after that are other agencies considered. The cosmopolitan response may be to consider what expertise is needed to deal with the issues and to consult those with the relevant expertise; local resources are considered second. The agrarian is more likely to see "community" as involuntary; it is those who were born there. The cosmopolitan is likely to see "community" in terms of voluntary membership, which are those who have chosen to become church members or members of the local Thrivent Financial Group branch or Book Club.

5. Other Elements It would be foolhardy to try to give a list here of all the elements of context that Pastor Ray might find himself interested in learning. Some of the best resources are the stories that members tell about the town or church. See the abbreviated list in *Discovering Hope*, for example.[6] It could be useful to give you a few questions that Pastor Ray might use to develop his understanding, however:

- What is the economic base of the community? How is that represented in the congregation?
- What resources are there in the community for people who are hurting—for example, victims of abuse, alcoholism, the poor, social groupings, etc.? To whom do these people turn for help?
- How is the church perceived in the community?
- What or who do the people in the congregation and community trust?
- What stories do people tell about their church? Their community? What structures their self-understanding?
- Whose voices are not heard in the community? How has the population shifted in the past decade? Do the police treat all members of the community alike?
- How do people feel about their congregation and community? Are they willing to make commitments to their civic and corporate life? Who are the church's partners in ministry?
- What is the place of youth, of gays and lesbians, of the elderly, of people of color, of young adults, etc.?
- Another good motif for analyzing the dimensions of a place is the notion of "capital," which can be translated as "asset." Cornelia and Jan Flora do a fine job of offering us categories of capital or assets that can be used to identify gifts and distinctive features of a place.[7]

LEADERSHIP IN A THEOLOGICAL FRAME

In considering the theological framework that informs the privilege of leading a rural congregation, the second section of this chapter begins by considering how it is that pastoral care and leadership intersect. Personal issues are always also social issues that require leadership to organize and mobilize the church and community toward ongoing healing and transformation, changes that produce greater health. Part of that intersection involves the theology that guides leadership in a congregational place. The leadership of the congregation (pastor and people) wishes to live out the narrative of the community of Jesus Christ, and a particular style of leadership is involved in practicing care and in building community. In a rural setting, the practice of public leadership is both the disciples' (church members) and the pastor's vocation. It is a matter of how the pastor and people build community in their context. Here the wisdom of leadership theory comes into view, especially as it has been developed within a congregational context.

Pastoral care and leadership are integrally related. One aspect represented in our case is the way in which our leadership styles make a difference in the care we offer. For example, we as Christian clergy and lay leaders certainly intend that our styles of leadership demonstrate care and respect. Usually they do reflect such care. However, a leader cannot express care and respect if he is continually telling other parishioners what to do and how to do it (dismissing their opinions and thoughts). Any of us will recognize the disconnection between the talk and the walk. What we say with our mouths may or may not match the way we operate. Thus, the pastor and leaders need to attend to their own spiritual well-being and care. They need both integrity and humility. Our leadership styles as pastors and lay leaders do express certain values and have the capacity to foster caring leadership in others and ourselves or to stifle caring leadership.

Yet, there is more to the connection between pastoral care and leadership than that of the style of the pastoral leader. Congregational care requires that we not only attend to the individuals who are in our communities of faith, but that we also extend that care by paying attention to the dynamics and cultural contexts that sometimes diminish life for our congregants. Part of the premise of this book is that care is never only about isolated individuals and their stories; rather, it is about the way in which the congregation—its staff and its members—attend to the dynamics and realities of people who live in rural contexts. The church has a public role to play. Thus, the dimensions of more interpersonal care have wider social causes; both call for our attention as pastoral leaders. The pastoral leader recognizes that the cultural aspects of living in smaller, rural communities make a difference in multiple ways on the lives of those individuals. Hence, Pastor Ray must be aware not only of those who are sick and lonely and who need pastoral care, he must also attend to the economics of the community or the lack of resources in the community or the differences emerging in the community in ways that will call him to take leadership. Recognizing that those who live in rural communities often experience isolation and marginalization, good pastoral leadership requires that pastors will have the ability both to recognize and analyze the impact of oppression on individuals and faith communities and to know how to utilize their prophetic role to bring healing, voice, and wholeness to the marginalized.[8] Good pastoral care requires attention to one's leadership.

In addition, one essential element of leadership and pastoral care is attention to our spiritual life. Despite what the pastor brings to the congregation, it is true that the web of relationships and expectations and church life has a history that is different from the pastor's. After all, the members of this congregation have been learning to live together for some time before the pastor arrives. They have developed ways of doing business, and have certain customs and norms. They have a *context*, a place that has been shaped theologically and practically. God has been present in that congregation, and will continue to be present. The newcomer, whether pastor or not, begins with the premise that God has been at work in that location. There are many spiritual gifts as a result of God's ongoing incarnation in that community. The pastor's task is to articulate the presence of God, to call others to see and do the mission of God, and to enter the world where God has been and will be.

One thing that Pastor Ray thought about for the week after his conversation was his own motives for entering ministry. He was clear that one of his motives at least was to follow the example of Jesus Christ in his caring and all-inclusive ministry. He wanted to be a leader who followed Jesus' teaching and who cared for people. Moreover, he thought, it is not just people in general but the particular people that God has led to the congregation where he had been called to be the pastor. His ministry was in this place and with these people and those who were attracted to this congregation. He realized that his ministry could not be solitary or standardized. Furthermore, his image of leadership did not include being hired to provide services. Building mission and community was a more challenging task in the field than it had seemed at seminary. It was indeed a high calling.

Leadership itself could be seen, he realized, as a part of group life that organizes and mobilizes God's people for ministry. Obviously in any social grouping there has to be some form of organizing. Without an organizing function, there is little mobilizing to fulfill the mission of the organization. He remembered his ministry professor talking about the internal life of the congregation and its external mission. They were not as separate as they might appear, his professor had said. But they were distinct. And they do get organized in some shape, whether by laissez-faire drift, authoritarian pronouncement, or careful and long negotiation/collaboration. He realized that this was another point of connection between pastoral care and the mission of what the congregation could be. All Christians are priests in understanding their gifts as being in the service of Christian discipleship. Mobilizing those gifts in a way that serves God's mission is a task of leadership, and exercising leadership has this practical as well as spiritual dimension. His vision was that of being collaborative. He came to the conclusion that he needed to learn how to guide that process through the mobilization of all the gifts of the laity, to the maximum extent possible. Thus leadership was related to pastoral care, both theologically and also practically, through how he carried out a mobilizing leadership. So he came to the conclusion that his leadership needed to be an egalitarian, collaborative style.

Collaborative theory is a postmodern way of thinking about therapy, leadership, and the work of communities. It is built around such notions as valuing the "local knowledge" or expertise of people, recognizing the importance of diversity, and developing ways of genuine collaboration that move beyond simply walking alongside one another in our decision making or our work. The narrative therapy movement parallels many of these same commitments.[9]

The organizing center that Pastor Ray does have, however, is knowing that the congregation is not just any organization, nor is it obliged to operate in a vacuum or depend totally on business organization techniques, however good those might be. Indeed, he realized that the specific local church was also part of a larger tradition, a tradition replete with saints and sinners, good organization and bad. The Christian faith tradition could guide and shape his leadership and the wider leadership of the whole congregation.

The first asset that the church has is its distinctive belief system and foundation in Jesus Christ. With this purpose and identity established in its self-understanding (and that is an ongoing process), that will begin to set the parameters of the shape of leadership. For example, the style of leadership is patterned on the style that we believe Jesus modeled in his life. Did Jesus demonstrate a style that centered on his own power and activity, or did Jesus while acting compassionately himself also send out the disciples to do ministry? It is clear that the latter was his course. Scripture after scripture suggests that the disciples are commissioned to go into the entire world to spread the good news and to heal, feed, and clothe people in need. The purpose of the organization is to worship and love God, and to love the neighbor as oneself. To the extent that the religious organization demonstrates this sense of mission and purpose, it is expressing its founding reason for being, its commission.

As Jesus said, "You are the salt of the earth. . . . You are the light of the world" (Matt. 5:13, 14). We can articulate what it is that God calls the church to be and to do, and can understand the leadership of the church as facilitating the purposes and calling of the church. We can say what the heart of ministry is. Exactly what is entailed in being the salt of the earth or the light of the world in this place is filtered through our cultural lens, of course, but it probably does not mean that we will become sought-after celebrities, rich, or powerful. It would tend to mean the opposite: that we are to be humble, persistent, and loving, God-bearing in our demeanor, and to continue to struggle with what that means.

One of the primary pointers to what leadership means in Christian theology has to do with "vocation" or "servant leadership." All disciples, all Christians, are called to show the grace of God in their professions or jobs. We are all—pastor, social worker, mechanic, waitress, doctor, teacher, and mail carrier—to mediate the grace of God in whatever vocation we are called. Usually that includes doing the best possible job we can, being as competent and effective as well as gracious in our interactions. We are called to be Christians, followers of the Christ. Part of what that means is that we are to be caring for all peoples, no matter their station or hygiene or income level. Certainly that is what Jesus demonstrated in his disregard for the culture's opinion of the people with whom he consorted. Another aspect is that the pastor is called to hold up the spiritual standards of social justice for all people and indeed for all creation. While it may be foolhardy to take a stand on one side or the other of the hog feedlot issue, it is clearly within the pastor's prophetic role to call for a public forum on the issue.

Reinforcing this egalitarianism is what can be seen as the central metaphor for what a church is called to be. The church is the "body of Christ," and the ministry of vocation is to build up that body. This is a particularly organic image and, as such, it expresses the fact that the church is about relationships—a relationship with God, with other people, with the earth, and with oneself. It is clear that this is a very general understanding but it is one that almost every Christian body would endorse. Furthermore, it is one that suggests that no one is any better than another, and all are called to play their part to become the members that God has called them to be. The pastor is one of those members who has a unique set of roles.

Some of what had seemed like abstract theology to Pastor Ray in seminary was beginning to become practical. To be sure, his reflections at this point were ones that applied to most congregations, but it was helpful to pull back and think about the mission of the church in all places and all times. His thinking was assisted by these other beliefs that bear on the theology of leadership.

- The church is to manifest Christ's own love. Instituted by Jesus Christ, the church is called to build up the discipleship of the baptized for the sake of the world. The church exists to extend the experience of God's love and concern. Thus the leadership of the church is called to exhibit that same love that Jesus Christ exhibited when he was incarnate. (That is why the church is called the "body of Christ.") The church is especially directed toward those who are hurting in any way.
- Ministry is shared among all believers. Every member of the body is a disciple and equally a minister of God's grace. Leadership in the congregation is designed "to equip the saints for the work of ministry" (Eph. 4:12). The ministry does not belong to the pastor but to Christ, and the professional minister is to teach others to be ministers as well, and to offer care to others. The pastor does have a particular set of skills and vocation, but is of equal status. All the members of the church have a vocation, not just the pastor.
- The church is concerned for the local community. The pastor is a public theologian; that is, the particular nature of the gospel is to work for the well-being of all others, the whole people of God, which includes all humankind and not only those who affiliate with a church. The pastor and other disciples are called to exhibit justice and compassion. The community in which the church is located has a particular claim on the mission of the church and its leadership. The proximity of the town, city, or countryside to the church calls for a special degree of attention to the well-being of the citizens there.
- The mission and leadership of the church are collaborative. It shares this mission with all the churches of Christ and especially with those in close proximity, and throughout the world. It is a visible symbol of faithful living committed to the welfare of fellow disciples and those who live nearby, and also those who share the global *communion* of Christians. Furthermore, it recognizes that so-called secular agencies are often used by God to carry out God's mission of care for all. The quality of life in a church's location is enriched by the justice standards of Christian churches.

PRACTICING CARE

An essential activity is thinking about the particular features of the context of the church interconnected with the benchmarks of Christian theology of leadership. But, important as context and theology are, unless they are lived out and experienced by the leadership (pastor included) and the community, they will be counted as "clanging cymbals." It is the way of life that people see and experience that builds discipleship and community.

This chapter suggests that one integrating motif that pulls together a lot of these perspectives into their implications for ministry is that of building community. The pastor is the leader in building community. This model will assist the pastor practically in knowing how to begin and proceed. The identification of "building community," as an appropriate shorthand for the role of the town and country pastors, builds on Chapter 3, and becomes more concrete in how to go about that.

Jackson Carroll speaks of the pastor as the builder or "producer of corporate culture" in the church.[10] This thought overlaps ours of "building community." Though it may take a pastor some time to be accepted into the community, even at the outset of his ministry the congregation may anticipate that the pastor will meet certain expectations: to preach well, to know scripture, to act with integrity, to keep confidences, to be compassionate, and so forth. As the pastor fulfills these expectations, he is more accepted into the community. As the pastor gains the respect of the congregation and community, he will find himself taken more seriously in shaping decisions that build community and shape the corporate culture of the congregation. The laity have a range of understandings of what community entails, which will be shaped by the pastor's vision and skill, but they might find it difficult or presumptuous to articulate those features themselves. Nevertheless, the pastor has the capacity to enlist the hopes and dreams of the laity in building community into the most God-bearing culture possible. He will do this by encouraging and networking and keeping a Christ-like vision before himself and the congregation.

As we describe what is entailed in building community, let us offer some general perspectives before turning to more practical suggestions for building community.

GENERAL PERSPECTIVES

1. It may seem strange to begin this section on community by speaking of differentiation, but being an effective leader (and this is especially true in the task of building community) involves the ability to differentiate oneself from others' struggles while at the same time

maintaining connection with them. Different degrees of each of these two qualities are called for in different situations. Being an effective rural leader may entail a greater degree of "joining one's own congregation."[11] At the same time, being able to take care of oneself, especially spiritually, and knowing one's limits, is essential to building community among other people, without becoming overwhelmed or overfunctioning oneself.[12]

Caring for one's own spiritual life and turning the results over to God is essential.

On the other hand, boundaries enrich one's abilities to do pastoral care and to perform the public role of the pastor. In this way, Pastor Ray could maintain contact with and care for others as well; this might prove especially useful in speaking to both factions in the conflict over the hog feedlot and in seeking a creative alternative.

As a pastor and the official leader of the congregation, Pastor Ray has the power to convene forums, to gather people together to talk, to invite sharing. These are significant events for those who may feel as though they are the only ones experiencing a potential threat. Furthermore, such forums might produce some avenues to ameliorate concerns. Gathering people together to discuss community issues is itself an event that would begin to shape the corporate culture of a congregation.[13] Parenthetically, Pastor Ray needed to realize that becoming part of the community would take a while. On the one hand, he has the authority as pastor to be intimately involved in intense situations in people's lives; on the other hand, he would need to maintain autonomy as a pastor, even a highly respected pastor, with all but a few trusted friends in the congregation.

Being alert to his own assets and the way that he had been called to use those assets in concert with others in the body of Christ led to the insight that Pastor Ray couldn't "fix" the church. He would need to learn to like the church, to enjoy being there, to encourage members of the church. He could fan the sparks that existed and he could join his assets to those of the laity in being the most very caring congregation possible. He could assist the Holy Spirit in God's work.

2. Second, as Pastor Ray began to interact more and more with members of the congregation, he realized that there were several leaders in the church who were interested in doing mission. There were other assets in this church. There were caregivers, he included, who were called to minister to the hurt, the lonely, the poor, the friendless, and the unheard. He realized as well that there might well be fairly affluent people in the congregation who also needed a chance to share their feelings and who might be empowered to act.

3. He also began to see beyond the walls of the church to those who had connections in the community, who could in fact introduce him to the associations and institutions of the town. Third, then, leadership in a rural community or congregation with few resources may necessitate more cooperation with social agencies, the school district, and other helping agencies (such as hospitals, police departments, and local businesses) to build up the community. The word "parish" connotes the responsibility that a church has to maintain or improve the quality of life in one's neighborhood. This is not the same thing as increasing the income of the congregants, but it might connote improving the quality of life in other ways (family relationships, opening childcare centers, after-school activities). Rather than being a liability, the necessity of such partnering may open up many ways that the church does caring leadership. Pastor Ray can see that such cooperation probably would strengthen his town and country congregations. His awakening to the fact that part of pastoral leadership had to do with partnering with those inside and outside the church to build community was encouraging to him. Also, it just might be that such community knowledge would be of assistance in convening a communitywide group to discuss the feedlot issue.

There were resources in the congregation that he had not discovered, resources in the community at large, and resources at the church regional governing body level. There were a myriad of books, DVDs, and websites that provided perspective on the sorts of issues that pastors face. He had access to a broad range of people and institutions that could be of help.

4. Rural communities have numerous similarities with other communities around the world that have few resources. We in the U.S. can learn from them. One of those is the theology that comes to us from countries of the South, which can then be modified and translated into our own vernacular. Theologically, we could learn from the theology of Nestor Miguez, a professor at ISEDET, a seminary in Buenos Aires. Miguez asserts that Christians can make a contribution to the transformation that is needed in our radically nonegalitarian world. One thing that is vital is an "alternative subjectivity." In the following quotation, listen for the way it might serve as a foundation for God's community:

> Our first message is this: it is possible to be human in a different way than that which is proposed by the greed, ambition, and selfishness of individual consumerism. But that requires not only a personal will to change but the construction of an alternative subjectivity, understanding subjectivity as not only what is in my mind, but also

the presence of the other inside me, of what I am in others, and what others are in me. When we say that "I live in Christ," and that "Christ lives in me," we are recognizing that our self is not complete by itself, but can only be a full self by the presence of the other, the transcendent Other, but also the other human being, for Christ is the human being, the needed neighbor.[14]

Specific ways of building community. There are some specific ways of building community that have been tested in rural congregations and communities and that might be of use in your situation. Pastor Ray might find in consultation with other pastors that some combination of these would be energizing.

> 1. One is the process of personally interviewing the members of the congregation either singly or with another church leader. This will allow the pastor and lay leader to become better acquainted with the interests, skills, hopes, and dreams of the church disciples. Combined with this level of caregiving might be a spiritual gifts inventory (perhaps done individually, in conversation, or at a churchwide meeting). A pastoral team might also ask about the meaning of the Christian faith and also of the church to the people visited. Such questions as "What's preventing or enabling your being able to receive the new life in Christ?" "What is the state of our soul?" is a question that will press toward reflection on the members' faith. This might need to be signaled ahead of the visit so that the person is able to think about it. Furthermore, specific ministries could be surfaced (a filmmaker's offering to share his/her craft with youth) or for groups with similar mission activities to network.
> 2. Another process is the small spiritual formation or Bible study group in which the congregational members can get to know each other better and begin to develop stronger faith relationships with each other. They might also develop friendships at deeper levels than is the social norm. The pastor or lay leader might want to convene the facilitators of such groups and train them in basic small-group skills, and then check back with the leaders every month or two. The leadership of those groups might change as well. It has been our experience that such groups come to care for each other and also serve to network the pastor or other lay leaders in. The pastor might find that her spiritual growth is promoted by participating in such a group.
> 3. Third, moving toward engaging the congregation in caring leadership with the wider community is the next step. One activity that has been very helpful in developing community is the use of an

asset-mapping exercise, which is both fun and instructive. It can be devised in such a way that the members' associations, skills, spiritual gifts, and activities in the community can be seen as part of the church's resources and scope.[15] In this way, the wider community comes to be seen more clearly as part of the congregation, and also the church begins to think of the community as its parish, where the quality of life there is part of the mission of the church. Finally, the sort of activities suggested in a Discovering Hope process can be used to help the church determine which mission and discipleship activities are both feasible for this congregation and also most likely to promote future growth.

Investing one's energy for mission in community actions can be spiritually fulfilling as well. There are any number of community activities in which a pastor can enjoy participating as an individual, which also permit his to get to know other people in the community. Not neglecting either the internal life of the congregation or the external life of the community is a continual tension that, if maintained, can increase the social capital of the parish. Partnering with other churches, agencies, and community development organizations can result in a sense of communal involvement and connectedness. Here the pastor can deploy his skills and abilities (perhaps with one or two other members) and get involved in a caring ministry. He, after all, is a disciple who needs to engage in mission himself. Besides, this sort of modeling (or witnessing) may attract others and/or result in some friendships. Finally, the sort of leadership that elicits discipleship in rural congregations is one of collaborative accompaniment—the pastor is one of the ministers with a special role, that of encouraging others to bring their best gifts to the congregation and communities. His or her caring leadership brings care to others and equips others to care.

Notes

1. Roy Oswald and Arlin Rothauge have made the theory that size of congregation shapes many other dynamics. See Arlin J. Rothauge, *Sizing Up a Congregation for New Member Ministry*, the Episcopal Church Center, 815 Second Avenue, New York 10017; and Roy Oswald, "How to Minister Effectively in Family, Pastoral, Program, or Corporate Size Churches" (Special Papers and Research Reports, Alban Institute, 1993).

2. For the concept of "going to the balcony," see Ronald A. Heifetz, Abraham Grashow, and Mark Linsky, *The Practice of Adaptive Leadership: Tools and Tactics for Changing Your Organization and the World* (Boston: Harvard Business School, 2009), 7–8.

3. Ibid., 47–48, passim.

4. The "thick web of relationships" is from James Hopewell, *Congregation: Stories and Structures* (Philadelphia: Fortress Press, 1987). Other books helpful in doing a diagnosis of the

rural context include James R. Nieman, *Knowing the Context: Frames, Tools, and Signs forPreaching* (Minneapolis: Fortress Press, 2008); Nancy Ammerman, *Studying Congregations: A New Handbook* (Nashville: Abingdon, 1998); and Jackson Carroll, *God's Potters: Pastoral Leadership and the Shaping of Congregations* (Grand Rapids: Eerdmans, 2006).

5. Consider anecdotally the experiences of Ronald Lischer, *Open Secrets: A Memoir of Faith and Discovery* (New York: Broadway Books, 2002), and Lenora T. Tisdale, *Preaching as Local Theology and Folklore* (Minneapolis: Augsburg Fortress, 1997).

6. David Poling-Goldenne, L. Shannon Jung, Evangelical Lutheran Church in America, and Wartburg Theological Seminary, *Discovering Hope: Building Vitality in Rural Congregations* (Minneapolis: Augsburg Fortress, 2001).

7. Cornelia B. Flora and Jan L. Flora, *Rural Communities: Legacy and Change* (Boulder, CO: Westview, 2012); Hopewell, *Congregation*; and Carroll, *God's Potters*.

8. This position reflects our collective view of the way that prophetic ministry is tied into healing and transformative ministry. While it is widely shared, one of the best statements of it can be found in a chapter constructed by Gary Farley, in the collaborative volume edited by Jung et al., *Rural Ministry: The Shape of the Renewal to Come* (Nashville: Abingdon, 1998), 57.

9. See Harlene Anderson and Diane Gerhart, *Collaborative Therapy: Relationships and Conversations That Make a Difference* (New York: Routledge, 2007); Michael White, *Maps of NarrativePractice* (New York: W. W. Norton, 2007); and Joretta Marshall, "Collaborative Generativity: The What, Who, and How of Supervision in a Modern/Postmodern Context," in *Reflective Practice: Formationand Supervision in Ministry* (2011): 151–65.

10. Jackson Carroll, *God's Potters: Pastoral Leadership and the Shaping of Congregations* (Grand Rapids, MI: Eerdmans, 2006).

11. R. Paul Stevens and Phil Collins, *The Equipping Pastor: A Systems Approach toCongregational Leadership* (Washington, DC: Alban Institute, 1992).

12. E. Friedman, *Generation to Generation: Family Process in Church and Synagogue* (New York: Guilford Press, 2011); R.D. Sisk, *The Competent Pastor: Skills and Self-Knowledge for Serving Well* (Herndon, VA: Alban Institute, 2005); J. Fred Lehr, *Clergy Burnout:Recovering from the 70-Hour Workweek* (Minneapolis: Fortress Press, 2005); and Anne Marie Nuechterlein, *The Dynamics of Exemplary Church Pastors*, a study done for the Lutheran Brotherhood Foundation, 1992, unpublished.

13. Gary Gunderson, *Deeply Woven Roots: Improving the Quality of Life in Your Community* (Minneapolis: Fortress Press, 1997).

14. N. O. Miguez, "Doing Theology in a Non-Revolutionary Situation," Cleaver Lecture, Saint Paul School of Theology, Kansas City, MO. For a similar point of view, see also the thought of Emmanuel Levinas, especially as interpreted by Corey Beals: *Levinas and the Wisdom of Love: The Question of Invisibility* (Waco, TX: Baylor University Press, 2007), especially chapters 3 and 4.

15. Luther Snow, *The Powerof Asset Mapping: How Your Congregation Can Act on Its Gifts* (Herndon, VA: Alban Institute, 2004).

4

Care Responding to Diversity

St. Luke's was one of the older, established churches in Plainsville. It had more resources than most of the ten churches in town and had long been a significant part of the social landscape of this small town. Its members served on the school board and city council. It provided meeting space for civic organizations and town meetings. In recent years, many of its members worked tirelessly to try to bring new growth to the town since its population and businesses had slowly diminished. Now, after years of decline, Plainsville is experiencing rapid growth brought about in conjunction with the meatpacking plant that opened outside town a year before. The people of Plainsville had hoped and prayed for something to revitalize their town, but they were not prepared for all the changes that were coming with that revitalization. The town was growing but looks very different from the town the longtime residents knew, a predominantly Euro-American middle-class community. With the new plant came scores of new workers who were primarily low-wage-earning Spanish-speaking Latino/as. The demand for new housing for the workers and the need for more desks for their children in the school were just some of the new demands that came with growth. The people of St. Luke's realized they didn't know what they had been praying for. How should the church respond to these new realities? That was the question before the church council at St. Luke's.

The people of St. Luke's have a history of outreach and concern for all the people of the community. They understand care for the poor and the stranger as central to the gospel message. It isn't that they don't want to be hospitable to their new neighbors or that they are unconcerned about their well-being, they are just unclear and at odds with each other about how to express that hospitality and care.

When the agenda turns to membership growth, Jan, one of the officers of the church who works in the public elementary school, says "It's high time we began to reach out more vigorously to the Mexicans who work for U.S. Beef. We invited their children to Vacation Bible School last summer and some of them came. They use our *clothes closet and our food bank, but hardly any of them have come to church on Sunday. I think we need to try to figure out how to be more welcoming and really invite them to join us." Jan sees the needs of the children every day at the school, and she also sees that many of their parents are hard-working and concerned like other parents in their town. She does what she can but feels frustrated by the slowness of the town to respond and the lack of social services for these new families.*

Chris, owner of the hardware business in town, replies: "I don't think they want to come to our church. We are here; we post our worship times. Not one of those kids who came to our Vacation Bible School brought their parents to church. And if a lot of them did come to church, would we have to do everything in Spanish? They seem content to be mostly with other Hispanics. I don't think we have to do more than we've done. We have a good church—if they want to join us they can, but I really think they would rather just go to their own churches." Chris finds it really difficult to appreciate the new growth in town. He thinks about how hard he struggles to keep his hardware business open even as his income keeps slipping. Now things are busy, but not with the kind of businesses that he thinks make the town a good place to live. He has always paid his employees well and they work hard, but he isn't sure the new folks hold the same values.

The situation looks a little different to Manuel and Emilia Gonzalez, who have recently arrived in town. They came because Manuel's brother had found a job here and told them that his boss said that since Manuel is a good worker they would also hire his brother. Manuel has a steady job at the packing plant but the wages are low and there are no benefits. Emilia works part time for a cleaning business. She tries to work around Manuel's shift so that he can be home in the afternoon with the kids, but her mother also lives with them to help out. At first they moved in with Manuel's brother and his family, but now they are renting a mobile home. Manuel and Emilia speak little English but want their children to have a better life, to learn English, go to college, and get good jobs. The children are Americans; they were born in the United States.

They were glad to get out of the big city and out to a smaller town where there are not so many gangs or as much violence. But they sometimes wonder if they made the right decision. The work is steady but the services that were available in the city are hard to access in Plainsville, and most of the Anglos there speak no Spanish at all. Manuel's work is hard, and so many of the men get hurt. Their children struggle to find their way in the school and to make friends. Few accommodations have been thought out by the school board in terms of language and increased desk-space. Other students regard their dress and their language and their customs with suspicion. Manuel and Emilia depend on their children to interpret for them, but they tend to stick close to other Latino/as and slowly they are becoming a community of their own. Some Latino families go to the Catholic church in town; others started their own small Pentecostal church.

When the Gonzalezes saw the notices for Vacation Bible School at St. Luke's, they thought it might be a good way to see if their children liked it there. They really want to go to a church that has both Anglos and Latino/as because they thought it would be better for the children. There were just a couple of other Latino families there. The children seemed to have a good time, but Manuel and Emilia felt out of place and the worship service was very different than their evangelico[1] *church at home had been. Emilia's mother and Manuel felt especially uncomfortable even though Emilia was willing to try it for the children's sake. So they have not been back to visit St. Luke's.*

*****

DIVERSITY IN RURAL AMERICA

In addition to being shaped by place, engaging community and including leadership, healing, and transformative care in congregations and communities means responding to multiple diversities such as those represented in the scenario above. Rural communities are not the first place that comes to mind for most people when diversity is mentioned, but it is an increasing reality for rural life. Rural United States is as diverse as the rest of the country. Though many people in rural communities have built their sense of community on homogeneity within their town, rural places themselves are becoming locally more diverse as well. In other words, the sense of being connected to, dependent on, and responsible for one another has assumed likeness—like-minded, like-looking, and like-backgrounded. The diversity of town and country life has become much more complex than most stereotypes of small-town USA lead us to believe. Sometimes diversity comes in the form of newcomers, perhaps immigrants coming to work in the meatpacking plant, as it did for the people of Plainsville, but it may also mean city people who move to the country for its quiet natural beauty, or the pastor who comes to serve for only a limited amount of time. These kinds of diversities often result in a town that is in transition, because of a changing economic base, and this change brings a sense of possibility for some but a sense of loss and disorientation for others. The struggles of small towns over issues of community and diversity, identity and change, hold particular wisdom and challenge for pastoral care.

Often people in small towns, as in other places, behave as though their community is threatened by, rather than enriched by, persons who are different from the majority. Chapter 3 explored the meaning of community for small places, and how for many people in the USA "rural" stands as a symbol for tradition and community itself. This chapter looks at the question of community in the face of diversity. To what extent is the close and supportive community of small towns based on an assumption of homogeneity that obscures the diversity actually present in the town? How does this obfuscation function in the face of changing populations and social conditions? Small towns can be places of ostracization and exclusion, unwelcoming to those who do not fit the majority norms; but they are also sometimes places where diverse peoples come together to form community.

Rural places struggle with maintaining tradition and identity while responding to new realities. The church can learn from these struggles to understand healing and transformative care as embracing diversity in ways that maintain integrity and identity yet see these as dynamic and changing. The opening scenario in this chapter presents one kind of change facing many rural areas, that of an increasing Latino/a and immigrant population. This chapter looks at ways that the rural United States is racially, ethnically, religiously, and attitudinally diverse. Small towns are often divided within themselves and from each other. It also explores an approach to intercultural care that can lead to more inclusive and integral community, one that celebrates the whole people of God, and faithful Christian discipleship.

RACIAL AND ETHNIC DIVERSITY

The situation in Plainsville is happening in various ways across the rural United States. The largest percentage increases in immigrant populations are in rural areas, and Latina/os are the fastest-growing immigrant group.[2] All signs point toward rural America becoming increasingly diverse in the future. While it appears that emigration has slowed recently, the growth rate of Latino/as in the U.S. has not. Kenneth Johnson and Daniel Lichter, rural demographers with the Carsey Institute, report that natural increase, the birth of children to Hispanic parents, is the leading factor in the growth of Hispanic/Latino/a rural population.[3] They state that "[c]urrent trends will remake the social and cultural fabric of communities for decades to come. They raise new concerns about ethnic conflict, flagging immigrant incorporation, and the burdens on local taxpayers (e.g., bilingual education, property taxes, health care, and social services)."[4] Statistics back this assessment up: the Hispanic population grew by 60.6 percent during the 1990s, while the overall U.S. growth was only 13 percent. That growth has accelerated since 2000, and by 2010 had already grown by 46 percent. Hispanics in 2010 constitute 16.3 percent of the U.S.

population and 9.3 percent of rural and small-town populations.[5] The increase in the proportion of Hispanic immigrants in rural locations from greater birth rates than non-Hispanic whites suggests that the population increase of Hispanics will continue despite a slowing of immigration trends. Furthermore, rural counties that have been declining due to an aging population and high death rates will experience a different demographic face to their communities. Sociologists William Kandel, Randy Capps, Heather Koball, and Everett Henderson report that "[r]apid Latino population growth in new rural destinations across the United States is occurring against a backdrop of an aging, native population. Regardless of current political debates, rural communities will increasingly rely upon the productivity, economic well being, health, and civic participation of settled Latino workers and their children in the coming decades. Consequently, integration of these newest residents is critical to the future of many rural communities."[6]

Churches like St. Luke's that are concerned about ministering to and with the people in their locales will be wise to consider the implications of these trends. The possibility of conflict emerging out of the threat to long-term residents and their perceived loss of community is a major factor. It will influence the shape of rural church. How the churches and communities respond will make a lot of difference as to which ones can continue to offer a high quality of life.

In one wide-ranging study of rural towns experiencing rising Latina/o population influx in Indiana, Michigan, Nebraska, and Ohio, researchers Ann V. Millard and Jorge Chapa found that while they may enjoy each other's foods (thus the title of their book, *Apple Pie and Enchiladas*) Anglos and Latina/os are rarely living in an integrated community; instead they live in segregated social networks.[7] They are separated by language, immigration policy, and economic status. Few Anglos understand what it means to work in food-processing plants or how the workers are exploited by their employers. Workers are paid low wages, given no benefits, and allowed only very short breaks in physically demanding and often dangerous jobs. Employers assume that government services will provide what they do not. The larger community then derides the workers for depending on government services.[8] Anglos in the Millard and Chapa study were generally disapproving of, suspicious of, or hostile to Latino/a newcomers, holding on to a stereotype "that Latinos arrive destitute and have come simply to live on welfare benefits."[9] There is little understanding among Anglos of the circumstances under which Latino/as live. Latina/os feel the derision and lack of understanding and the social power of the

Anglo long-time residents; thus they tend to socialize with each other, further reinforcing some of the stereotypes Anglos hold.

Although religion was not the focus of their research, Millard and Chapa found that churches could be a resource for transforming this situation of exploitation and segregation. As a central social institution in rural communities and in Latino/a life, churches can "play the crucial role of mediating between marginalized groups and institutions for the dominant society."[10] As demonstrated in the Gonzalez family, Latino/a families do not always agree on where to go to church; some want traditional Spanish-speaking worship and others want mixed congregations where they can assimilate more into local culture. In both cases, however, worship seems to be a place where Latino/as hope to maintain connection to their heritage, meaning that worship may need to include more movement, a range of contemporary music, more time for *testimonios*,[11] and acknowledgment of days like Cinco de Mayo or the feast of la Virgen de Guadalupe. Churches in Plainsville can be crucial to establishing a healthy stable new future for their town if they are willing to engage in expanding their traditions. St. Luke's church council is wrestling with what it means to live in the midst of rapid change into a more ethnically diverse community. Because the United States is so divided on issues of immigration and ethnic difference, emotions run high. Jan, Chris, and others of the church have personal investment and identities embedded in this town. They may be tempted to see the new people as primarily a means to their town's survival, or a way to increase membership and the survival of the church, without really wanting to engage the cultural differences or paternalism that often characterizes interactions between white persons and others. People like Jan may have to face the possibility that the new Latina/o people in town do not want to worship at St. Luke's for a variety of reasons, and people like Chris may need to find the inner courage to face fears and loss if they want to maintain the strong community they have had in the past and their desire for the future. It will be important to identify the social forces that are impacting their lives and the history of this place. The Gonzalezes and the new immigrant families will be more aware of the social and cultural forces that separate them from the Anglo longer-term residents of the town, but they will also experience feelings of loss, anxiety, and confusion as they seek a way to make this town their new home. The rapid change that is facing this town means that everyone is experiencing the stress of locating themselves in a new place. Both groups need pastors and other religious leaders to guide them in ways that honor their inner discomforts and move them toward healing and transformative care for one another.

Racial and ethnic diversity is not only about the recent increase in Latina/o migration, immigration, or birth rate. Like many Euro-Americans, the white people of St. Luke's may forget that at one time their families were also new to this land. Before European Americans, Latin Americans, or African Americans diversified the racial and ethnic landscape of what is now the USA, the land was inhabited by indigenous peoples. Native Americans were living and working here until they were forceably removed to serve the colonial interests of European nations. Europeans did not "discover" the Americas; there were people here long before they arrived.[12] It is important to remember also that God did not arrive with the frontier settlers and Christian missionaries—God was already here.

The history of the United States' indigenous peoples is a story that rural congregations cannot afford to forget. The mid-nineteenth century saw a brutal movement to "civilize" Native Americans by taking their land, changing their names, forcing their children to attend English-speaking Christian boarding schools, massacring their people, and eradicating their culture. Eventual treaties with the federal government "reserved" land for the sovereign use of American Indians but it did not begin to represent what had been taken from them. American indigenous peoples were, and still are, treated as outsiders, as foreigners in their own land.

Indian reservations remain under the sovereign authority of many tribal governments. There are 310 Indian reservations in the U.S, and about one-third of all Native Americans live on those reservations, which make up about 2 percent of all U.S. land.[13] About 2 percent of the non-metro population is Native American, about two-thirds of whom live in the non-metro counties of seven states (Oklahoma, Arizona, New Mexico, Arkansas, North Carolina, South Dakota, and Montana).[14] The rural Native American regions of the Dakotas, Oklahoma, New Mexico, and Montana hold the most persistent poverty in the United States. Health issues—diabetes, tuberculosis, pneumonia, gastrointestinal disorders, and such—have more frequent rates of occurrence among rural Native Americans. Distance from major health facilities probably exacerbates these illnesses. Lower educational attainment among children and social problems like alcohol abuse and child neglect are also associated with severely crowded housing conditions. In almost every measure of disadvantage, Native Americans are the poorest of the poor.

Over time, the tribal cultures of American Indians have been compromised and lost under the pressures of the immigrant masses.[15] Efforts are being made to retrieve and preserve Native American cultural perspectives of the communal good and value of spatiality, in contrast to western European individualism and focus on temporality. Transgenerational grief and trauma, the complexities of identity and relationship to the Christian church of Native American peoples bring particular challenges to rural congregations who seek to practice healing. Rural communities' attachment to land may be a starting place for reconciliation between Native Americans and Euro-American rural peoples, which is not to say that they have the same understanding of the land but that it might be a beginning.

There are two significant movements that have been reshaping life for Native Americans: one is the tribal casino business that has been thriving in the past twenty years. It is difficult to say whether gaming sources of revenue can help alleviate health, housing, and education issues. It does appear that during the first decade of the twenty-first century there has been some progress in addressing housing, restorative justice, natural resources, and law endorsement.[16] Gaming also brings another layer of complexity to the relationship between Native Americans and Christian congregations, who may see gambling as a moral problem while some Native Americans see it as destructive of cultural norms. The second movement is the Tribal College Movement, which offers residential programs and seeks to maintain traditional languages and cultures while also offering sustainable skills.[17] Native Americans are significantly present in rural areas, and they continue to experience racism and discrimination in this country. Rural congregations are especially well placed to work in solidarity with Native Americans.

It might be interesting for the people of St. Luke's to engage in a storytelling of their own immigrant history and the early relationships with the American Indians. This storytelling should include the affirmations and strengths of this history but also the struggles and less pleasant aspects. These ancestral stories, and the values they reveal, can shape their experience of current immigrant realities in Plainsville. A pastoral caregiver will want to make sure that every voice is heard and that the whole story comes to the surface, including the parts that are often excluded because they are embarrassing or painful. The multiple and ambiguous truths in the personal stories will be necessary for healthy transformation in the community.

Much of the story of the United States' race relations is tied to the painful history of enslaving Africans. Almost every rural county in the USA has some African American families living within it, and in the South some rural counties are almost entirely African American. While most African Americans find their U.S. roots in the rural South, many left for the urban areas of the North in the "great migration" of the early 1900s. A second migration took place in the 1970s.[18] There are few African American farmers left, but there are rural areas in which rural African Americans continue to live, with a high concentration in the southeastern U.S. and parts of Texas, often referred to as the "Black Belt." There are many rural counties along the Mississippi Delta that are more than 50 percent African American.[19] These counties remain relatively stable in population, but little more than one-half of working-age people had jobs in 2000, and in 2004, 29 percent of residents were living in poverty.[20] The Black Belt holds almost half of all African Americans and more than a third of the nation's poor.[21]

African American presence in rural regions cannot be understood apart from its roots in slavery and a long history of racism in the United States. Prior to the 1900s, 90 percent of all African Americans lived in the rural South, but they were farming land that did not belong to them.[22] Even after "emancipation," under the sharecropping system, black farmers farmed the land for a share of the profits but increasingly grew in debt to white owners. Land ownership in the rural South did not come easily for African Americans and often required finding a white person who was willing to work as an agent on their behalf to hide the fact that it was a black person who was actually buying the land.[23] The early plantation system of inequality in the rural South may no longer exist per se, but inequality based on racial difference remains strong. African Americans still suffer from the effects of limited access to education, health care, property ownership, and employment.[24]

bell hooks describes the ambivalence that African Americans might hold toward their roots in the agrarian South, which holds both the historical memory of slavery but, hooks argues, also holds the hills that gave rise to an "oppositional consciousness."[25] In general, the history of the black farmer has been forgotten and the African American farmers of the present are invisible. As hooks says, people should remember, "For they are the ancestors who gave to black folk from slavery on into reconstruction an oppositional consciousness, ways to think about life that could enable one to have positive self-esteem even in the midst of harsh and brutal circumstances. Their legacy of self-determination and hard work was a living challenge to the racist stereotype that claimed blacks were lazy and unwilling to work independently without white supervision."[26] The African American church arose in this setting, in many ways turning the Christianity of white folks into a liberating message for African Americans.[27] In the hills and fields of the rural South, black people gathered to sing, pray, and engage in rituals of resistance to the messages of white supremacy that shaped their living situations and threatened their inner core. Rural communities and congregations cannot escape the history and current realities that racial and ethnic diversity hold in the United States.

They are especially suited to bringing to the forefront certain aspects of the present situation. Pastoral caregivers in rural ministry must take into account the ancestral and sociopolitical history of African Americans as it continues to influence people's sense of entitlement and value, or lack thereof. The deconstruction of white privilege and liberation from racial oppression is an essential ingredient of care in all places, including rural, though the nature of responding to diversity should take into account the local context.

SUBURBAN/URBAN NEWCOMERS

In addition to racial and ethnic diversity, small towns and rural places may experience the diversity of ideas and worldviews brought in by newcomers through suburban sprawl or retiree migration. As metropolitan areas continue to grow, the suburban edge moves further out and in the process may encompass places that were previously more autonomous communities. Families move to the growing suburbs because of perceived increased safety for children, improved education, access to parks and recreation, and access to a range of goods and services. They may move away from the urban core, which they perceive as the site of all that is not safe, high quality, or desirable. While these newcomers may be model citizens, one cannot ignore the possibility that this movement may also involve "white flight" away from nonwhite communities, supported by a complex system of racism in the U.S. While in earlier times, people of these towns lived, worked, played, and worshiped in town, these newcomers often live in town but may work, worship, and use the services of the city.

In addition to metropolitan sprawl, rural areas are experiencing an influx of retirees, whose incomes are not tied to a specific place and may either be seeking the scenic amenity-rich areas like the Rocky Mountains or the quieter and less-expensive small-town life. The Economic Research Service of the USDA reports: "The analysis finds a significant increase in the propensity to migrate to non-metro counties as people reach their fifties and sixties and projects a shift in migration among boomers towards more isolated settings, especially those with high natural and urban amenities and lower housing costs. If baby boomers follow past migration patterns, the non-metro population age 55–75 will increase by 30 percent between now and 2020."[28] More remote counties, according to the report, will see the most dramatic increases.

Some small towns immediately resent the "takeover" of "their" town by these newcomers, but many small towns see these migrations as an answer to their prayers for economic survival and future thriving. Often neither the old-timers nor newcomers are prepared for the effects of the different worldviews that come with them. Indeed, it is likely that most of the boomers who are moving to rural and small-town areas in search of amenities and a slower pace are Anglos. These are likely people who look the same as members of traditional Euro-American churches. However, they may have a quite different outlook on life—one that is more "cosmopolitan" and contrasts with an "agrarian" mindset. In some ways, these migrants may be as strange to the old-timers as those who bring a different ethnic ancestry.

The "agrarian" worldview that often characterizes small towns and rural areas tends to be more relational than functional. As described in Chapter 2, place shapes people's identities in individual and communal ways. An agrarian paradigm emphasizes place, tight-knit social networks, cooperation, loyalty, and egalitarianism. A cosmopolitan worldview emphasizes individual privacy, functional roles, competition, efficiency, and material wealth over social networks. Agrarian norms emphasize looking for the common good, which downplays difference, while cosmopolitan norms emphasize individual freedom and potential. Agrarian-based churches may seek out local sources of wisdom and work while cosmopolitan churches engage specialists and professionals, programmatic and age-based activities.[29] One study of the effects of suburbanization found that long-time residents and newcomers clashed over the direction for the town's schools. Long-time residents saw the school much like a community center for children and youth. They used informal methods of governance through relationships with parents and school boards. Newcomers accused them of emphasizing athletics over academics; they wanted a more formal, "professional" approach to school management.[30] They had very different understandings of what constitutes good schools, and they may bring similar competing views of what constitutes vital church.

Anthropologist Sonya Salamon studied the dynamic of newcomers and suburbanization in six small towns in southern Illinois.[31] Salamon wanted to understand more about what happens to the sense of community when newcomers arrive. Based on comparisons in four dimensions—use of space, interconnectedness, access to social resources, and relationship to the youth—Salamon found that in the context of rapid change, small towns can incorporate newcomers and maintain a sense of community when they already had diversified economies, the proportion of newcomers is low, the newcomers have similar economic status, and expectations are realistic. Only two of the towns managed to thrive and maintain their agrarian ideals and this was done through incorporation, not acceptance and accommodation.[32] The others were to varying degrees engulfed by the "rural growth machine," as Salamon calls it, into post-agrarian suburban towns. In most cases the long-term residents met the newcomers with resistance and though they may originally have been hopeful that new residents and new workers would help the town survive, they were not ready to accept the changes in culture and community identity that would be required. Those towns that were more receptive to newcomers tended to strengthen their communities.

Sometimes nonmetropolitan and metropolitan newcomers experience differences in sociopolitical viewpoints, but this also may be linked to false generalizations both groups have about the other. The fact that in general rural regions are known to be more conservative may obscure the diversity of views within small towns, the regionality of those views, and the relationship to factors other than geographic location. A Carsey Institute study found that there is significant difference in the level of social conservatism between Southern, Midwestern, Western, and Eastern nonmetro areas, with the Southern regions being the most conservative based on religious involvement, and views on abortion and same-sex relations.[33] One interesting result of this study, however, is that there is little difference between metro and non-metro attitudes toward abortion and same-sex relations when religious involvement is taken into account. In other words, this conservatism appears to be more of a function of religion than geography. Rural areas tend to be more religious. In addition, the study suggests that views of same-sex relations may be based on age more than geography, with younger persons taking a more accepting attitude than older persons. Rural populations tend to be older. Each of these findings also show significant difference based on region, with Southern regions tending to be more conservative, followed by the Midwest, with the West and Northeast often shifting between the third and fourth positions.

RELIGIOUS DIVERSITY

In contrast to metropolitan areas, in most small towns there is no more than one church in a particular denomination, but remarkably there may be several small churches representing several denominations. In rural communities, joining with other churches almost always means working across denominational lines, which seems to be easier for mainline Protestant churches, such as United Methodist, Presbyterian, UCC, Disciples of Christ, or the Evangelical Lutheran Church of America, but harder when the other church holds a quite different belief system. For instance, when the Christian community wants to join together for worship but one of the churches does not recognize the baptism of the others; or when one will not include the other in Holy Communion; or when one church does not believe in the ordination of women or gays and lesbians and therefore will not support the leadership of another church's pastor; it is more difficult to collaborate with each other across denominational lines. Pragmatic immediacy, rather than theological commitment, is often the motivating force behind ecumenical alliances in rural places, but small-town pastors expect to engage the challenge and gift of ecumenical ministry in ways that many metropolitan pastors never have to. The practice of ecumenical ministry can lead to insights into what it means to be community as the body of Christ, but it also requires careful examination of what it means to live in loving community when even our most deeply held values are challenged by the other.

Ecumenical alliances are common in rural areas, at least across mainline Protestant congregations, but religious diversity presents its own kind of challenge in small towns. Increasingly, small towns include Jewish, Muslim, or other religious groups. As the United States becomes more religiously plural so do small towns; as rural places rapidly increase in racial and ethnic diversity they also increase in religious diversity. A group of Hasidic Jews moved to Postville, Iowa, and opened a kosher meat-processing plant, which brought not only a jump in religious diversity but also an increase in Latina/o populations who came to work in the plant. African immigrants may also bring the religious practices of the Muslim faith, which can include stopping for prayer in the middle of a workday, such as happened in Emporia, Kansas. Sociologists Dianna Shandy and Katherine Fennelly studied two groups of African refugees who moved into a small Minnesota town looking for jobs and the safe quiet pace of rural life, many of the same reasons that anyone moves into a rural area.[34] They found religion to be a major factor in how the two groups integrated into life of the community. The African Christians found it much easier to make connections than did African Muslims, who generally felt more excluded in a place where churches are central to civic life.

Religious tensions in these small Midwestern towns have been the subject of media and academic reports, which sometimes present rural people as less tolerant or open-minded than those in large cities; however, the very nature of being fewer in number requires an intensity of experience between persons that may certainly bring conflict but can also be a strong impetus for finding ways to be loving community in the midst of, even celebrating, difference. Pastors in rural churches are called to care for those within congregations as well as for the community as religious diversity becomes more widespread. Pastoral theologian Kathleen Greider, using Paul Knitter's framework, suggests that there are four ways that Christians commonly think about other religions.[35] First, some believe that Christianity should replace all religions. Second, many believe that Jesus Christ is the fulfillment of all religions. Third, many argue that God is the same in all religions and see Jesus Christ as one among many. In a fourth approach, one that Greider supports, Christians may simply aim to accept difference, engaging in dialogue but also seeing the limits of that dialogue. Encounters with religious diversity will challenge Christians' assumptions and self-understanding as well as the boundaries of tolerance, respect, and love for the other. It is important for congregations to think deeply about what forming community across religious difference means for them in seeking to care for the people in their towns but also for people in their congregations who are living in the midst of religious diversity.

DIVERSITY IN A THEOLOGICAL FRAME

Though much of our sense of community in any place is based in our sense of being with others like us, community in the way of Christ calls for being with others who are different from us. Community in the richest sense means not only tolerating diversity but seeking diversity because it is more authentic and life-giving. But is diversity always life-giving? Does that mean one should embrace everything that other cultures, other ideas, or other religions bring with them? Clearly diversity in community should also have limits—not everything that is different from us is honorable. But how does one know that appropriate limits are being set rather than simply generalizing out of our own narrow perceptions and assumptions? The question for Christians is what in our faith guides us toward diversity in community in a way that both stretches us toward embracing the other and at the same time maintains integrity within our faith?

Dynamic interrelatedness is the very essence of creation. God has created us in deep relationship to all others in such a way that what happens to one affects us all, though a person may not, at any one point in time, notice or comprehend that effect. Our love and care for one another, all others, is central to the Christian message and way of life. Love of the other is required not only for the well-being of the other but for our own well-being as well. This is the premise upon which Christian encounter with difference begins.

Many alliances are entered into for pragmatic or economic reasons; we can get more done if we join with others. We are suggesting that the Christian priority of loving relationship points beyond pragmatic support for alliances to *insistence* on those alliances. Connection across difference is needed, not only for its instrumental value, but for its inherent place in the kin-dom of God. In general, people live in societies segmented by sameness, acting as if what happens on one side of the city does not affect the other. People in small towns are increasingly unable to live in places of sameness, and for them the move toward a more diverse place is front and center, encountered regularly in the one school, the one grocery store, or the one restaurant in town. Proximity of difference matters; it makes the encounter unavoidable.

The churches, their leaders and caregivers, are key to framing these changes in ways that can lead either to conflict or to richer and more meaningful community. This is perhaps one of the greatest challenges of our time: how to live together peacefully in a world of otherness. As Emmanuel Lartey puts it, "This attempt to respectfully maintain the otherness of the Other and the integrity of the Self, while also working out an ethical way of being in relation with the Other is, in my view, the dilemma of the age."[36] This finely tuned interaction of "embracing" the other,[37] moving beyond tolerance to actually incorporating others into one's self and community, and also maintaining one's own identity and integrity is required if a peaceful and abundant life in the way of Christ is to be sustained. We cannot opt out of our need for one another, but we often try to live as if we can be wholly self-sufficient.

Life itself depends on us finding ways to live together, not in separate enclaves but in community, in engaged care for one another. Yet Lartey's statement identifies the challenge raised above in the discussion of interreligious encounter: Does this mean that we have to like everything the other does? Does this mean we have to agree? Does this mean that we have to tolerate everything? Bonnie Miller-McLemore and Melinda McGarrah-Sharp take up this question in light of conflicts that can arise between feminist and multicultural commitments.[38] For example, feminists strongly support women's rights to education but some cultures see it as inappropriate. The challenge is to maintain an "ethical way of being in relation," to embrace and yet to also know our limits, to live passionately in our beliefs and commitments and yet live peacefully and respectfully with those whose passions are different, and sometimes opposed to ours.

Difference is both a manifestation of God's creation and a construct of human life. The earth and its creatures come in a variety of characteristics, but human beings give meaning to those differences and often structure them in hierarchies of value. Though persons are created in a wide range of colors and shapes, it is human beings who created the categories of race as a means to distinguish and then structured those racial categories in ways that privileged some over others. We often forget that human beings, not God, set up those meanings and built those structures of value. Even when we have done so with the best of intentions and interpretations of God's desire, we are yet human. Our understanding is finite and partial, but we have a tendency to generalize from our own experience. As Peggy Way says, "Along with the duty to acknowledge that one is not God goes the obligation to recognize that there are other truths in the world than my own."[39] This means that we are required to live into the reality that we might be wrong, even as we also draw lines of accountability around injustices and make passionate pleas for inclusivity. We must be willing to listen and seek to understand those whose realities are not our own.

As liberation theologians urge us, this also requires that we become astute at seeing the dynamics of power and how it is exercised. Jesus taught that the stranger, poor, outcast, and marginalized are of primary concern to Christian life. Iris Young suggests five criteria for assessing oppression and identifying the way power is used to oppress: exploitation, marginalization, powerlessness, cultural imperialism, and violence.[40] Those who are less powerful, less privileged, and therefore less able to influence the forces such as political and economic systems that shape human life, not only have a viewpoint that is different from those who live in more powerful circumstances, but they have a viewpoint that those with more privilege need in order to be self-critical and to grow. In the face of external forces, people tend to see themselves as less powerful than they actually are and see others as having more power to change and influence situations than they actually do. Encounters across differences of power and privilege, often ascribed by race or ethnicity but also by gender, sexual orientation, economic status, or religion, help us get a broader view.

Enriching communities by embracing difference requires deconstructing privilege so that we might live into the peace and justice of God's kin-dom. Greider insists that looking at Christian privilege in the United States is essential in our encounter with other religions. Nancy Ramsay picks up this theme when she suggests that in the reality of complex and multiple layers of race and gender oppression, to which any number of oppressions can be added, we must deconstruct privilege.[41] Peggy McIntosh's well-known inventory of white privilege[42] reminds us that privilege based on race is not something that persons carry with them that can be discarded or left behind. It functions in a system of racism that permeates U.S. culture. In the Millard and Chapa study referred to earlier in this chapter, the Anglos they interviewed considered themselves to be fair-minded open people, certainly not racist; however, "every Latino reported having received clear-cut discriminatory messages, ranging from 'Go back to Mexico' to actually getting beaten up."[43] Anglos tended to equate racism to blatant hostile acts of aggression and failed to see the more subtle and covert types of racism involved in "small negative comments, avoidance, and distrust."[44] They failed to see the connection between racism and what they describe as "deficiencies" in education or English. When personal relationships can be formed across difference, then Anglos begin to see more clearly the depth of the U.S. culture of racism. Churches seem a likely place for these kinds of relationships to develop.[45]

Taking the call to diversity seriously means that rural encounters across difference are a blessing, though not necessarily an easy one, to the community and to the church, enabling us to see ourselves and others more clearly. Though always limited by human finitude and sin, this can also move us to see more clearly God's ever-present creative Spirit in our midst, embracing us in love and calling us to account.

PRACTICING CARE

Healing and transformative care in diverse communities requires attention to the needs of all persons in the communities, indigenous peoples, immigrants, newcomers, long-term residents, Muslims, Christians, and Jews. This care must keep in mind both the needs of individuals and the broader needs of the community, as well as our faith commitment to the life-giving use of power and the vision of a peaceful diverse society in which all life flourishes. A pastoral care perspective can be a helpful lens with which to address diversity within rural churches and communities. Commitment to diverse community requires congregations and their pastors to become adept at intercultural care, not unlike that which Lartey argues for, care that is *contextually* based, requires attention to *multiple perspectives*, and *authentic participation* of all involved.[46] It asks us to see the other as one who knows, as one who has wisdom about what she wants and needs. This approach begins with deep concern for the well-being of all involved, an understanding of the internal dynamics that often make change difficult for individual persons, and attentiveness to relational interaction and to sociocultural systems that impact the situations of persons and families.[47] It also helps us live "creatively with extremes rather than by extremes" and invites us into the tension of "opposing positions."[48]

Meaningful and healthy engagement across difference requires first an environment of care and respect for all involved, Christians *and* non-Christians, newcomers *and* old-timers, or Euro-Americans, Native Americans, Latina/os, *and* African Americans, the whole community. Ramsay, drawing on the developmental psychology of Robert Kegan, reminds us of the "important role of intentional communities who offer *confirmation* of emerging recognitions around the need to reconstruct our identities and agency in relation to privilege and oppression; *continuity* as we try on new self-understanding and behaviors;

and *contradiction* when we misstep in our process of reconstructing our sense of self and related practices."[49] Communities of care are needed for both those engaging in deconstructing privilege and those deconstructing internalized oppression. We need support from groups "like us" and times when we are with people who are different from us. We are socialized into ways of relating through oppression and privilege; change requires socialization into new identities and relationships of mutuality and justice. This means allowing plenty of time for Jan, Chris, and others at St. Luke's UMC to process and reflect on their experience of the change in the community. They will need to care for one another in a way that allows fears and unpleasant thoughts to be voiced without fear of being rejected or abandoned. Meaningful and effective movements toward justice for the oppressed require patient respect for the deep internal struggle this can provoke in persons.

The "shock of otherness"[50] often moves people into reactivity out of fear, ignorance, and insecurity. Pastors often make one of two moves in response to this reactivity: supporting retreat or pushing more encounter. A more helpful response might be to assist persons in a process of "conscientization"[51] that begins with a spiritual practice of self-reflection and growing self-awareness. Jan and Chris mirror the complexity of persons who have multiple layers of identity. None of us fit into just one category of identity, and most of us want to be recognized for the multiplicity that makes us up. No one is simply white, or Latina, or Christian. As we look at our own histories we find that we are a mix, a kind of pluralism of our own. Lartey offers one model, a "cycle of social therapy,"[52] which begins with "recognition" of who is involved in the process and requires a self-awareness on the part of all involved, including the pastoral caregiver. As someone who comes into contact with Hispanic and other migrant children every day as a result of her job, Jan may need to recognize that Chris has not been exposed to new migrants to the extent she has been. Well-meaning pastors often encourage groups to work together or to get to know one another across difference, without attending to the need for self-knowledge, which includes growing recognition of our own totalizing assumptions and a capacity for self-critique. In the case of Plainsville, there does need to be time when groups gather with others like themselves and then other times when they gather across difference.

"Befriending" the other requires willingness to engage in storytelling about our lives across differences of privilege and oppression. It means getting to know one another for the sheer joy of the relationship, not to change the other but simply to understand each other. The church council at St. Luke's could initiate this. Two cautions must be made here. First, this kind of storytelling does not end with the stories themselves; they must be reflected upon for the ways in which we have been enculturated for privilege and oppression, for the cultural messages that we have internalized about our self and others. This kind of storytelling and reflection moves toward clarity about what values we live by and enables us to see our choices more clearly.[53] Second, storytelling across difference may require us to recognize the "limits of empathy" and the "irreducibility of difference."[54] It is quite tempting, especially for the privileged, to see more commonality than can be claimed; there are ways in which we each are like no other and, though we may seek to know another as deeply we can, there is always the difference that cannot be known. This kind of practice entails vulnerability and risks that persons need to be prepared for, not simply thrown into. Acknowledging differences and stretching one's identity and routine can be frightening but may also prove exhilarating. A pastoral caregiver is working at multiple levels through this kind of process, in personal relationship to each of the persons or groups involved, within each group and between groups. The intensity, vulnerability, and potential for hurt suggests that pastors who engage this kind of ministry need to have persons who can support her or him through the process.

Saint Luke's Church in Plainsville has already begun creating a caring, diverse community. They have tried to reach out and they are having the conversations about their changing community. As church leaders, they and the pastor can engage the congregation in raising awareness and education about the realities of life faced by Latino/a newcomers and the cultural heritage they bring. They can share with one another their own struggles about change and, while reasserting their Christian call to care for all others, they can also encourage one another in the self-critical work it takes for Anglos to join in true community with their Latino/a neighbors. They may want to discuss ways they can befriend their neighbors, not in order to get them to come to church, not as objects of charity, but for the sake of caring relationship that will enrich them all.

Manuel and Emilia, while not responsible for helping Anglos deconstruct privilege or educating them about ethnic difference, may find that they can also find the abundant life they want in befriending Anglos such as those at St. Luke's, even if they decide not to go to church there. Forming these kinds of alliances and relationships will take courage and vulnerability for Latino families, but it can also be empowering for them. It may be that together the Gonzalezes, Jan, Chris, and others like them can work together to advocate for change in the social policies and corporate practices that have exploited workers in the local plant. Healing and transformation of lives and communities requires caring and courageous attention to the diversities in our midst.

Notes

1. *Evangelico* is a Spanish term used for Protestant churches.

2. *Race and Ethnicity in Rural America* (Housing Assistance Council, April 2012).

3. Kenneth M. Johnson and Daniel T. Lichter, "Population Growth in New Hispanic Destinations," Issue Brief no. 8 , Carsey Institute, University of New Hampshire (Fall 2008): 1.

4. Ibid.

5. *Race and Ethnicity in Rural America.*

6. Kenneth M. Johnson, "Rural Demographic Change in the New Century: Slower Growth, Increased Diversity," Issue Brief no. 44, Carsey Institute, University of New Hampshire (Winter 2012); *Population Change and Rural Society*, ed. William Kandel and David L. Brown (Dordrecht: Springer, 2006).

7. Ann V. Millard and Jorge Chapa, *Apple Pie and Enchiladas: Latino Newcomers in the Rural Midwest* (Austin: University of Texas Press, 2004).

8. For more about the meatpacking industry, farm workers, and other issues related to the increasing Latina/o population in the rural U.S., see Philip Martin, *Importing Poverty? Immigration and the Changing Face of Rural America* (New Haven: Yale University Press, 2009).

9. Millard and Chapa, *Apple Pie and Enchiladas*, 204.

10. Ibid., 194.

11. *Testimonios* are personal stories shared in Latino/a churches. See Miguel A. de la Torre, "Pastoral Care from the Latina/O Margins," in *Injustice and the Care of Souls: Taking Oppression Seriously in Pastoral Care*, ed. Sheryl A. Kujawa-Holbrook and Karen Brown Montagno (Minneapolis: Fortress Press, 2009), 59–72.

12. WCC Executive Committee, "Statement on the Doctrine of Discovery and Its Enduring Impact on Indigenous Peoples" (Bossey, Switzerland: WCC, 2012).

13. David L. Brown and Kai A. Schafft, *Rural People and Communities in the 21st Century: Resilience and Transformation* (Cambridge, UK/Malden, MA: Polity, 2011), 131.

14. See Janice C. Probst and others, *Minorities in Rural America: An Overview of Population Characteristics* (Columbia: South Carolina Rural Health Research Center, 2002), 14–16.

15. George E. Tinker, *Spirit and Resistance: Political Theology and American Indian Liberation* (Minneapolis: Fortress Press, 2004).

16. The basis of this description comes from Mary Beth Mattingly, Kenneth Johnson, and Andrew Schaefer, "More Poor Kids in More Poor Places," Policy Brief, Carsey Institute, University of New Hampshire (2011).

17. Reported at greater length in Brown and Schafft, *Rural People and Communities*, 131–36

18. Ibid., 130.

19. Probst and others, *Minorities in Rural America.*

20. Joel Hartter and Chris R. Colocousis, "Environmental, Economic, and Social Changes in Rural America Visible in Survey Data and Satellite Images," Carsey Institute, University of New Hampshire (2011).

21. Rosalind P. Harris and Dreamal Worthen, "African Americans in Rural America," in *Challenges for Rural America in the Twenty-First Century* (University Park: Pennsylvania State University Press, 2003), 35.

22. bell Hooks, *Belonging: A Culture of Place* (New York: Routledge, 2009), 41.

23. See hooks's own experience of this, ibid., 50.

24. See Harris and Worthen, "African Americans in Rural America."

25. bell hooks, *Belonging*, 43.

26. Ibid.

27. See Edward P. Wimberly, "The Bible as Pastor: An African American Perspective," *Journal of Pastoral Theology* 16, no. 1 (2006).

28. John Cromartie and Peter Nelson, "Baby Boom Migration and Its Impact on Rural America," ed. United States Department of Agriculture, Economic Research Report (Washington, DC: Economic Research Service, 2009).

29. Shannon has used this typology often in preference to an urban-rural classification. These values need not be seen as better or worse than one another. They simply represent the way that two kinds of people tend to see the world. Pastor Barney Wells was the original source of this device.

30. Aimee Howley, "The Poor Little Rich District: The Effects of Suburbanization on a Rural School and Community," *Journal of Research in Rural Education* 20, no. 9 (2005).

31. Sonya Salamon, *Newcomers to Old Towns: Suburbanization of the Heartland* (Chicago: University of Chicago Press, 2003).

32. Ibid., 185.

33. Michele Dillon and Sarah Savage, "Values and Religion in Rural America: Attitudes toward Abortion and Same-Sex Relations," Carsey Institute, University of New Hampshire (Fall 2006).

34. Dianna J. Shandy and Katherine Fennelly, "A Comparison of the Integration Experiences of Two African Immigrant Populations in a Rural Community," *Journal of Religion & Spirituality in Social Work* 25, no. 1 (2006).

35. Kathleen Greider, "Soul Care Amid Religious Plurality," in *Women Out of Order: Risking Change and Creating Care in a Multicultural World*, ed. Jeanne Stevenson Moessner and Teresa E. Snorton (Minneapolis: Fortress Press, 2009), 293–313.

36. Emmanuel Yartekwei Lartey, *Pastoral Theology in an Intercultural World* (Peterborough, UK: Epworth, 2006), 131.

37. This term has been popular after being used by Miroslav Volf in *Exclusion and Embrace: A Theological Exploration of Identity, Otherness, and Reconciliation* (Nashville: Abingdon, 1996).

38. Bonnie Miller-McLemore, "Are There Limits to Multicultural Inclusion? Difficult Questions for Feminist Pastoral Theology," in *Women Out of Order*, ed. Moessner and Snorton.

39. Peggy Way, *Created by God: Pastoral Care for All God's People* (St. Louis: Chalice, 2005), 96.

40. Nancy Ramsay, "Where Race and Gender Collide," in *Women Out of Order*, ed. Moessner and Snorton, 332.

41. Ibid.

42. Ibid.

43. Millard and Chapa, *Apple Pie and Enchiladas*, 103.

44. Ibid., 113.

45. See models for this in Joseph R. Barndt, *Understanding & Dismantling Racism: The Twenty-First Century Challenge to White America* (Minneapolis: Fortress Press, 2007); Joseph R. Barndt, *Becoming an Anti-Racist Church: Journeying toward Wholeness* (Minneapolis: Fortress Press, 2011); Eric H. F. Law, *The Wolf Shall Dwell with the Lamb: A Spirituality for Leadership in a Multicultural Community* (St. Louis: Chalice, 1993), Eric H. F. Law, *Inclusion: Making Room for Grace* (St. Louis: Chalice, 2000).

46. Emmanuel Lartey, *In Living Color: An Intercultural Approach to Pastoral Care and Counseling*, 2nd ed. (London: Jessica Kingsley, 2003); Lartey, *Pastoral Theology in an Intercultural World*.

47. Models for this kind of work from a pastoral care perspective include Lartey and Pamela Couture, *Child Poverty* (St. Louis: Chalice, 2007); Pamela D. Couture, "Feminist, Wesleyan, Practical Theology and the Practice of Pastoral Care," in *Liberating Faith Practices* (Louvain: Peeters,

1998); Larry Graham, *Care of Persons, Care of Worlds: A Psychosystems Approach to Pastoral Care and Counseling* (Nashville: Abingdon, 1992); Christie Cozad Neuger, *Counseling Women: A Narrative, Pastoral Approach* (Minneapolis: Fortress Press, 2001).

48. Lartey, *Pastoral Theology in an Intercultural World*, 127.

49. Reference to Kegan in Ramsay, "Where Race and Gender Collide," in *Women Out of Order*, ed. Moessner and Snorton, 339.

50. Way uses this phrase in *Created by God: Pastoral Care for All God's People*.

51. Paulo Freire, *Pedagogy of the Oppressed*, 30th anniversary ed. (New York: Continuum, 2000).

52. Lartey, *In Living Color*.

53. See Christie Cozad Neuger, *Counseling Women*.

54. Greider, "Soul Care Amid Religious Plurality," in *Women Out of Order*, ed. Moessner and Snorton, 307.

PART II

Healing and Transformative Care in Rural Contexts

Healing and transformative care in the context of rural congregations emphasizes the four themes we have talked about in this text thus far: Place, Community, Leadership, and Diversity. The chapters, up to this point, highlight the ways in which each of these themes represents something unique about rural ministry. They also suggest that these themes are theologically enhanced by our attention to the rural context. In other words, pastoral theology is expanded as we recognize the unique gifts of place, community, leadership, and diversity in rural contexts.

Concrete acts of care offered by persons related to the church—laity and ordained—result in the community of faith embodying gifts of healing and transformation for the members of its congregations as well as for those in the surrounding areas. Such care is often most evident in moments of struggle and chaos. In order to examine how these themes emerge in the concrete ways that people and churches care with and for one another, it is helpful to examine specific issues that emerge in the rural community. The situations, themselves, are not unique to rural life; rather, what is unique is the way in which rural contexts shape the realities of these issues in particular ways.

In what follows, we will do two things. First, we will talk about three issues we see as significant in rural communities. Again, these are not the only issues, nor do they represent issues that are found only in rural contexts. Instead, what we want to illustrate is how taking contextual realities seriously changes the way in which we experience the issues and how our response to them as those offering pastoral care on behalf of the congregations changes. The three issues—poverty, violence, and health care (in its broadest form)—are issues that often press upon rural congregations in unique ways.

Second, to illustrate how the themes outlined earlier in this text come alive in pastoral care, we will use the four themes to suggest concrete responses to cases presented in the following chapters. You will find in what follows a diversity that emerges among the three of us and our understandings of healing and transformative care. What we hope to illustrate by such difference is that there is not one way to respond to any issue in rural parishes; rather there are multiple perspectives and realities that converge to make care particular to the persons involved in the cases we present and to the uniqueness of the community itself. The discernment of a community and its pastoral leadership will determine how best to respond to any situation. The four themes, however, can become one perspective from which to offer healing and transformative care.

Ultimately, we suggest that concrete responses to issues in rural contexts can encourage movements toward healing and transformative care. Healing is one of those words that can capture multiple images and possibilities. We believe that pastoral care in rural contexts—and in other communities, as well—is at its best when it encourages the healing and flourishing of human lives, communities, the earth, and the world. This is not the individualized or therapeutic healing that many of us confuse with pastoral care; rather, this is the kind of healing that invites people, communities, the earth, and the world to live into the fullness of God's abundant grace and care.

Healing cannot be separated from the public and prophetic witness of communities of faith and their leadership. Because we want to expand notions of care beyond individualized and therapeutic contexts, we are convinced that good pastoral leadership in rural communities—whether offered by laity or ordained leaders—has to be attentive to the social structures that impede the flourishing of all God's world. In other words, pastoral care at its best confronts and challenges injustices and oppressive structures that impede abundant living, and works toward the transformation of souls, lives, communities, and the earth.

5

Rural Poverty, Class, and Care

Sue and Hank were respected in the Appalachian town where they lived. Sue's family had been members of the church for years and Hank was a hometown boy as well. Their children were growing into elementary school age and all seemed well. Sue had been the church council president and was regularly a member of the governing board. Hank was a regular churchgoer along with the family. They were good solid citizens.

Sue had known that business was off at the furniture store in the small Kentucky town and that her job as the only full-time salesperson was in some danger. She had worked at the store ever since high school, and even though the salary was not wonderful, it was enough to keep the family provided for, with the money Hank brought in from working in the mine. Like his father before him, Hank loved mining and every year was going to be the one when life would get easier. In a way, her job was what enabled him to keep mining.

When Hank's dad and mom had died within six months of each other, some of the floorboards were knocked out from under their financial arrangements. They had to find other childcare options. Sue's job had enabled them to do okay. Working in the mines was often bone-wearying, and Hank knew that one day he would have to give it up.

When the economic downturn came, people stopped buying whatever they didn't absolutely need or could make do without. The discount store that went into business out on the highway did nothing to bolster business at the furniture store that employed Sue. Then one day the couple who owned the store, and worked alongside Sue, called her into the office and said that they would have to let her go.

Sue and Hank had known that their financial situation was hanging by a thread, but it was manageable. The job loss cut the thread. How could they economize? Who could they tell? They felt ashamed. They knew that their story was shared by others who had to be let go, but that didn't seem very comforting. It wasn't something one talked about freely, even in the midst of a long-term recession. Before long, their neighbors began to wonder why Sue wasn't leaving the house at her customary 7:15 in the morning. They asked the owners of the furniture store. Soon the pieces began to fall into place, and they hinted to their lay minister at the next Sunday service that maybe she might want to visit Sue and Hank.

The lay minister has some inkling of just how serious this situation is, and of what the consequences could be for Sue and Hank, their children, and those who are their friends and relatives in the church and community. What the lay minister may not have realized was that this job loss represents a crisis of life-changing proportions. For one thing, it changes Sue's relationship to her employers, people she has been close to. For another, it affects the whole family's relationship to the community. How might the lay minister proceed? As she thought about how to accompany them through this crisis, the minister began to realize that this sort of blow was one that involved the pastoral care of the whole congregation. Others in the congregation and community had to fight their inclination to distance themselves from Sue and Hank because they felt that their own situation was not much more secure.

The lay minister does call Sue and Hank and asks if she can drop by that evening. When she arrives, it is clear that Sue has been crying and Hank looks distraught. "I just don't know whether I can continue to be on the church council, or even go to church anymore," Sue said. "People at church will talk, if they aren't already, about how we just aren't very capable and that we are failures. We already feel that way at least some of the time."

*****

Talking about one's economic situation is not something that Sue and Hank do very easily. It is not uncommon for people in rural communities to blame themselves if they face financial hard times. It is easy to fall from a respectable blue-collar lifestyle into a lower level of income. Poverty can seem to be a failure, no matter what the causes might be. This can be especially difficult for people like Hank and Sue who have a place in the community that other people count on. They feel as though they have let down the whole town or congregation. Furthermore, it does threaten their place of leadership or even membership in the congregation or community.

One of the distinctive features of rural poverty is that poverty cannot be nearly as anonymous in small-town and rural locations as in the city. Lack of anonymity generates a fear of the future that may make associating with those who are in a hard financial place difficult. Those whose own financial situation is not too secure fear that this could happen to them. Other features of rural poverty are that the children of lower-income families may suffer from tainted reputations, and be assumed to be lazy.

This chapter looks at the extent and context of rural poverty in order to understand what is going on with Sue and Hank, and many other rural residents. This case comes to us from the coalmining region of Appalachia and is distinctive to that context in some ways. In others, it could have come from the fishing towns of the Gulf states where the fishing industry has been decimated, or from farming communities.[1]

POVERTY AND CLASS IN RURAL CONTEXTS

Although there are distinctive dimensions of rural poverty, it is also clear that the rural scene displays many of the problems that characterize poverty in general: inequitable distribution of wealth, lack of availability of viable employment, wages, debt, downward mobility, child poverty, the feminization of poverty, homelessness and housing issues, the social distance and alienation of people from each other, and the ways that race and gender inequalities intersect with social class systems. Revealing the structures that contribute to and sustain inequalities and poverty as well as the complexities and nuances of poverty is a crucial step in the struggle to create a just world. Community health care may be less accessible and more tied to ability to pay in rural America. Gender stereotypes and pay inequalities may hang on longer in rural America. Feminist scholars and activists have demonstrated that one cannot isolate gender (or class) alone, but must consider the extent to which gender, race, class, and other lines of inequality intersect and feed into the experiences of individuals and communities. Similarly, scholars increasingly acknowledge connections between multiple social problems. The sort of poverty that Sue and Hank are experiencing is very personal and deserves the careful presence of the pastor *and* congregation; it is also a systemic issue that generates poverty for many in rural America. We need the careful presence of pastors and congregations who can see beyond Sue and Hank's perception of being merely personal failures. Poverty is clearly a systemic issue that impacts persons.

Attending to what is distinctive about poverty in rural town and country places is crucial to understanding Sue and Hank's situation. Compared to the urban poor, the rural poor have both similar and somewhat different characteristics. They do face unique macroeconomic circumstances and exhibit dissimilar economic survival strategies. As we have noted, place makes a difference. "The unique nature of rural poverty needs to be better understood if we are to tailor realistic policy options for rural areas," write Leif and Eric Jensen.[2] One of those features is that there are now fewer resources in rural congregational and community places than there once were. Clearly, understanding rural poverty is also essential for congregations and pastors if they are to respond caringly.

The image of poverty that is dominant in the U.S. is that poverty is primarily an urban phenomenon, but some scholars report that as many as 95 percent of the "persistently poor" counties in the U.S. are nonmetro or rural.[3] Being persistently poor involves having a poverty rate of 20 percent or more for the five decades from 1960 to 2010. A brief look at some statistics will emphasize the extent of rural poverty. The poverty level in 2010 was $22,113 for a family of four.[4] The use of newer measures of poverty would produce an increase in the number of people counted as poor. Even so, the rate of poverty by residence has been staying roughly the same for forty years or so—nonmetro rates remain just above the 15 percent rate; metro rates are somewhat below that, at 15.2 and 13.2 percent respectively in 2010.[5] There are pockets of poverty in the United States that are hidden by these averages. If we consider the "persistent poverty" counties in the U.S., we find that 340 of the 386 counties thus classified are rural counties. Those counties, in Appalachia, in an arc from the rural Carolinas into the Mississippi Delta, the Rio Grande Valley southwest, and the agricultural Northern Plains are distinguished by the fact that there are high concentrations of racial and ethnic minorities living there. They are also distinguished by the fact that those persistently poor counties tend to be or have a history of being agricultural.[6] There is a broad swath of states down the middle of the country that are agricultural and have higher-than-average rates of poverty. Poverty rates are also higher in more remote counties.[7] Roughly 10 percent of whites lived in poverty, 12 percent of Asians, 26.6 percent of Hispanics, and 27.4 percent of African Americans in 2010. Those rates are probably higher now.

Some of the causes of poverty point to other factors that rural congregations and their pastors will want to take into account. Educational levels tend to be lower among rural residents, and rural minorities tend to have higher rates of poverty than their urban counterparts. There are fewer female-headed families among the poor in nonmetro areas, a factor that makes the greater poverty of rural people even more striking. There are also more elderly people in town and country America. These individual characteristics are shaped by structural characteristics of the rural location. One important structural component of rural poverty is simply that there are not as many economic opportunities or positions that pay a living wage in rural locales. Sue's job at the furniture store paid not much better than minimum wage. Economies that are heavily dependent on extractive industries—mining, fishing, farming, even tourism—are impacted when those industries experience a downturn. Manufacturing industries in rural settings do not pay well. There is, furthermore, the factor of the "permeability of the local social hierarchies."[8] Who you know, your family of origin, and your own reputation determine the extent to which the community is open to your success. In rural communities, the local social hierarchy may be fairly closed or inaccessible. So, economic control, centralized industries, and blocked access are factors that can affect a downward drag on the economy. There are more or less open (or closed) economic structures, and sometimes prejudice and discrimination operate to increase poverty.

Sociologists Leif Jensen and Eric Jensen, in analyzing the "comparatively low education of rural residents," suggest that, among other factors, it may be linked to "the possibility that rural residents, sensing a local economy that yields a low payoff to education, rationally underinvest in their own human capital."[9] This correlates with the hypothesis of Patrick Carr and Maria Kefalas.[10] Their conclusion is that rural communities (and congregations) tend to invest most heavily not in their future leaders, but in those who will leave the rural community. Those who do well academically tend to leave the community, but then those who tend to do well academically may come from comfortably fixed families who themselves value education, and can free their children from having to take dead-end jobs.

In 1986, Walter Brueggemann preached a sermon at the height of the farm crisis. He asked an urban congregation to imagine a giant sucking sound, which was the sound of the urban industries of this country drawing the resources out of rural communities into themselves.[11] Certainly, this image applies to coalmining communities, where Sue and Hank are living, whose earnings and product leave town destined to fuel other industries and households. In Brueggemann's words, the value-added industries are "parasitic" on the resources—grain, youth, and values of hard work, minerals, and talent—which rural communities produce cheaply. Rural sectors have been impacted by the economic recession that began in 2008. But it is clear that, even relative to the rest of the nation in this current "downturn," rural America has been especially hard hit.

Social Class and Community. One axiom of social science claims that socioeconomic status is the central determinant of human behavior. Within rural communities there is a social stratification that varies with social class. According to William Thompson and Joseph Hickey, "It is impossible to understand people's behavior . . . without the concept of social stratification, because class position has a pervasive influence on almost everything . . . health, happiness, and even how long we will live."[12] There are upper middle and well-to-do classes in rural America. These may be younger professionals, entrepreneurs, retirees, and even older settled populations, often living off a fixed income (which does not necessarily equate with "low" income) who could be called the "respectable." They are often people who have sufficient means to travel, to live well, and who have disposable incomes. It is sufficient to remember that there are people of means living in rural America who have the capacity to contribute a great deal. There is also a lower middle class made up of semi-professionals and craftspeople with an average standard of living. These classes are often the members of traditional historic churches, either Protestant or Roman Catholic, which is why the poor often feel so alienated when their status has shifted.

The two groups on whom we wish to focus are the working class and the poor. These may be clerical and blue-collar workers, whose work is highly routine. Their standard of living varies depending on the number of income earners, but is commonly just adequate. Often there is low job security, and couples "live from pay check to pay check" with little margin for crises. They may have some high school education. Farmers, miners, and fishermen probably tend to fall into this category; they share many characteristics with blue-collar workers. In rural communities, these citizens have manufacturing positions, many of which are typically not at the upper end of the wage scale. The working poor are service workers, lower-rung clerical workers who have high economic insecurity and risk of poverty. The underclass or the poor are those with limited or no participation in the labor force who rely on government transfers. They fall officially under the poverty income definition, which is, as we noted, somewhat artificially low already.

Social status is a dimension that can get lost in the quantification of income. It is especially significant in rural areas where many still espouse the myth that this is a classless society. One's reputation and behavior are associated with status—how others see, classify, and treat others. Income *tends* to produce different styles of living; for example, some are categorized as "respectable middle class," and others derogatorily labeled "white trash." While some rural residents may pretend that there are no class divisions, it is clear that these gradations of respect and honor, as well as status and income, are well established.

Ethnicity and Income Status in Rural America. One factor deserving attention that enters into status is the ethnic and racial makeup of the poor and working poor. The 2009 income averages for all white non-Hispanic households living alone or in combination was $81,272; for Asian households living alone or in combination it was $100,562; for Hispanic households the figure was $54,074; and for African Americans $53,228.[13] These figures reflect the average household income levels for ethnic groups across the United States. It is important to note that household averages are less reflective of the typical household than median income figures, because "average" income figures tend to inflate the living standards of their referents. Thus, Warren Buffett and other wealthy people's incomes are "averaged" with poor people's incomes. Median figures (half above, half below) offer a more accurate image.

According to the Carsey Institute, in 2006 there were more than 3 million low-income white children living in rural areas, or nearly twice the number living in central cities. The largest share of low-income children in rural areas was white, although the rate of poverty among Native American children was over 50 percent. Even though the racial and ethnic makeup of low-income children in rural areas and central cities differs considerably, children who are members of racial and ethnic minorities are at greater risk of living at or near the poverty level in both metro and nonmetro areas of the United States. In rural areas in 2010, most minority children had rates of low income that were nearly twice those of white children. In central cities, rates for minority children were 2.5 times higher than for white children. In short, we can extrapolate from the percentage of children living in poverty in rural areas and from the average national income figures that racial and ethnic minority peoples are quite overrepresented among the rural poor. While it is difficult to get trustworthy figures on the income level among minority groups living in rural America, it is clear that the status of such groups is not high.

Somewhat more revelatory are the sort of data that Cynthia M. Duncan collected.[14] Through a series of narrative interviews, Duncan studied three rural communities—one in Appalachia, one in the Mississippi Delta, and one in rural Maine. She discovered that the Appalachian coalminers of Kentucky are in the same position as African American people in the Mississippi Delta. Her interviews reveal an implicit system of two social classes in both communities: the owners of the coalmines and their workers in Appalachia, and the owners of the Delta farms and their laborers on the Delta farms.

Little has occurred in the mining community to alter the power structures, which explains why rural poverty persists there. Employment is more a matter of who you know rather than what you know; one's surname is significant. Workers are dependent on owners, and the system continues in part through the diversion of school funds to subsidize the schools that owners' and managers' children attend. Some of Duncan's descriptors are "high unemployment," "welfare dependency," "drug and alcohol use" and attendant abuses; and "a general sense of hopelessness." Social class is socially constructed in Appalachia. Clear cultural criteria define people as "belonging" to the broad American middle class, and include such things as having all your teeth, being able to speak in standard American English, knowing how to dress for work or a job interview, knowing the demeanor that is appropriate to a job, and having the literacy skills to know about life beyond one's hollow.[15] A second component of this social class is the social ideology that allows the middle and upper class to maintain its control. The just-world hypothesis claims that those who want to work and who get ahead deserve that; those who don't work or don't get ahead deserve their misfortune in life. Another component is that owners often felt as though they were in fact doing the workers a favor by hiring them.

In her interviews of African American people in the Delta community of Dahlia, Mississippi, Duncan found the same structures she discovered in Appalachia. The large landowners or farmers (= mine owners) hire field hands (= coalminers) and the wealthy send their children to private academies rather than city schools. The insidious issue of race is added on to the process. The patron-client relationships, the corruption, the two-tier class system, and the sense of despair are analogous to those in Appalachia. What is striking about both these situations is the fact that the poor have little voice or participation in the political or economic system in either locale; the system works to systematically disadvantage and exploit them. To be sure, in both Appalachia and the Delta there are glimmers of hope that come with the change agents who have seen the wider world and who return or arrive with greater proficiency and who also have some economic independence.

Duncan's interviews in Maine offer a contrast to the poverty lifestyles she experienced in Mississippi and Kentucky. The poverty is less severe, the system of patron-client exploitation is missing, and the prospects for getting out of poverty are better. The paper mills that underwrote the economy there needed skilled workers, and a greater degree of egalitarianism developed. Children went to the same schools. Furthermore, there developed a degree of social capital within the community that translated into a sense of civic participation and a more open sense of the future. Duncan's findings in Maine give evidence of the importance of people's interacting with more widely diverse groups. The sense of participation in the public arena was greater in Maine; for example, students from many families went to the same public schools.

Charles Murray, in his book documenting the rise of the white underclass, suggests the importance of degree of integration of diverse groups.[16] One of his findings suggests that people of the same race and income group tend to be segregated from others and from the dominant society. That is, people who live in homogeneous neighborhoods tend to act the same; they tend to be overweight or healthy, rich or poor, watch the same number of hours of television, and so on. This suggests that those who are segregated by race and income fail to develop contacts or customs that would lead to their being able to grow and advance out of poverty. They develop their own enclaves, which are sometimes at variance with the dominant values of achievement and middle-class presentability.

Another dimension of rural America is the ethnic and racial varieties of people who live there, but whose economic status is no more economically stable than the Mississippi and Kentucky communities Duncan studied. If we turn to some of the realities of Native American life, we find that there are an estimated 2.4 million Native Americans, and they are among the most impoverished of all ethnic groups. According to the 2000 Census, an estimated 800,000 Native Americans reside on reservation (largely rural) lands. While some tribes have had success with gaming, only 40 percent of the 562 federally recognized tribes operate casinos. According to a 2007 survey by the U.S. Small Business Administration, only 1 percent of Native Americans own and operate a business. Rural Native Americans rank at the bottom of many social statistics: lowest per capita income, an unemployment rate of 65 percent, and many in deep poverty.[17] A summary comment from the President of Catholic Charities USA, Larry Snyder, states that "African Americans, Hispanics, and Native Americans are about three times as likely to live in poverty as whites.[18] In 2010, 16.7 percent of Americans living in rural areas were poor, but they accounted for more than 33 percent of the total increase in the number of poor Americans from 2003 to 2010 . . ."[19] One suspects that the statistics today are not much less depressing. Rates of child poverty, alcoholism, sexual abuse, and drugs tend to be accentuated on reservation communities.[20]

Hispanic people represent yet another ethnic minority who live in rural communities—often in communities that depend on meatpacking industries, also those who depend on migrant, seasonal labor. To be sure, within the high-poverty counties Hispanic poverty rates remain high, but have dropped from 41 percent in 1990 to 32 percent in 2000 to 23.2 percent in 2008. They increased to 39.6 in 2010.[21] An element that enters into the situation of the Hispanic minority group is immigration law. It is difficult to get accurate statistics, but more than that, it is easy to exploit workers whose continued residence in the U.S. is threatened if they are discovered to be undocumented. Furthermore, there is evidence of the law enforcement system operating to maintain a sense of instability. The specific situation of Hispanic people varies widely, and specific investigation of the local realities can replace generalities. There are many other ethnic minorities who reside in rural communities. Often such communities are attractive to those whose primary income is government transfers or fixed-income programs, for example Social Security payments. The cost of housing is considerably lower in most rural communities. Many immigrants who come from rural communities and small towns are more comfortable in that atmosphere. There is a "rural underclass" that develops among those who are attracted by the low cost of housing and the isolation of rural areas. Our focus here is on those who are poor, but it should be noted that the proximity of the well-off may intensify the sense of relative deprivation and poverty of the poor. Sometimes those who are relatively well off belong to what we might call the historic Christian churches in town.

For Sue and Hank, the loss of Sue's job entails their family's actual fall into a rural underclass that is stigmatized by both long-term residents who are middle class and by newcomers who are comfortably set. Thus the fact of absolute poverty is exacerbated by the threat of becoming part of the disreputable underclass. The culture of mainline congregation members involves some exclusion or hesitant welcoming of the rural underclass. Thus the question arises for Sue and Hank as to whether they can still belong to "their" church. They have moved from being in one culture to another, and voluntary associations that used to welcome them may feel differently now. At least they are conscious of this possibility.

When the community and the congregation are healthiest, there is a level of diversity where people work, learn, and interact together. Diversity produces an equilibrium that, in turn, enables low-income people to escape the trap of poverty. Furthermore, the church has a theological perspective to offer that promotes access for all, because it believes that all people are valuable and God wishes all people to flourish.

POVERTY IN A THEOLOGICAL FRAME

While there are many beliefs that followers of Christ could choose to articulate their concern for the well-being of the poor, and also for the necessity of the well-being of the poor for the affluent, we will concentrate on three: mutuality of care; economics as a theological agenda; and stewardship.

1. Mutual care. In speaking of the stratification of society into rich and poor, Jesus said, "It ought not be so among you." Christians are called to "uplift the downtrodden," "to feed the hungry," "to attend to the widow and orphan," and to "love the neighbor as oneself" (Matt. 20:26; Matt. 25:35; James 1:27; Matt. 22:39). This is not just about helping the poor; mutuality of care flows out of God's desire that we build vital communities of care in which no one is disadvantaged. The witness of scripture is clear that hunger, the pain of poverty, and the ill-health of others are matters of concern to those with resources; others' suffering is our suffering. Prejudice, discrimination, and exploitation are sins against God, who "hears the cry of the poor." There is no doubt that the Christian churches, throughout their history, have worked hard to relieve the suffering of the poor. There are countless organizations and church groups (every denomination has a "hunger program" and a "relief agency," for example) that attempt to encourage ethnic-minority people and offer low-income people a way out of poverty. To be sure, some of those are relief agencies but others are developmental in focus.

While congregations recognize the enormity of the problems associated with rural poverty, and are often overwhelmed by them, they can sometimes ignore the biblical injunctions and pretend that poverty has nothing to do with them. This is a dangerous tendency in town and country settings, because economics is so close to the surface and so central to the health of rural people. The whole congregation is called to care about the financial and social well-being of parishioners, community residents, and the town itself. Caring for the well-being of people necessarily involves caring for the whole person, and thus a congregation might be open to care that extends beyond what is thought of as "spiritual" care.

The mutuality of care extends to an inclusivity that promotes access to opportunities. The communities Duncan studied in Mississippi and Kentucky were closed; they would not allow the poor to improve their education, job opportunities, and standard of living. By contrast, it was the greater openness to others in Maine that changed the nature of the community she studied.

2. Economics is a theological matter. Why, in the midst of poverty, can the rural church not talk about money? The Christian perspective on money is at odds with that of the culture, but the church seldom explicitly addresses that difference. James Hudnut-Beumler, Dean of the Vanderbilt Divinity School, suggests that talking about the meaning of money in church is a taboo and that "[w]herever there are taboos, one can be reasonably sure that idols are nearby."[22] So, this taboo stems from "money's central role as an expression and index of worth."[23] There are doubtless other factors that make the discussion of money a taboo topic in church, and make us dread the stewardship sermon. It is better for the pastor and congregation to integrate a concern for sharing throughout the church year, and to promote sharing as a gift given to the giver. Giving is in fact a way we receive.

Not seeing social class and poverty as a theological issue may derive from the fear rural people have of falling into the situation of Sue and Hank. They may fear differences in social class and social acceptance; those characteristics may be associated with Hispanics, African Americans, or Native Americans. So it may be fear that keeps economics a taboo in church. Not seeing economics as a theological matter comes at a high cost.

Ignoring people's financial circumstances suggests that God is not concerned about people's economic or material well-being. Nothing could be further from the truth. Indeed, God wills the best for all people and desires that we structure our economy in such a way that the needs of all are met. God will not govern the economy but expects us to exhibit justice, compassion, and sufficiency for everyone concerned.

When Sue loses her job and the family's finances are jeopardized, it would mean a great deal if the pastor were to come and be with the family and to signify that their situation is not beyond God's care. Indeed, God desires that the church constitute a community of mutual benefit, and exhibit neighbor-love that extends to people's material needs. Kathryn Tanner suggests several ways that Christian and secular values can and do intersect. Adopting policies that promote such mutual intersection is one principle that can guide financial policy. One of her examples is the way that public parks and community centers and highways are considered legitimate projects for communitywide action.

In fact, the scriptures mention money and related issues as being quite powerful. So Jesus warns his disciples that it is easier for a camel to go through the eye of a needle than for the rich to enter the kingdom of heaven (Luke 17:25). In the U.S., we church people (and especially church people without money) wish to have money. Sometimes our desire for money crowds out our desire for a relationship with God. Consumption turns out to be a false god, but its power to throw our lives (and Sue and Hank's) into chaos is forceful. Falling into poverty can be a source of shame.

It may be that there are affluent members in the same pews as ethnic and racial minorities. It may even be that the affluent contribute to the poverty of the Latino, African American, or poor white families in the congregation, or in the racial and ethnic communities of the town. The affluent need to be challenged to examine their hiring and salary policies as a theological or faith issue. Ignoring Jesus' mandate to love the neighbor certainly extends to a concern for their economic and thus physical well-being. The moral minimum that our Christian theology implies is that everyone has a decent or subsistence standard of living.

Sue and Hank's situation helps us to see that theology is in fact practical! An open and frank discussion of money from the perspective of faith may help dissipate the sense of shame and the secretiveness that Sue and Hank feel. Furthermore, it increases the possibility that they could receive real help from the congregation—if not employment leads or similar tangible help, at the least a supportive and encouraging environment where they will feel less alone in their financial woes. More broadly, people might recognize that their own financial situations are not beyond God's care. It might give the congregation a different perspective on those in poverty.

3. Stewardship. The belief that articulates how faith and money are related is that of stewardship. Stewardship is of course a matter of all the ways in which we respond to God's love, how we live out all of our lives. It is a way of doing God's work. It is seeing our lives as a gift and disposing of our time, energy, and money in response to God's gift. As a matter of worship and of giving, it is one way of sharing with others what God has given us. Tanner quite rightly writes that there is no way that we can repay God for the giving that God unconditionally keeps on giving to bless us.[24] The essence of God is that God gives, and gives, and gives, no matter what, no matter how little we deserve it. However, that does not mean that God does not desire that we enter into relationship with God by passing on some of that love and care. Thus, the very way we live our lives as disciples involves stewardship. Calvin could speak of wages as being a means of grace; Wesley advised his disciples not only to "earn as much as possible," but also "to give as much as possible." The foundation of God's essence, being that of giving, is the basis for our seeing our lives as a blessing from God. God has gifted us, and thus we respond in gratitude. How we can compound the blessings of our lives for other people? How can we be a blessing to them? One of the Christian promises is that in giving we receive.

Stewardship is also a corporate matter. It intersects with the case of Sue and Hank in that it begins to move into the congregation's concern for the whole quality of life in their locale. Insofar as money is a prerequisite for living, the congregation can examine its context: Who are the lower-income and financially insecure people who are living there? Who are the racial and ethnic minorities who are part of the town? How is their parish involved in working to ensure a quality of life for all in the community? Are we alert to the needs and gifts of other ethnic and racial groups in our communities? The pastor can take the lead in articulating and sharing care, and in providing means of building the church's capacity to do that. In this regard, we think of community development efforts, or other ways of sharing the pastoral care throughout a congregation as well as, possibly, convening the business people in the congregation to address the community economy.

PRACTICING CARE

Returning now to the four themes of rural life that our team discovered to be characteristic of the rural context, we will use them to develop an integrative approach to pastoral care for congregations and pastors. We emphasize the practical implications for ministry.

SHAPED BY PLACE

Rural communities have distinctive and dynamic senses of place. What has become very clear in this chapter is that any effort to do pastoral care needs to attend to the quite specific dimensions of unstable financial situations (the blue-collar and poverty classes) in that context. Rural communities are quite different from each other; each community is its own distinctive web of life and socioeconomic factors. There is a rich sense of place in many rural communities, a feature we described in detail in Chapter 2. A large percentage of people live in rural communities because they want to be there; they like the natural capital and the neighborliness and the sense that life is manageable there. In a way that sounds almost anachronistic, they love their place.

This love of place sometimes translates into a difficulty when rural places change, as they are changing now. The extents of poverty and of new populations who are seeking to make a better life for themselves contrast with the settled and apparently unchanging ethos of the town or countryside. So Hank and Sue find themselves in the position of being resident in a place where retirees are living comfortably on fixed incomes and are changing Hank and Sue's place. A community's attachment to place can become an idol that impedes change and growth, which can be especially pernicious when it blocks adaptation to changes in a place.

Enter economics. Over and over, it has been emphasized that the number one need in rural communities is decent-paying jobs. This is a reflection of the loss of good-paying jobs and the decline in extractive industries like mining or farming. The financial health of the community and its economic future are aspects of place. The changing circumstances of the Appalachian town make Hank and Sue's slide into a lower-income status even starker. They are beginning to experience relative deprivation.

Like many others, they look to their church to help them understand how they should respond, but it has always been difficult for congregations to talk about poverty. Add to that the reality of new populations moving into rural communities, and there are several barriers to considering change. The strong identification of work (and income) with worth in rural America makes it especially difficult for a church to deal with the poor, and perhaps even more with those like Hank and Sue who had had a decent income before losing their jobs and becoming members of the poverty class. Dealing with poverty is an issue that town and country congregations and their pastors are encountering as a pastoral care issue. Furthermore, the role of the congregation in the community includes a concern about the financial health of the community structurally. Hank and Sue's dilemma has wider dimensions that the congregation may be reluctant to face.

There are many resources in the Christian tradition that could be used to engage the congregation in thinking about the economics of their community and how they could enable more people to have a decent standard of living. Simply talking openly about economics and finance would be a gigantic and vital step. Especially important would be exploring the reasons behind the economic stigma attached to poverty, and how that comports with the Christian faith. The first step might be a forum exploring the relation of economics and faith, perhaps using James Hudnut-Beumler's book *Generous Saints*.[25] It would have been useful to Hank and Sue if this discussion about the reasons behind rural poverty, how to think about poverty from a theological perspective, and how the stigma surrounding poverty might be weakened, had occurred before Sue's being let go.

This is an instance where the changed place presents a pastoral care issue for Hank and Sue, but also for the whole congregation. There are ways to strengthen the local economy that assist low-income people to develop incomes that allow a decent standard of living.

Though it is not an immediate answer to the dilemma that Hank and Sue face, it may be one task that a congregation or cluster of communities could take on. They might attempt to increase the number of opportunities that are available within easy commuting range of their town, or capture some of the "value-added" processes that could remain within their communities. Keeping businesses local could lead to higher salaries. There is a growing "localism" movement in the U.S. and particularly in the rural sections of our country.[26] It might also mean that Sue could find employment within the community, as could other financially fragile households in the congregation.

What pastoral care entails, in this view and in rural places, is both an exploration of attitudes surrounding poverty in light of faith, and also what sorts of practical steps might be brought to light to help in circumstances of immediate need. If this outreach activity were to be seen as part of the church's mission of supporting the quality of life in this place, one suspects that that might rebound to the church's growth and spiritual vigor as well. Being a conduit for immigrants' finding employment opportunities would be a powerful means of extending hospitality. Furthermore, it is clear that dealing with poverty and finances is an issue that the rural congregation and community will be struggling with for some time.

ENGAGING COMMUNITY

Town and country locations have a strong sense of community that expresses people's connectedness to each other. As we saw in Chapter 3, this is a theme that still exists in rural places, though its strength can no longer be simply assumed. How can the congregation address pastoral care issues with the aid of community? The sense of being connected with each other has been the strength of rural communities, but that social network requires ongoing attention. Sue and Hank have long felt themselves to be a respectable part of the community, but their new situation threatens their standing.

In a culture as individualistic as ours, and this is especially true in rural communities, it is easy for men and women like Sue and Hank to feel as though their poverty is their own fault. They may feel as though if only they had done something differently, they might have averted their financial problems. Many, many families who are experiencing hardships may feel this way, each of them assuming that what is happening to them is their own fault, rather than recognizing the structural and societal dynamics that are impacting them. Hank and Sue feel this. Minority persons who are mired in blue-collar or poverty situations may wonder why they cannot get ahead. We each assume, I think, that the other families on our block are doing better than we are, or we find a way to rationalize the financial hardships as being justified in some way. The much-touted "rugged individualism" of town and country America has contributed to the sense that we get what we deserve. Even Christian churches in town and country settings can reinforce this notion, however theologically wrongheaded it is. How can the pastor address this threat to community and overcome the invisible class lines that may stymie the church's ministry?

The whole church has a vital role to play in the development of social capital both within itself and in the wider community.[27] There are assets that can be counted on for this development, but the church is one of the leading institutions in these towns and is often looked to for leadership in coordinating resources and bringing people together to plan for the health of the community. The pastor has a vital role to play here; she must address the issue of how to build community. The church can initiate forums for many groups in the community to discuss what is happening there. One of the dimensions of social power that may go unnoticed is the way that churches coming together to discuss school issues or working conditions or public works can have clout.

Social capital and the extent to which we are connected to other people is a prime component of happiness, and rural towns could capitalize on this dynamic. Being unemployed threatens the loss of these connections. According to Nobel laureate Joseph Stiglitz, "You might say, if we have unemployment, don't worry, we'll just compensate the person. But that doesn't fully compensate them."[28] Harvard professor Robert Putnam suggests that losing a job can have repercussions that affect a person's social connections for many years. As a prime driver of human happiness, social connections are very important. Putnam suggests that the "damage to this country's social fabric from this economic crisis must have been huge, huge, huge."[29]

The economic downturn that the whole country has been experiencing since 2008 has been with the rural community for quite some time; it is little wonder that the social fabric of rural America has become tattered. Macro structures that impact food costs, the environment, and rural communities' economics have wrested control from local communities. It is vital that the church step into this gap, not only for Sue and Hank, but also to deal with the consequences that macro structures are producing at a communitywide level.[30]

INTERSECTING WITH LEADERSHIP

In this situation, it is especially important for the church to provide leadership in discussing the theology and ministry of social class, which will support the fabric of the community. Sue and Hank's situation illustrates the vital role that the church can play, now that they feel their standing as community leaders is eroding. Rural church leaders, pastors and laypeople, have developed a particular style of public leadership that is well suited to rural churches and their pastoral care. As public theologians, pastors can assist congregations and communities to focus on ameliorating poverty. Pastoral care involves relaying God's care to Sue and Hank; it also involves promoting the growth of care to those within and outside the congregation, especially in the rural community.

It may seem that this task of leading the caring congregation is a tall order for pastoral and congregational leaders to take on. Indeed. Nevertheless, it is part of the church's mission to its community that it seek to maintain and build as healthy a place to live as it can. That is why we call one of the roles of the pastor that of being the "public theologian." The nature of leadership, as we discussed in Chapter 4, is anything but standard for all communities. There are also many partners who would welcome church leadership and contribute their resources in this endeavor. Sue and Hank might benefit from partners who could assist them on the journey they are experiencing. Pastors need to network with other groups who have compatible goals; many of those partners will be part of church communities and thus there are many points of entry into community development and vitalization efforts. It may be that there could be such a group for Sue and Hank.

Most rural congregations that exhibit vital pastoral care have a networking and relational style of leadership. They recognize that relationships supersede functions in rural congregations and communities. Thus, being visible and accessible, being a community broker who knows what is happening and how people's interests intersect, are valuable assets. A highly appreciated characteristic of town and country pastors is that she or he be an "encourager" of others' dreams and mission ideas. Furthermore, the pastor is capable, in a way that others may not be, of initiating conversations and of listening to the deep hurts and concerns of people.

Another tool that we have already alluded to is the educational capacity of the church. The church could investigate the role of the faith it confesses in relation to the economy. Thinking about the relation of faith and money can best begin when there is either no immediate crisis or when the issue is only coming into view. So, for example, if your church were to take the case with which we began this chapter and discuss it as though Sue and Hank were members of your congregation, then your church might be better prepared to deal with similar cases. That might best be done before Sue and Hank become the objects of the discussion, of course.

It is possible for the churches in a rural community or region to take on the task of establishing a regional development foundation whose jobs might be to pull together a team to work on economic issues and to think about improving the quality of life in an area. The foundation would have an economic dimension, but would not be limited to that. It might very well look at the ways in which the quality of life in a town or region could be improved without any economic cost or at relatively minimal cost. There are any number of nongovernmental and even some governmental agencies that could be engaged in that effort.

RESPONDING TO DIVERSITY

Rural communities are becoming increasingly diverse; this is a factor that congregations and communities need to address. It is an aspect of pastoral care, which formed the body of Chapter 5. One of our emphases in this book has to do with diversity. Communities, once monoculture and rural, are experiencing a wave of immigrants who are important to the future of those towns. It is part of the church's communal role and its faith mandate to welcome the stranger and to assist them in becoming part of the congregation and community. Doing so is one way that the church builds community and can provide economic health for the future. However, Sue and Hank may be feeling anything but welcoming. Their own boat is being swamped, and they may find that the new Walmart on the edge of town is one reason Sue has lost her job. It would be easy to become resentful of this diversity and the talk about welcoming newcomers.

The dilemma for Sue and Hank, the lay pastor, and the congregation involves how much to address fear, accommodate change, and hang on to the traditions that have made their Appalachia town a treasured community. Could it be that the generally low income levels of the new immigrant populations also present some opportunities for long-term residents like Sue and Hank? Sue and Hank might see that such diversity could result in new employment possibilities for them. Maybe that is getting ahead of the pastoral care story. The first emotional reactions may be fear of losing their community as it used to be, and grief at the anticipated loss. Sue and Hank may symbolize the first wave of this changed reality. The pastor can enable her congregation to realize what is happening and what the stakes of reaction are. That is, the pastor can help people deal with their grief, recognize what has enduring value, and move on to address pressing emotional and life issues.[31]

Some rural congregations have found ways to incorporate the leadership of indigenous peoples. Some are multicultural and multilingual. Others are still struggling to find a way to genuinely welcome their brothers and sisters in Christ. Attending to family life, to youth, to the school system, and to the economic situation in town are all areas of importance that the church can help initiate. There are many partner agencies and people that are vital to achieving a basic level of justice for all. They may be useful to Sue and Hank as well.

LIVING OUT OF ABUNDANCE: CONCLUSION

Many rural communities do not think they have many resources, and economically this may be somewhat true. However, those very same communities may have many other assets that go unnoticed. For example, the small school system that many rural residents consider inferior is able to lavish huge amounts of time and attention on their kids' education, and same for the church. The fact that there are only four high school students in the church can be seen not as a liability, but an asset. Those students are seen as treasures that the people in the church cherish. They are the recipients of the congregation's care and they are in fact caregivers themselves.[32]

Perhaps those assets are harder to see because the lens we are using is so much influenced by the urban-oriented media, which fails to appreciate the human touch and the holistic care that churches can provide for others. We need to think through the ways that God's grace operates through money and other resources. Perhaps the first step is educational:

1. How does the church view economics now? How does it address stewardship?
2. On what assets could the pastor and congregation build?
3. What sorts of attitudes and actions are theologically implicated?
4. What rewards are the congregation and community liable to experience through sharing God's love and gifts?

In summary, as the lay minister who comes to visit with Sue and Hank, you see a number of things. First, simply being there with them in their distress is a significant signal that God cares about their whole selves. Do not put off these visits as though they were less important than visiting those who are sick or dying. Second, by beginning an educational project in your church that begins to put the economy and people's poverty (and other financial standing) in conversation with the faith, you can set a framework for addressing personal and corporate finances. Rural pastors can deal with poverty, economics, and diversity. Third, you can initiate a conversation in the community that takes the initiative in offering people wider opportunities than previously offered. You realize that this is not just Sue and Hank's issue but an issue that affects many more people, both in and out of the congregation. Physical and mental health is such an issue. Finally, it is important to put all of your own and your congregation's money matters in the hands of God by thinking about them but also praying about them.

Notes

1. See, for example, the *New York Times* story "Cleanup Hiring Feeds Frustration in Fishing Town," July 17, 2010, page 10, about what happened in Bayou La Batre, Alabama, following Katrina, or happened to Plaquemine Parish as a result of Hurricane Isaac.

2. Larry Jensen and Eric Jensen, "Poverty," in *The Encyclopedia of Rural America*, ed. G. Goreham (Millerton, NY: Grey House, 2008), 774.

3. Kathleen Miller and Bruce Weber, "Persistent Poverty Across the Rural-Urban Continuum," Rural Poverty Research Center, Oregon State University (2003). Accessed at www.IDEAS.org. 9-13-12. Lance George extends this statistic into 2012. See "Persistent Poverty in Rural America," Shelterforce Blog, National Housing Institute (2012). Accessed at Housing Assistance Council, www. hac.org. Accessed 9-14-12.

4. National Poverty Center, "Poverty in the United States FAQs," University of Michigan, April 13, 2012, based on U.S. Census 2010 data. Accessed at www.npc.umich.edu/poverty/ on September 10, 2012.

5. See Larry Snyder, *How Poverty in America Affects Us All* (Maryknoll, NY: Orbis, 2010), 36.

6. See Marybeth Mattingly, Kenneth M. Johnson, and Andrew Schaefer, "More Poor Kids in More Poor Places: Children Increasingly Live Where Poverty Persists," Issue Brief no. 38, Carsey Institute, University of New Hampshire (Fall 2011). Accessed at www.carseyinstitute@unh.edu, August 20, 2012.

7. See Jensen and Jensen, "Poverty," 775.

8. See this discussion in Cynthia Mil Duncan, *Worlds Apart: Why Poverty Persists in Rural America* (New Haven: Yale University Press, 1999), passim, but see especially the chapters on Dahlia and Blackwell.

9. Jensen and Jensen, "Poverty," 777.

10. P. J. Carr and M. Kefalas, *Hollowing Out the Middle: The Rural Brain Drain and What ItMeans for America* (Boston: Beacon, 2009).

11. Walter Brueggemann, "The City and the Land: Monopoly and Marginality," Riverside Church, New York, 1986.

12. W. E. Thompson and J. V. Hickey, *Society in Focus: An Introduction to Sociology* (Boston: Allyn & Bacon, 2005).

13. U.S. Census Bureau (2012), "2012 Statistical Abstract of the United States." Retrieved August 7, 2012 at www.census.gov.

14. Duncan, *Worlds Apart*.15 Ibid.

15. Ibid.

16. Charles Murray, *Coming Apart: The State of White America, 1960-2010* (New York: Crown Forum, 2012).

17. See Calvin Beal, "Distinctive Characteristics of High Poverty Counties," *Amber Waves*, a publication of the USDA Economic Research Service, 2004. Of the 444 nonmetro counties classified as high-poverty counties in 2000 (based on 1999 income), three-fourths reflect the low income of racial and ethnic minorities and are classified as Black, Native American, or Hispanic high-poverty counties. The remaining quarter of high-poverty counties are mostly located in the Southern Highlands, and the poor are predominantly non-Hispanic whites.

18. Larry Snyder, *Think and Act Anew: How Poverty in America Affects Us All and What You CanDo About It* (Maryknoll, NY: Orbis, 2010). See also "American Indians in Rural Areas," in David L. Brown and Kai A. Schaftt, *Rural People and Communities in the 21st Century: Resilience and Transformation* (Cambridge: Polity, 2011), 131–36.

19. See also "The Concentration of Poverty Is a Growing Rural Problem," *Amber Waves*, December 2012, Economic Research Service, United States Department of Agriculture. Accessed at www.amberwaves/gov/usda on December 11, 2012.

20. See, for example, the website "Alcohol Information." Retrieved August 22, 2012 from http://www.alcohol-information.com/. See especially "Alcohol Abuse in Native Communities." Retrieved August 22, 2012, from http://www.alcohol-information.com/ Alcohol_Abuse_in_Native_Communities.html.

21. *Amber Waves*, December 2012, Economic Research Search, USDA. Accessed December 11, 2012.

22. James Hudnut-Beumler, *Generous Saints* (Herndon, VA: Alban Institute, 1999).

23. Ibid., 2–3.

24. Katherine Tanner, *Economy of Grace* (Minneapolis: Fortress Press, 2005).

25. Hudnut-Beumler, *Generous Saints*.

26. Rena Froohar, "Go Glocal," *Time* magazine, August 20, 2012, 26–32.

27. See Cornelia Flora and Jan Flora, *Rural Communities: Legacy and Change*, 4th ed. (Boulder, CO: Westview, 2012).

28. Quoted in Jon Gertner, "The Rise and Fall of the G.D.P.," *The New York Times Sunday Magazine*, May 16, 2010, 60–71. Quote is from 68.

29. Ibid., 68–69, quoting Robert Putnam, *Bowling Alone: The Collapse and Revival of American Community* (New York: Simon & Schuster, 2001).

30. For a review of how this happened, see L. S. Jung, *Hunger and Happiness* (Minneapolis: Augsburg Fortress, 2009).

31. Sonya Salamon, *Newcomers to Old Towns: Suburbanization of the Heartland* (Chicago: University of Chicago Press, 2003).

32. For one way of identifying assets, see Luther Snow, *The Power of Asset Mapping: How Your Congregation Can Act on Its Gifts* (Herndon, VA: Alban Institute, 2004).

6

Rural Violence and Care

Amanda and Jennifer are members of Trinity Church in Ranchville, a small western town. Many in the town work in service jobs in a larger town fifteen miles away where there is a grocery store, Walmart, a school, and a few other businesses. Most families live on small ranches in the area.

Mitch, the pastor of Trinity Church, serves the church part-time while he also teaches history at the high school. He and his spouse, Anne, and school-age children moved from a large city to Ranchville a few years ago when they decided they wanted small-town life for their children. Anne teaches at the elementary school.

One Sunday Jennifer and Amanda, active women's group members, stopped Mitch after church and asked to speak to him for a minute. Jennifer and Amanda tell Mitch that they are quite worried about Dawn Grady, another member of the church. Jennifer and Amanda tell him that Dawn missed the women's group meeting this month and was not in church today. They did see her and Michael Grady, Dawn's husband, at Walmart last weekend. They think it is "time somebody did something." They are pretty sure that Michael hits Dawn. When they saw her at Walmart they noticed a bruise on her neck, and she had a large bandage on her arm. Dawn has become less involved than she used to be in the women's group and other church activities. She gave "some lame excuse" for not helping with the potluck last month. There were always rumors about Michael's father being mean and violent to Dottie, Michael's mother. If Michael and Dawn are having trouble then they need help, according to Jennifer and Amanda. They think that, as the pastor, Mitch should do something to intervene.

Mitch is acquainted with Michael and Dawn Grady and their three children, Althea, age five, Jason, age seven, and Caleb, age nine. They live about twenty miles down the highway from town, on Michael's family ranch left to him by his parents when they moved to a larger town about an hour away near Michael's older sister and her family. Michael has another sister who lives in another state with her husband and children. Dawn and Michael dated in high school and married soon after graduation.

Michael grew up in the church that Mitch now pastors and Dawn grew up in Jefferson, a town about forty miles away. Her father died in a car accident when she was twelve. Her mother and younger brother still live in Jefferson, where her mother is a hairdresser.

*****

Many people, like Mitch and Anne, think of small-town life as safe and wholesome, in contrast to what they perceive as urban problems of crime and violence. As stated in previous chapters, sometimes trying to live into the image of being a "safe" place can obscure the actuality of everyday life, including violence. Households like the Gradys' reveal but one kind of violence present in rural areas and small towns to which the church must respond. Pastoral care often requires responding to persons who have been victimized by and who have perpetrated abuse, assault, theft, hate, and a myriad of other kinds of violence. This chapter will demonstrate first that rural areas are not immune from violence and second that violence in rural areas may require different kinds of responses. In circumstances like these, the ways toward healing and transformation of the persons involved and of the communities of which they are a part are complex yet of vital importance as we seek to live into God's vision of peaceful relationships. Scenarios like the one that opens this chapter necessitate attention to what pastoral caregivers have learned about the dynamics, effects, and most helpful responses to situations of violence. They also necessitate attention to the distinctiveness of the rural context in which the violence occurs and how the context may demand new ways of thinking and doing in response. This chapter will frame the pastoral care called for from Mitch and Trinity Church, by first exploring rural crime and violence in general and then proposing an approach to care for the Grady family that is shaped by place, engages community, includes leadership, and responds to diversity in ways that can move everyone toward more healing and justice.

Violence in Rural Contexts

Most people assume that town and country areas are safer than large cities and metropolitan areas. Generally close-knit community and high civic involvement are thought, even by the experts, to lower rates of crime; thus they conclude that rural communities and small towns will have lower rates. Overall this is true; crime *is* lower generally in small towns than in urban/metropolitan areas. However, some criminologists have found that in the most remote rural places, crime rates *equal or exceed* metropolitan areas.[1] In other words, crime decreases as a function of population size to a point, and then it begins increasing again. In Canada, rural homicide rates are higher than in cities.[2] In a broad study of rural crime in the United States, Ralph Weisheit, David Falcone, and Edward Wells found that more than half of the counties with the highest homicide rates were nonmetropolitan.[3] Across age ranges, rural DUI arrests are more than double the rates of larger cities.[4] The rates of methamphetamine use are higher in rural areas than in metropolitan.[5] The state with the highest rate of rape is the largely rural state of Alaska.[6] Evidence suggests that rates of domestic violence, especially domestic homicides, may be significantly higher in town and country places than in other areas.[7] Crime exists in rural USA, and some kinds of crimes, including some violent crimes, seem to exist in higher numbers than they do in larger cities.

Rural criminologists and others continue to study rural culture and social organization for deeper understanding of the differences in rates and kinds of violent crime that affect rural areas. Rural crime is different, not entirely but significantly, and the theories that have been developed to understand and prevent crime do not always translate easily to town and country contexts. Distinct features that impact crime and violence in rural areas include the high levels of community bonding, lack of anonymity, economic change, mistrust of government, geographic isolation, cultural norms of noninterference, widespread availability of guns, and high use of alcohol. Some of these contextual realities appear to function in exactly the opposite way that they function in more populated areas. High levels of community involvement, for instance, are thought to help prevent crime, but in the case of small towns, it may actually tend to facilitate more crime rather than less, especially in domestic violence cases, which will be discussed later in more detail. Not all of these features are present in every rural place, nor do they function in exactly the same way across regions of rural USA, yet if rural churches and pastoral caregivers want to increase the safety of their communities, they will need to understand how these cultural realities and others function to support or deter crime and violence.

The strong sense of connection to one another and lack of anonymity can lead town and country people to resist upsetting the social balance by reporting crimes committed by others in the areas.[8] In small towns as compared to cities, there seems to be a larger margin between reported crime and actual crime; but as Weisheit, Falcone, and Wells point out, this does not necessarily mean that they are more tolerant of crime; in fact they are less tolerant of crime than their metropolitan counterparts.[9] The same study that reported Canada's high rural homicide rates found that the communities report a strong sense of connection and high levels of trust in one another.[10] While knowing your neighbors may help deter crime in metropolitan areas, in small towns it may function more to deter addressing or reporting crime publicly, thereby functioning as more a support for than deterrence against.

One kind of criminal activity for which lack of anonymity does seem to deter crime in rural areas is crime related to youth and youth gangs. Rural youth are faced with fewer job possibilities and recreational opportunities in small towns but they also have less anonymity, meaning that in many ways they have more adult supervision. Though they do exist, rural youth gangs are distinct from urban gangs.[11] The theories developed from studying urban gangs indicate that factors of social disorganization such as high neighborhood mobility, poverty, and low civic participation contribute to the development of gangs. However, small towns where youth gangs develop tend to have solid economic bases and highly organized, close-knit communities.[12] The gangs that develop in rural areas tend to be small, transient, and unstable and more likely to develop during economic recovery. There is not enough of a population base to sustain them over time.[13] The popularity of "gangsta" culture may even have some youth labeled as gang members when there is actually no more than one or two young people who find the media image appealing. Small towns seem to be fairly effective at maintaining safety for their youth when it comes to violent crime; and unlike in larger cities, when youth do get into criminal trouble it tends to coincide with positive, but rapid, economic change.

Many studies have shown links between poverty and crime, but those studies have almost always been located in cities even though the persistently poor more than likely live in rural areas. Weisheit, Falcone, and Wells found that in rural areas there is not as strong a link between poverty and crime as there is in urban areas. They state that "the level of economic resources had no effect on violent crime in rural areas. In contrast, rural areas with more economic resources had more property crime, but for urban areas more economic resources mean lower levels of property crimes."[14] Small communities experiencing rapid growth, such as those with new food-processing plants discussed in Chapter 5, often see higher crime rates even though the economy is improving; the rate of change is disorienting and small-town infrastructures are rarely prepared for rapid growth.

The people of small towns rely more on "informal social control," handling things themselves, in part due to the inaccessibility of services and a distrust of government.[15] Geographic isolation and a rural distrust of government can also support citizen militia groups that thrive on secrecy and often try to merge violence and religion. These groups can exist somewhat "off the grid" in rural areas, and while most rural people do not support or belong to these groups they often tolerate and take a nonintervention approach to their existence, even though the potential for violence because of these groups is high. Many rural areas in the South have long histories of lynchings and other forms of racially based hate violence. The isolation of rural areas seemed ideal for producing meth and growing marijuana without notice, and until recently methamphetamine use and rural production was on a steady increase.[16] The unpopulated, and unpatrolled, areas of the country can be prime locations for those who seek to be "under the radar" of law enforcement, and the strong culture of self-reliance, live-and-let-live, and noninterference in some rural areas can actually help sustain criminal activity.

Stereotypes associated with gun racks and holstered pistols and the ongoing assumption that rural people continually block gun control laws might suggest that rural people would show a higher rate of gun violence than other areas. The Weisheit, Falcone, and Wells study shows, however, that while small-town people are more likely to own guns, they are less likely to use them in commission of a crime.[17] Guns are more likely to be used to commit suicide in rural areas but less likely than in metropolitan areas to be used to hurt someone else. Guns mean something different to rural people; they are a symbol of surviving on one's own.[18] Hunting remains a common recreational activity in rural areas and in some areas still provides a regular source of food. In one small town in Alaska, people rely on hunting for their food, but police are not allowed to have guns because if police had guns "somebody might get shot."[19] In rural areas and small towns, gun possession does not seem to increase gun violence in terms of threats or intentional harm to the other, but it does increase the likelihood of accidental injury and suicide.

VIOLENCE AGAINST WOMEN AND CHILDREN

While in general crime is lower in small towns and rural areas, violence against women and children in families, which includes intimate partner violence, incest, and child maltreatment, occurs more frequently in these places than in metropolitan areas.[20] All of the characteristics of rural life identified above—bonding, lack of anonymity, economic change, isolation—contribute to problems with domestic violence in rural communities. One of the results of the move of meatpacking plants to rural areas is a rise in crime, with the most significant increase occurring in domestic violence and child abuse. Some of this increase is related to the changing demographics, but the presence of meatpacking industry itself seems to be correlated to increases in rape and sexual assault specifically.[21] The rate of violence against women and children is no doubt higher than criminal justice statistics suggest because rural folks tend to report crimes like child abuse and domestic violence even less often than those in cities. When there is violence in rural areas, it is more likely to be violence against a family member.[22]

In places where anonymity is unlikely, the perpetrator is more than likely someone the victim knows, which often leads to victims deciding not to call the police or press charges. In the cases of domestic violence and child abuse, knowing the police officer or social worker who may respond to the call results in fewer reports being made. This may be due to the fear that the officer will side with the perpetrator, with whom the officer is also likely to be acquainted; fear that the incident will be made public or that there may be social consequences of exclusion and stigmatization; or it may be due to the reality that not much will be done to protect the victim because of lack of services and training on the part of responders.[23] In a significant study of rural women who left abusive relationships, over 80 percent of the women reported that they could not count on their neighbors for help and experienced an extreme lack of help from their community.[24] There remains in rural United States a norm of nonintervention in what many still see as "private family affairs." While many times people think of small towns as places where everyone helps everyone else, this does not seem to hold when those in need of help are women and children being victimized in their families.

Over the last forty years of focused efforts to end domestic violence, many theologians, theorists, and activists have identified male domination as one of, if not *the*, primary contributing factor to intimate partner violence.[25] Gender norms in rural communities develop in ways somewhat specific to small towns and rural communities. DeKeseredy and Schwartz identified three characteristics of rural men who sexually assaulted their partners—peer support, a belief in the male as head of the household, and use of pornography.[26] These characteristics may apply to metropolitan men as well, but they develop in certain ways in rural communities that may contribute to the fact that there is more domestic violence there than elsewhere. Alcohol use is particularly high in rural areas and if other recreational opportunities are limited, men often gather at the local bar.[27] Assaults on women are often supported by male peers in settings where objectification of women, sexist jokes, and misogynist stories go unchecked and are even reinforced by laughter and support of other men. The presence of adult superstores enjoying the isolation of rural places and the prevalence of pornography can serve to "strengthen male misogynist bonds" and promote a distorted understanding of sexuality.[28] In addition, feminism may be one of those "city" values that small-town people see as disrupting their community, even though women have always played a significant role in agricultural economies.

As pointed out above, rural distrust of government, intense social cohesion, and lack of services contribute to low reporting of crimes, but these and other rural norms may foster higher rates of violence in families. As we have indicated throughout this book, rural areas suffer from lack of available, accessible, and affordable services from government and nongovernmental organizations. In the case of violence against women and children in families, lack of training for criminal justice and health-care workers means they do not always know how to assess and respond appropriately to domestic violence situations. Battered-women's shelters and foster care for children may not be readily available near home, school, or family. Women who leave abusive relationships find it difficult in rural areas to establish a violence-free life in their hometown because of lack of affordable housing, lack of public transportation, and lack of economic opportunity. If a mother is required to stay nearby because of custody arrangements, she is not free to relocate and will see her abuser on a regular basis. This means she is also exposed to ongoing violence or threat of violence. When victims of intimate partner violence are killed by their abusers it is, in the vast majority of cases, after or during the time when a woman decides to try to end the relationship. Intimate partner homicides are higher in rural areas than in metropolitan or metropolitan-adjacent places,[29] probably in part due to the higher rates of gun possession combined with the high rates of domestic violence.

Overall rates of child maltreatment, which includes both neglect and abuse, in rural areas are about the same as metropolitan; but families in rural areas are more likely to show signs of family stress and financial needs.[30] Children who are abused, either directly or by witnessing the abuse of a parent, face barriers to help similar to those of abused women. Isolation, limited access to social services, lack of anonymity, reluctance to intervene in "private" matters, and fear of communal ostracism sustain child abuse in small communities. Rural women and children who are victims of violence need the help of family, friends, and the community; and when they get assistance it seems to have an even larger impact toward the reduction of violence than in larger cities.[31] Churches have a role and a responsibility to help make sure that abused women and children get the help they need and to do all they can to make small towns and rural places safer.

PRACTICING CARE

The scene that opens this chapter raises the issue of domestic violence, even though as the story is presented we do not know for sure whether or not Michael is battering his wife, Dawn. The possibility that that situation might involve violence means that those who want to care for the Gradys need to think about what that possibility means for how they will proceed. The goal of pastoral care in the context of partner violence is to foster resistance to violence in the victim, perpetrator, and the community; to protect the most vulnerable, often the children; and to create an environment of safety wherein all persons can grow in relationships of mutual love. Intimate partner abuse is a pattern of behavior in which one partner exercises power unilaterally to coerce and control another. The many tactics for this abuse of power include pushing, shoving, rape, humiliation, threats, restricting access to money, and destruction of household objects. Even when physical violence is not immediately present there is an atmosphere of fear, and the constant threat of violence keeps the abuser in control of the relationship at all times.

The basics of pastoral response to situations of intimate partner violence are these:

1. assert that intimate partner violence is never okay;
2. attend to issues of safety for the victim, including children;
3. empower the victim;
4. hold the batterer accountable.

First, Pastor Mitch will want to make it clear to Jennifer and Amanda and to others that violence in families is never acceptable. There are no valid justifications for abuse. Dawn and Michael must also hear this message loud and clear. If the congregation and community have not heard this message through various public means, then that should be a priority for the ministry of Trinity Church. Second, safety for victims of violence should be the number one concern. In the situation with Dawn and Michael, there is potential at least that violence is present in their household; this possibility should frame any response Mitch or others might make. For instance, confronting Michael directly could result in his retaliating against Dawn or against whoever dares to intervene. Extra attention from Mitch toward Dawn, or a surprise visit from the pastor, could also have this effect. Since violence often increases when a victim attempts to leave or gives signals that she is preparing to leave, insisting that Dawn leave her home may put her and the children at increased risk. Mitch, Jennifer, and Amanda must think carefully about the risks involved in intervention and prepare their responses to help Dawn make informed choices about her relationship and her future.

Those who are interested in caring for victims of violence do not want to replicate the dynamics of abusive power and control by telling a victim what to do and insisting that they know what is best for her. Instead, focused and careful responses that provide information, connection, material support, and respectful listening can lead to healing and just outcomes for all involved. The pastoral caregiver must remember that, in this case, Dawn is the expert on herself and her life. She may benefit from information about domestic violence and available services, but she needs the respect that is expressed by letting her define what is happening and what she wants to do about it. Pastoral caregivers may help by engaging in conversations that can shift narrative interpretations by attending to exceptions, exclusions, and alternative explanations.[32] For instance, if Dawn were to say, "Michael just loses control," further conversations might talk about how Michael *gains control* through his actions. There must also be plenty of space for tolerating ambivalence and ambiguity.[33] Outsiders often find it difficult to tolerate that victims of domestic violence express love for their partners or return to them after brief separations. However, demonizing batterers and idealizing victims does not help either party heal or change behavior.[34]

SHAPED BY PLACE

The above standards for care are appropriate across contexts but take on different characteristics depending on the particular place. As highlighted in Chapter 2, the rural context teaches us that place shapes pastoral care. Place is impacting this particular situation, and Trinity Church can take this into account as they care for the Gradys' in ways that can foster healing and transformation. Place, including the land, geographical location, and meanings ascribed to it, forms persons' sense of identity. The people of Ranchville who have grown up there, like Michael, may feel that they *are* Ranchville. The vast open ranges and the rugged mountains symbolized the freedom of the frontier for early homesteaders and reinforced the values of rugged individualism, self-sufficiency, and perseverance. The cowboy image in the local culture may serve to promote a masculinity based on toughness and strength to conquer and control.

Sheep, cattle, and horses need wide-open spaces to graze; thus many of the homes in this region are miles apart. People from this region may have a strong need for space, but this space can also exacerbate domestic violence, isolating the victim and supporting a notion of family privacy that makes others unaware of what is happening in the Grady home or reluctant to intervene in someone's personal affairs. Isolation is known as one tactic of abusers for keeping control over victims, but it is a fact of life in remote rural areas, making it less evident as a sign of abuse.

Though rural life may be isolated, its small numbers mean it also lacks anonymity. In the most remote places, people may not see each other often but when they do see someone, they are recognized. As the conversation between Jennifer, Amanda, and Mitch indicates, Michael's and Dawn's personal histories are known to many in the community. It is impossible to hide in a small town like Ranchville. In small towns and rural areas, there are simply not as many options for safe anonymous retreats, nor are there as many support services to assist in doing so.

If Dawn is experiencing physical abuse in her home at the hands of her husband Michael, then her and the children's safety should be the first concern. Victims of intimate partner violence are often encouraged to have safety plans in place for escaping especially dangerous times; but in cases like Dawn's, domestic violence safehomes may be hours away and if they are more local, they are not likely to be in confidential locations.

Safety plans for victims of domestic violence may include finding shelter, calling the police, or going to a neighbor's. In a rural context, there may not be a domestic violence shelter; the nearest neighbor may be miles away; public transportation is not available; cell-phone service may be nonexistent; the sheriff may not arrive very quickly and could easily be one of Michael's friends. Planning for safety, whether temporary or long term, should be carefully thought through. A direct confrontation or intervention could put her at more risk. Statistics consistently show that women are in more danger of being killed when they leave a relationship, and abusive behavior often continues even after a relationship has officially ended. Dawn and the children would need cash, transportation, and a place to stay. If the risk of lethality is great, anyone that helps Dawn could be in danger as well. Unless her life is in immediate danger, this kind of coordination will take careful planning, and Dawn and those who want to support and care for her will find it helpful to consult a network of resources, such as Internet and hotlines, before making any moves. It is especially important to find this information and make the plan without arousing Michael's suspicion.

Dawn may have to face the hard reality that ending the abuse will require ending the relationship and moving to another region. Additionally, having the choice to leave a relationship is an important aspect of empowering victims of intimate partner violence, but in rural areas, more often than in metropolitan areas, leaving a relationship means going farther away from the place called home. There is no doubt in this case that Dawn would be the one to have to move since the very land is Michael's family land; even if the court system were to award the ranch to Dawn, in Ranchville it would always be the Grady place. She will need financial support, job training, and legal advocacy, especially as related to custody of children. If she has to, or wants to, stay in the area then she will need to be able to count on the whole community.

Michael's deep ties to this place can be both barrier to and resource for changing his behavior. If indeed his father did abuse his mother, that contributes to his having a model for abusive relationships between spouses, but it is not a determinative factor. Most children who witness abuse do not grow up to become abusers. It takes a confluence of factors to support abusive behavior, including supportive male peers, a justice system that does not respond, and a community that does not intervene. Michael will need clear messages that he must stop his behavior. Michael might be encouraged to draw upon the strength of mountains and legends of homesteader tenacity to give him the strength and tenacity it will take to stop abusing. His ties to the ranch, and the threat of losing it, could also serve as impetus to change.

Dawn, Michael, and the Grady children are isolated by geographic space and a prairie that demands much of their attention and strength. The cattle and horses depend on them; the oil pumped from their land provides financial support, but they are also part of a human community that will need to show rugged perseverance and strength if they are to help this family and others who face the ravages of domestic violence.

ENGAGING COMMUNITY

Pastoral care that fosters resistance to and healing from intimate partner violence requires participation of the whole congregation; it requires daily acts of ordinary care. In the case of the Gradys, two members of the congregation, Jennifer and Amanda, go to the pastor with their concern. Some might see their actions as perpetrating rumor and gossip, and no doubt their motives are mixed, but gossip and rumor can also be understood as a means of expressing concern and sorting through moral questions. They are triangulating the pastor into the issue, and while some might see this kind of triangulation as a problem, it may also be an expression of real concern. In systems theory, triangles function to reduce anxiety between members of a system by shifting the focus to someone or something else. In other words, Jennifer and Amanda are not sharing their anxiety with Dawn and Michael directly; instead they are trying to reduce it by bringing in the pastor. Triangles can be rigid and work to avoid conflicts that need attention, but they can also be useful. In this case Jennifer and Amanda, perhaps seeing their lack of expertise and their uncertainty of how to proceed, and possibly some hope that they can avoid getting involved, ask the pastor to do something. A pastor could respond to Jennifer and Amanda by saying that he cannot engage in speculation about Dawn and Michael and cannot do anything unless Dawn herself comes for help. In part this is a helpful response; the pastor should not engage in speculation and does need to think carefully about making interventions that have not been requested and could be dangerous. However, Jennifer and Amanda are also pastoral caregivers in this situation and in fact may be the best hope for reaching out to Dawn. They may be better positioned than the pastor, Mitch, to do what is needed. All three of them will need to be extremely careful about talking to others about their concerns or in any way raising public scrutiny of the Grady family, which will only make it less likely that Dawn would confide in them or ask for help.

If Dawn is being abused by Michael, then Jennifer, Amanda, and Mitch might think together about how to create an environment in which Dawn, and others like her, can feel safe enough to ask for help and receive the support she needs. Because the possibility of domestic violence is present, they will need to be very careful to keep Dawn and the children's safety in mind as they proceed. As established above, a confrontational visit from the pastor would likely escalate any violence, and since extreme jealousy is often a tactic of abusive control, in this case the fact that the pastor is a man makes a pastoral visit or phone call even riskier. There are some primary needs at this early point—check for the level of dangerousness, connection to others for support, and information that can expand Dawn's options. Jennifer, Amanda, and Mitch can find information about domestic violence on the Internet, in books, and through national and local agencies that work in the area of sexual and domestic violence. A call to the closest battered women's program or hotline may provide consultation in how to proceed. Discussing, or even mentioning, the topic of domestic violence and sharing information in a general way, such as posting important hotline numbers in the restrooms, in the congregation, and the community can begin to set the tone for Trinity Church to be seen as a safe place for disclosure. A caution is needed here: in a small congregation when these kinds of actions happen all at once and all of a sudden, people may begin to speculate about who or what prompted this action. Drawing attention to an issue is always important but also heightens anxiety for victims and abusers. A slow, gentle, consistent approach is preferred, and victims should not feel coerced into disclosure; such coercion simply replicates the dynamics of abuse.

This does not mean that Jennifer and Amanda should not connect directly with Dawn.

If Dawn is being more and more isolated, it is important for others to find safe ways of connecting with her. Jennifer and Amanda might say to Dawn that they noticed her bandages and were concerned about her, and assure her that they have kept their concern to themselves. Their ties to Dawn and Michael in the community and in the church can serve as basis for care. It is then up to Dawn to share what she wants about how she got those injuries. If they are the result of domestic violence, it is Dawn who must lead the way, but having information and consistent ongoing support from friends can encourage her. Caring friends and family often find it difficult to stand with victims and abusers over the long haul of change, and they are often putting themselves at some risk by doing so. Engaging a whole community with information about the dynamics of abuse and appropriate responses can reduce the risk to any one or two individuals, creating an environment of safety, support, and accountability that victims can trust.

The closeness, sense of community, and lack of anonymity can serve as both a barrier to and resource for changing dynamics of intimate partner violence such as those that may be present in the Grady home. Dawn may hesitate to seek help from those in her community because of the sense that if someone knows, everyone will know, and there is still a stigma against women who are victims of domestic violence. She may not feel able to call the sheriff because of the closeness of the community, and Michael's deep roots in the community may make the sheriff reluctant to make an arrest. Mitch and the members of Trinity Church have a Christian obligation to care for the whole of the Grady family, which includes holding Michael accountable for his behavior. If Michael is abusing Dawn, he will need his whole community to give the clear message that this is not acceptable, that he will be prosecuted for criminal behavior, and that he will also receive the support he needs to change. Pastors are often easily manipulated by abusers into believing that they are the real victims or that they have changed.[35] If Michael admitted to Mitch or another member of the congregation that he was abusing Dawn, Michael needs to receive care toward accountability and change. Directing Michael to a batterer's intervention program and making sure that he attends and participates might be one way of caring for Michael. Helping him to move out of the family home, attend another church, and assuring him that his friends and family will call the police if he violates a restraining order can also help Michael toward healing. Batterers of intimate partners, according to statistics, find it very hard to change because there is little that forces them to, but there is the possibility that with enough assistance from various parts of the community Michael can change.[36]

INTERSECTING WITH LEADERSHIP

Care for the Grady family should involve not only the immediate support necessary to ensure the safety of Dawn and the children and the intervention necessary to stop Michael from abusing, but also a whole community response to stop domestic violence. The church is called to care for the whole community, not only the people in their own congregations. Caring for the Grady family, and other families harmed by domestic violence, requires leading a community response to domestic violence. In rural congregations, the church is a central social institution and the pastor a caregiver and theologian for the whole town; as such they should see themselves as called to organize and mobilize the church and community to stop domestic violence. Trinity Church may want to begin raising awareness on the issue of intimate partner violence by holding public education events. They may want to volunteer at a nearby agency or begin efforts to establish a safehouse network in their area. Women's study groups can become good places for education and sharing. Mitch and other men in the congregation may think about finding ways to be explicit about what masculinity means from a Christian perspective. Men's groups that talk specifically about how to challenge their peers who engage in demeaning behavior toward women can begin to change the gender norms that support male violence against women. They may want to raise funds to train the local law enforcement in how best to respond. If Trinity Church takes the lead on this issue, they can be sure that other persons in need of care will emerge; healing and transformation can then spread.

RESPONDING TO DIVERSITY

Diversity is always present, and healing and transformative care must always respond to these diversities. There are several ways that diversity must be attended to in the illustration of the Grady family and Trinity Church if the church is serious about inclusive respect for difference and just relationships. Mitch and Anne are relative newcomers to the community. They are city raised and educated and may have brought with them a false idealization of small-town life. Even though they have been there for two years, the long-time residents of Ranchville may still not see them as "one of us." If Mitch brings with him some of the cosmopolitan values of specialist expertise, professional distance, and social privacy, then he might misread the expectations of the community that sees it as their obligation to involve themselves in the Gradys' problems but resists bringing in professional outsiders to help. His seminary pastoral care training might not have prepared him for the challenges of making a referral when there are so few nearby services, or negotiating a culture where everyone expects to know what is going on with the others. Mitch will need to use his education but also listen carefully for the historical traditions present in Ranchville and in Trinity Church. He can respect the tradition, affirm values within it that are consistent with Christian discipleship, and at the same time help people to challenge themselves where the tradition is not functioning to further the kin-dom of God.

Intimate partner violence is one form of violence against women rooted in the historical oppression and objectification of women. The fact that nearly all victims of intimate partner abuse are women and that nearly all the perpetrators are men highlights the intensely gendered nature of this issue. One of the first things that Mitch will need to realize is that in this case his maleness matters. Men who want to assist in stopping violence against women have to attend to the way that male power and privilege operate; and Mitch will want to understand the cultural gender norms in Ranchville. DeKeseredy and Schwartz found that "male peer support" and "rural norms of patriarchy" strongly supported domestic violence in rural communities.[37] Intimate partner abuse is a pattern of power exercised by one, usually a man, to coerce and control another, usually a woman, over a period of time in the context of an intimate relationship. Male privilege has historically supported woman abuse by asserting deep divisions in gender roles and men's authority over women. Though, as a country, the United Sates has made great strides toward more equality for women and more models for what it means to be a man or woman, these norms are still deeply ingrained in the culture and social inequity still exists. Research consistently shows that male abusers of their female intimate partners have strong commitments to gender roles in which men have the right, and responsibility, to exercise authority over women.

As a male pastor, Mitch can model what it means to be a man who works to end violence against women by using his power and authority as a pastor and community leader to give voice to the women in the community on this issue and to follow their lead. He will want to watch his own tendency to shift into roles that disempower women even if they seem to be benevolent impulses. He may experience an urge to go and rescue Dawn or to serve as her protector, but these actions can diminish Dawn's strength and authority over her own life. Mitch can use his position and identity as a man to help other men begin to deconstruct their own privilege and offer alternative peer support to men like

Michael, one that encourages mutually respectful relationships between men and women.

If Mitch, Jennifer, Amanda, and others in Trinity Church engage in the process of conscientization across gender, as described in Chapter 5, on the issue of domestic violence, they will need to proceed care-fully attending to the deep identity issues that are at stake and the deep wounds that can open up. It requires self-knowledge and willingness to be vulnerable but with special attention to how vulnerability functions. It takes much trust for women to open up about these issues with other women and even more so with men. Men must be careful to acknowledge what they cannot know about being a woman and must be willing to grant epistemological privilege to the experience of women on issues of woman abuse. Women also need to be able to listen to the struggles of men, as even their best of intentions can be undermined by norms so deeply ingrained that change involves reconstructing their very identity. None of this process is recommended for those like Michael and Dawn, who are in the midst of abusive relationships, because the inequality and the risks are so great. More appropriate response in a time of crisis is to provide same-gender assistance for each of them, but the power dynamics of gender are a significant factor as Mitch and others care for the Gradys at this time.

Healing and transformation for more love and justice in this family, this congregation, and in this community calls first for acknowledging that things like domestic violence happen in small towns. Well-informed care will follow some of the best practices of care established by the church and other helping professions, but this care must be responsive to the context of rural communities. Situations of intimate partner violence face rural challenges such as lack of services, lack of anonymity, and geographic isolation. These same challenges can be the impetus for engaging the congregation, rather than the pastor alone, to act in care for families and to change the community to reduce domestic violence. Care shaped by place will engage the community and require Mitch and others to work at the intersection of healing care for persons and leading communities toward transformation.

Notes

1. Joseph Donnermeyer, "Crime in Rural Communities: The Impact, the Causes, the Prevention," in *International Conference on Rural Crime* (University of New England, Armidale, New South Wales, Australia: 2006).

2. Ibid.

3. Ralph A. Weisheit, David N. Falcone, and L. Edward Wells, *Crime and Policing in Rural and Small-Town America*, 3rd ed. (Long Grove, IL: Waveland, 2006).

4. Ibid., 75.

5. Joseph F. Donnermeyer and Ken Tunnell, "In Our Own Backyard: Methamphetamine Manufacturing, Trafficking and Abuse in Rural America," in *Rural Realities* (Columbia, MO: Rural Sociological Society, 2007).

6. NSRV.

7. Walter S. DeKeseredy and Martin D. Schwartz, *Dangerous Exits: Escaping Abusive Relationships in Rural America*, Critical Issues in Crime and Society (New Brunswick, NJ: Rutgers University Press, 2009).

8. See Donnermeyer, "Crime in Rural Communities."

9. Weisheit, Falcone, and Wells, *Crime and Policing in Rural and Small-Town America*, 40.

10. Donnermeyer, "Crime in Rural Communities."

11. James C. Howell and Arlen Egley, "Gangs in Small Towns and Rural Counties," Office of Juvenile Justice and Delinquency Prevention, *NYGC Bulletin* (June 2005); Ralph A. Weisheit and L. Edward Wells, "Youth Gangs in Rural America," *NIJ Journal* (2004).

12. Maria T. Kaylen and William A. Pridemore, "A Reassessment of the Association between Social Disorganization and Youth Violence in Rural Areas," *Social Science Quarterly* 92, no. 4 (2011).

13. See Weisheit and Wells, "Youth Gangs in Rural America," and Weisheit, Falcone, and Wells, *Crime and Policing in Rural and Small-Town America*.

14. Weisheit, Falcone, and Wells, *Crime and Policing in Rural and Small-Town America*, 31.

15. Ibid., 40.

16. Donnermeyer and Tunnell, "In Our Own Backyard."

17. Weisheit, Falcone, and Wells, *Crime and Policing in Rural and Small-Town America*, 27. Gun violence is higher in rural areas than in small towns.

18. For interesting discussion of the role of guns as cultural symbols and the implications of that for the gun control debate, see Donald Braman, Dan M. Kahan, and James Grimmelmann, "Modeling Facts, Culture, and Cognition in the Gun Debate," *Social Justice Research* 18, no. 3 (2005): 283–304; and Donald Braman and Dan M. Kahan, "Overcoming the Fear of Guns, the Fear of Gun Control, and the Fear of Cultural Politics: Constructing a Better Gun Debate," *Emory Law Journal* 55, no. 4 (2006): 569–607. For a theological approach to gun violence, see *Gun Violence, Gospel Values: Mobilizing in Response to God's Call*, Presbyterian Church (U.S.A.), 2011.

19. Tomas Alex Tizon. "Stop—or We'll Shout," *Los Angeles Times*, October 7, 2004, quoted in Weisheit, Falcone, and Wells, *Crime and Policing in Rural and Small-Town America*.

20. See Walter S. DeKeseredy, Joseph Donnermeyer, Amy J. Fitzgerald, Linda Kalof, and Thomas Dietz, "Slaughterhouses and Increased Crime Rates: An Empirical Analysis of the Spillover from "the Jungle" into the Surrounding Community," *Organization and Environment* 22, no. 2 (2009): 158–84; and Susan H. Lewis, *Unspoken Crimes: Sexual Assault in Rural America* (Enola, PA: National Sexual Violence Resource Center, 2003).

21. Amy J. Fitzgerald, Linda Kalof, and Thomas Dietz, "Slaughterhouses and Increased Crime Rates: An Empirical Analysis of the Spillover from 'the Jungle' into the Surrounding Community," *Organization and Environment* 22, no. 2 (2009). This study was exploring the question of whether or not the violence required of workers in slaughterhouses resulted in more violence in the community. They found a direct effect between slaughterhouses and increases in rape and sex offenses, and they found that when other kinds of industries move into towns they have the opposite effect; violence decreases.

22. Weisheit, Falcone, and Wells, *Crime and Policing in Rural and Small-Town America*, 85.

23. Christina Lanier and Michael O. Maume, "Intimate Partner Violence and Social Isolation across the Rural/Urban Divide," *Violence Against Women* 15, no. 11 (2009). This study found that the strength of ties between people in rural areas may foster more intimate partner violence, in contrast to the theory that "collective efficacy" mitigates violence. Another study of rural communities (Arlene Haddon, Marilyn Merritt-Gray, and Judith Wuest, "Private Matters and Public Knowledge in Rural Communities: The Paradox," in *Understanding Abuse: Partnering for*

Change, ed. Mary Lou Stirling et al. [Toronto: University of Toronto Press, 2009]) found that fear about the lack of confidentiality, even from service providers, fear of being the object of public conversation, and fear of losing privacy and control over one's life are major factors keeping abused rural women from disclosing abuse or asking for help. DeKeseredy and Schwartz made similar findings in *Dangerous Exits*.

24. DeKeseredy and Schwartz, *Dangerous Exits*, 91.

25. For some pastoral theological approaches see Carol Adams and Marie Fortune, eds., *Violence against Women and Children: A Christian Theological Sourcebook* (New York: Continuum, 1995); Pamela Cooper-White, *The Cry of Tamar: Violence against Women and the Church's Response*, 2nd ed. (Minneapolis: Fortress Press, 2012); and James Poling, *The Abuse of Power: A Theological Problem* (Nashville: Abingdon, 1991).

26. DeKeseredy and Schwartz, *Dangerous Exits*.

27. Rural DUI's are more than double the rate of larger cities (Weisheit et al., *Crime and Policing*, 75). In rural areas, one in four boys aged thirteen to fourteen consume pornography, a rate higher than urban boys (Dekeseredy and Schwartz, *Dangerous Exits*, 68).

28. DeKeseredy and Schwartz, *Dangerous Exits*.

29. Lanier and Maume, "Intimate Partner Violence," 13–14.

30. See Marybeth J. Mattingly and Wendy A. Walsh, "Rural Families with a Child Abuse Report Are More Likely Headed by a Single Parent and Endure Economic and Family Stress," Carsey Institute, University of New Hampshire (2010). Poverty is not a legal basis for removal of a child from a home, but there are many ways that biases against poor parents add to the likelihood that poor children will be removed from their homes. See Lisa R. Pruitt and Janet L. Wallace, "Judging Parents, Judging Place: Poverty, Rurality and Termination of Parental Rights," in *Missouri Law Review* (2011) for an in-depth look at how rural poor families are even more vulnerable to biased child welfare decisions.

31. Lanier and Maume, "Intimate Partner Violence," 13–22.

32. For a narrative pastoral approach to domestic violence, see Christie Cozad Neuger, *Counseling Women: A Narrative, Pastoral Approach* (Minneapolis: Fortress Press, 2001).

33. For more on ambiguity and ambivalence in the context of intimate partner violence, see Jeanne M. Hoeft, *Agency, Culture and Human Personhood: Pastoral Theology and Intimate Partner Violence*, Princeton Theological Monographs (Eugene, OR: Pickwick, 2009); Poling, *The Abuse of Power*; and James N. Poling, *Rethinking Faith: A Constructive Practical Theology* (Minneapolis: Fortress Press, 2011).

34. Ibid.

35. See Jeanne M. Hoeft, "Seeing Power: Pastoral Recognition and Response to Intimate Partner Abuse," *INTAMS Review* 17 (2011): 152–61.

36. For more on batterers and batterer intervention, see Evan Stark, *Coercive Control: The Entrapment of Women in Personal Life*, Interpersonal Violence (New York: Oxford University Press, 2007).

37. DeKeseredy and Schwartz, *Dangerous Exits*.

7

Rural Health and Wholeness

Pastor Miguel enters into his morning meditation time, conscious of the parishioners he serves. He describes his congregation as two distinct fellowships united by a common belief in Christ: one that primarily worships in Spanish and a second that actually was the original congregation and worships in English. The fellowships worship at different times in the same church building, coming together once in a while for shared celebrations. This is the only church building left in this small, Southwestern community. Having grown up in this area close to the Mexican border, Pastor Miguel's bilingual heritage has been a gift to the congregation. He is pleased to serve this church because of his commitment to the people of the area and to his denomination. The area is fairly isolated; it is about thirty miles to the nearest medium-sized community that has grocery stores, a public high school, gas stations, and other essential services, and another thirty miles beyond that to a city that has more amenities. Because it is a small church and they cannot afford a full-time pastor, Pastor Miguel is a bi-vocational pastor whose full-time job includes work as a coach and teacher for the school system.

This morning the pastor's list of prayer concerns is full. He remembers the Hopper family who is taking care of the matriarch of their family, Jeannette. She has advanced Alzheimer's and the family continues to try to maintain her in their family home. Mrs. Hopper stays home and cares for her while Mr. Hopper (Jeannette's son) commutes to the neighboring community to work as an electrician. The Hoppers used to work the family's small ranch, but sold most of the property several years ago when a neighbor wanted to expand and it was clear that none of their family wanted to continue. They did negotiate to remain in the house, which had been built by the Hoppers. Multiple complexities are present for the Hoppers: there are few resources for the family in the local community, Jeannette has no insurance other than Medicare/Medicaid, and the closest specialist and treatment center is sixty miles away from where they live.

Pastor Miguel also remembers Mrs. Miguez and her eleven-year-old son, Raphael. Raphael's teachers are concerned about him because he seems to have problems focusing in school, is easily distracted, and often seems isolated from the other children his age. The school has recommended that Mrs. Miguez seek counseling for her son. She is a single mother who works a minimum-wage job in addition to doing housekeeping for some of the elderly folks in the community. Her jobs, of course, do not offer insurance, but Raphael's teacher has suggested they call the public mental health clinic in the town about thirty minutes away. Mrs. Miguez's first and primary language is Spanish, and she is most comfortable having Raphael interpret for her when there is a need or when there is something she does not understand. It is difficult to get an appointment with the counselor at the mental health clinic, and when she does take Raphael to the clinic, the counselor explains in English that she is not a specialist in working with adolescents and would like Raphael to see someone in the city, another thirty miles away. Mrs. Miguez does not completely understand what the counselor is saying and Raphael interprets for her. The counselor will help get Mrs. Miguez and Raphael on the waiting list for service, although Mrs. Miguez is aware that driving to the city will probably not be possible because it would mean losing another day of work and she is not convinced there is really anything wrong with Raphael. She doesn't say this to the counselor they see because she doesn't think that the counselor will understand. And, she doesn't want to talk to anyone in the fellowship because then everyone will know what is going on. Pastor Miguel knows about the situation largely because of his connections in the school system.

As the prayer list continues, Pastor Miguel is mindful of Jerry, whose life hangs in the balance as he struggles with cancer. Jerry teaches school in the same school system as Pastor Miguel. He is in his late fifties and developed signs of lung cancer several months ago. In the last few weeks his health has declined considerably. There is a local care clinic in the community thirty miles away where he has been able to get some of his treatments, but for the most part he has had to travel to the larger community sixty miles away where there is a small clinic that serves the area. A specialist comes in once a week from the larger city to the clinic, and Jerry has to be there on the one day the doctor comes to the clinic. People from the English-speaking fellowship have been helpful in transporting Jerry to appointments, but everyone is beginning to feel the tiredness of arranging transportation, treatments, and the hopelessness of impending death. There is a tri-county hospice resource with nurses and a staff located around the region in order to provide service to a large land area that has a small population. Pastor Miguel is grateful for the resource and also aware that the staff cannot be present in ways that might always be helpful.

And finally, Pastor Miguel lifts up the primary care doctor, Dr. Ramon, who serves the area. Dr. Ramon also grew up in the borderlands and came to this community because of her desire to serve the underserved, particularly those for whom English is not a primary or first language. She is feeling the burden of being the only Spanish-speaking physician in the area as well as experiencing some of the isolation of being a single female in an area that is remote and distant. Her closest friends live in the larger metropolitan area about ninety miles away, and she finds herself wondering whether she can continue to serve this area. She has sought out her pastor, Pastor Miguel, for guidance in thinking about her vocational choices.

Pastor Miguel understands that his role as a pastoral care provider in this community is to foster the wholeness of individuals, families, and of the community itself. Because of this, he is deeply invested in the physical, mental, and spiritual health of his parishioners. While he understands his primary role to be one who embodies God's healing, sustaining, guiding, and reconciling presence to his congregation, he is also aware that the needs of the community he serves extend beyond what he can offer by himself. He has been in the community for three years and is beginning to see the need to work collaboratively with various partners in offering physical, mental, and spiritual care. Yet, he is also aware of the overwhelming feeling of isolation as he begins to think about the task at hand.

*****

RURAL HEALTH AND WHOLENESS

Participating in the healing of people's lives has always been a primary function of pastoral care and those who minister on behalf of the church.[1] Pastor Miguel cannot escape the way in which the physical and mental health needs of his congregation are deeply related to his responsibilities as a pastoral and spiritual leader. Nor can he deny that the quality and quantity of health-care resources for his community have a direct impact on the physical, mental, and spiritual health of the members of his fellowships. Wanting to nurture wholeness through pastoral care in any community of faith requires that leaders attend to the health needs of individuals and families, as well as of the community in general.

The individuals and families in Pastor Miguel's church represent normal situations in many congregations, and at one level there is nothing unique about the interconnection between pastoral care and the physical and mental health needs of a congregation or community. People everywhere wrestle with issues of aging populations, dying patients and their families who deserve quality care, the specialized needs of mental health care for adolescents and children, or the recruiting and retaining of qualified and dedicated physicians, emergency personnel, nurses, dentists, and mental health providers. Pastoral caregivers are often on the front lines as they sit with families in the midst of many of these struggles. And, as they hear the stories of parishioners, they often find themselves in places where they become part of the healing presence as well as part of a team of advocates in the health-care context.

Rev. Miguel's ministry is focused not simply on the individuals and families in his congregation; rather he is aware that his concern for the health of the whole community reflects pastoral care that is more than individualistic in its endeavors. The rural context also offers a glimpse into how physical, emotional and mental, and spiritual care requires the efforts of multiple partners. The presence or absence of services, and the many partners who make care possible, make it easier or harder for people to access quality care for their physical or mental health on the other, compromising or putting more pressure on their emotional and spiritual lives.

The context also illuminates the strengths and vulnerabilities for small communities in rural areas. On the one hand, Pastor Miguel recognizes the incredible support of parishioners for one another, even across cultural lines at times. Likewise, he is aware that he knows more about the stories of a larger percentage of the population in his area than he would ever know in a larger community or city. At the same time, he is aware of how the particular struggles of being rural add to the challenges of health care: the isolation and distance from services, the financial hardship for small communities to provide even minimal services, and the difficulties that come with parishioners who never feel like they can remain more anonymous about what is going on in their families. It is also true that his context of the Southwest creates a different kind of complexity than rural living on the shores of the Gulf, the expansive farmland of the Midwest, the timbered regions of the Northwest, or any other region.

Ultimately, the way in which congregations and pastors meet the challenge of nurturing wholeness in the lives of individuals, families, and communities can offer insight into pastoral care practices in general. For the purposes of this chapter, it is important to look at two specific dimensions of wholeness and health care: physical and mental/behavioral health. By examining the uniqueness of the rural context in each of these arenas, it is possible to begin to see the relationships between the presence—or absence—of such things as health-care resources, mental health providers, diverse spiritual leaders, and the quality of life of the people within rural communities. The end of the chapter will return us to the particular themes we have looked at in this text as we move toward integrative pastoral care in a rural context.

WHAT IS PARTICULAR ABOUT RURAL HEALTH CARE?

As we are well aware, the United States has been struggling with issues related to affordable and adequate health care for a very long time. At the beginning of this century, the United States government initiated a project called "Healthy People 2010," targeting matters important to the health of the nation.[2] All of the issues they identified were true for both rural and nonrural populations. However, differences between rural communities and urban or metropolitan areas seemed significant enough for the Office of Rural Health Policy, in collaboration with the Southwest Rural Health Research Center at Texas A&M University, to identify specific needs of rural communities. Their work included identifying models of care from various rural contexts in the United States in order to illustrate "best practices" toward addressing some of the needs. As the authors of *Rural Healthy People 2010: A Companion Document to Healthy People 2010* point out, "Rural areas frequently pose different, and in some instances, greater challenges than urban areas in addressing a number of HP2010 objectives. There are rural-urban disparities in health conditions associated with particular preventable or chronic diseases and disparities in infrastructure or professional capacity to address health needs."[3] Such differences are important for pastoral leaders to recognize if they hope to be effective in their pastoral care.

The researchers, along with national and state rural health experts, identified access to health care—including such things as emergency medical services, workforce (doctors, nurses, technicians, etc.), health services in general, health insurance, and access to primary care—as the highest rural priority. The second-highest overall category, mental health services, was followed by the need for attention in the area of oral health. In other words, access to health care, to mental health practitioners, and to dentists and hygienists, constituted the highest needs identified by rural experts.[4] In fact, almost every text that deals with rural health care, whether from the perspective of physicians and doctors, hospitals, nurses, governmental agencies, or mental health practitioners, consistently notes the difficulties for rural communities to provide broad health-care services.[5]

Attending to the various segments of health services, including public, environmental, and occupational health, requires not only hospitals and doctors, but the infrastructure and support staff needed to offer such things as screening and disease surveillance; emergency treatment; transportation services; diagnostic, treatment, and curative procedures; disease management; and rehabilitation services.[6] Human resources—nurses, physicians, specialists related to all areas of health care, dentists, oral hygienists, mental health providers, pharmacists, spiritual and pastoral caregivers, and more—are needed for the systems to function. The presence of these resources in a region carries a financial cost that is often impossible to meet in rural communities, and the lack of resources exacts an emotional, physical, and spiritual cost for everyone related to the region.

Rural communities differ in what is most needed in a particular region. In one area, the most significant need might be addressing the harmful effect of tobacco, while in another location it may be creating responses to occupational or safety hazards that arise in the most prevalent work environments in the area. The role of government at all levels and the development of policies are often quite helpful and important, but as one set of authors notes, "In approaches to health promotion and disease prevention, investigators should recognize that lifestyle choices and adoption of healthy behaviors are influenced not only by governmental policies but also by individual, social, geographical, and climatological factors."[7] Various factors that make for wholeness differ and interact within each context and community.

Many pastoral leaders are among the first in rural communities to become aware of struggles that are not only physical in nature, but that have mental and behavioral components as well. Because of this, it is helpful to briefly reflect on five areas related to health care: the role of occupations and work, human resources, financial factors, specific health issues, and the uniqueness of mental and behavioral health.

OCCUPATIONS AND WORK

Factors such as employment patterns, the availability of needed job skills, the value placed on workers who are not paid or who receive financial remuneration, and the presence or lack of benefits such as insurance, have a deep and abiding impact on health care. In a chapter related to rural nursing, Kathleen Long and Clarann Weinert note that "[h]ealth is assessed by rural people in relation to work role and work activities, and health needs are usually secondary to work needs." They go on to suggest that persons in rural contexts often define health as "the ability to work, to be productive, to do usual tasks."[8] Hence, illness or pain (whether physical or related to mental health) might be tolerated as long as it does not interfere with functioning and with productive work. Preventive care and treatment for minor difficulties are often put aside, especially if they interfere with work or productivity.

Rural areas are also unique because of the kind of occupations and work related to their contexts. As noted elsewhere in this text, the economic status of rural communities varies across geographic locations and is often connected to natural resources that are available within a region. For example, oil and gas industries are predominant in the rural Southwest where Rev. Miguel's church is located, with ranching and agriculture following closely behind. Other parts of the Southwest close to the Gulf of Mexico may depend more on industries related to fishing, hunting, or tourism, while still other areas depend economically upon ranching and the ancillary businesses required for that enterprise. Opportunities for meaningful work are an important ingredient in every community, and in the lives of the individuals and families who live there.

Many occupations in rural areas demand hard physical labor under sometimes harsh conditions, thereby compromising the health of those employed in those jobs. Difficult and labor-intensive work is not limited only to those who are paid, but also to spouses, partners, children, and others who participate in the work and who are often in situations that some would describe as dangerous. For example, in the area of Rev. Miguel's church there is a great emphasis on petroleum production. Such work carries with it hazards such as blowouts, work-related injury and death, as well as potential environmental hazards. Several occupations across the rural United States—mining, logging, farming, fishing—involve extracting natural resources. Evidence suggests that "fatality rates for each of the extractive industries have exceeded the national average every year."[9]

Such work takes its toll not only on the physical lives of employees, but on the mental health of themselves and their families as well. "Stress results from the large number of uncontrollable factors: weather, storms at sea, or market prices. There can be significant isolation at work. . . . For farm families the demands related to debt, the cyclical nature of farm prices and income, and the juggling of farm and off-farm jobs produce stress."[10] No matter the region in which people live, the emotional and mental anxiety that accompanies work in rural contexts is always present.

Relational issues can also become part of the stress that people experience in their work lives. Again, this is true whether one lives in the city or in a small community. What is distinct about rural life is that it is difficult to avoid someone or to remain distant. Boundaries are more permeable and fluid in rural areas as individuals and families often connect in smaller public arenas. For example, the only Protestant or Catholic church or the only synagogue in town may be the place where bosses sit next to their co-workers, physicians or counselors sit behind clients and their families, the social worker responsible for investigating allegations of abuse is the Sunday School teacher for one of those children, or underpaid service staff worship with those responsible for their checks. The underpaid or unpaid migrant worker's family in the Spanish-speaking fellowship of Rev. Miguel attends one service, while the boss attends another. The various stratifications and the way in which power emerges and is negotiated are unique for rural communities. The boundaries that are more easily maintained in urban or suburban contexts are more permeable realities in rural contexts.[11]

Finally, several researchers raise concerns about the environmental risks that arise in rural areas. Often the dangers for the most vulnerable of the population, such as children and the elderly, are underreported or underexamined. As researchers in the field of health care, Wade Hill and Patricia Butterfield note that "[f]or more than 200 years, rural areas have been considered the 'dumping ground' of a production-based economy. Items (e.g., nuclear waste, antiquated military supplies) and activities (e.g., mining, smelting) considered dangerous, distasteful, or requiring large plots of land have preferentially located in remote parts of the country. Contaminants from such historic activities have left a legacy of risks for local residents."[12] The potential for harm not only to the environment, but to rural residents and, in particular, to those who are most vulnerable, are painful realities for many rural communities.

It would be a mistake to oversimplify the work life of rural people, to treat the type and kind of occupations they engage in as insignificant, or to suggest that rural persons simply ought to find other ways that are less dangerous or more compatible with environmental concerns in order to make a living. The economy of local areas, the desire to support a particular lifestyle, the generational reality of being tied together through vocational choices, and the market demand for certain products all are interwoven in the way that people understand the meaning of their work. All of these factors contribute to a contextual reality that has an impact on the wholeness—physically, spiritually, mentally—of congregations and communities of faith in rural areas.

HUMAN RESOURCES

For some in rural communities, working in the health-care profession as a nurse, mental health worker, dentist, pharmacist, or physician provides meaningful work. Yet, the reality is that for rural communities, the smaller population base means that there are simply fewer resources in the form of personnel. At one level, it makes sense that there are fewer physicians located in rural communities simply because of the financial resources it takes to pay for that person's services. Yet, while many communities at least have some access to general practitioners (although fewer in number per capita than might be found in urban or suburban settings), the more remote a community is, the less likely they are to have specialists of any kind. Recruiting practitioners and their families is of tremendous importance to rural communities. Whether trying to fill positions as mental health specialists, personnel for a county health agency, or doctors and nurses to serve as primary caregivers, the challenges are sometimes daunting. Not only is there a financial cost in order to secure adequate salaries and benefit packages, there are also the complications for families of providers who are looking for employment for spouses in the area or adequate school systems for their children.[13]

Often the family physician is met with multiple issues for which she or he may not be adequately trained. At one moment the family doctor may be treating someone for depression while, at another time, the physician may be asked to help with a child who has developed a rare form of cancer for which there are no treatment options locally and for whom there is no insurance other than Medicare or Medicaid. The need for one person to treat multiple issues requires more ongoing educational opportunities for those who serve rural communities, yet that often entails financial resources to travel to meetings and workshops as well as leaving practices unfilled for a time. Those who serve in rural areas are often drawn to such work because of their histories or their commitments to serve the underserved.

The presence of new technologies and advances in communication hold out much promise for rural communities. Consultations to rural physicians, mental health providers, or others can occur with specialists in larger urban hospitals or mental health centers. The government and others are particularly interested in how information technology will make a positive difference in the lives of those who practice in rural areas, as well as in the quality of and access to care.[14]

While being a practitioner in a rural community is daunting, it can also be rewarding. For those who are eager to know more about those to whom they offer care, or to know something of the kinship systems and networks of care that sustain people, rural communities offer something unique to health-care professionals. For the parishioners in Pastor Miguel's church, knowing more about their doctors, nurses, counselors, and pastors can bring a more meaningful connection to their lives.

FINANCIAL REALITIES: COMMUNAL AND INDIVIDUAL/FAMILY

In examining the challenges related to the behavioral and mental health of rural populations, psychologists Pamela Mulder and Warren Lambert suggest that there are three kinds of stressors that have an impact on the health of those living in rural areas: socioeconomic, sociocultural, and other concerns related to specific health issues. As they point out, these stressors should not necessarily be interpreted as causative of poor health in rural communities; rather they ought to be understood as intimately connected to the quality of living in the rural United States.[15] In addition, these are not simply challenges that have an impact on the wholeness of individuals and families, but on the wellness of the communities themselves.

As noted elsewhere in this text, the economies of local communities are dependent on various factors that, in turn, determine the adequacy or availability of quality health care. As one report notes, "In general, the smaller, poorer, and more isolated a rural community is, the more difficult it is to ensure the availability of high-quality health services. Compared with urban communities, rural communities tend to have fewer health care organizations and professionals of all types, less choice and competition among them, and broad variation in their availability at the local level."[16] Such differences can create a devastating, or at the very least a challenging reality for rural communities.

One of the determining factors for the financial status of health care in rural areas rests in the small population base available to create revenue through tax dollars or payment for services. There is no doubt that the sparse population centers of rural communities cannot financially support a quantity of health-care options in ways that are commensurate with urban areas.[17] Such financial realities are often indicative of fewer hospitals, fewer multiple-level care centers, fewer mental health resources, fewer emergency rooms or trauma centers, fewer physicians and dentists, fewer pharmacists, and fewer public health options for those on Medicare or Medicaid.[18] The lack of emergency rooms is a particularly poignant case to examine. As is pointed out in *Rural Healthy People 2010*, "injuries in rural areas tend to be greater in severity than in urban areas. Only one-third of all motor vehicle accidents occur in rural areas, yet two-thirds of the deaths attributed to these accidents occur on rural roads."[19] Deaths from unintentional injuries increase by over 80 percent in rural areas. Higher fatality rates occur in areas that are more remote.[20] Adequate and appropriate resources for multiple levels of care are costly, and the consequence of the lack of these resources in rural areas is remarkable.

Hospitals in rural areas often rely more on Medicare and Medicaid funding and are more likely to be government-owned or fall into the nonprofit sector.[21] While there are cultural changes occurring around their funding, many rural areas have depended upon larger communities (not necessarily urban areas, but county population centers) for their hospital resources. In those communities, the hospital often provides significant financial support for the community as they become one of the larger employers for the area.

Financial issues related to health care are compounded by the socioeconomic challenges of individuals and families in rural areas. For example, because of the various kinds of work and occupations related to rural living, a higher percentage of rural persons are uninsured (about 20 percent in rural areas and 17 percent in urban areas in 2000). Uninsured percentages rise among African Americans and increase even more for Latinos, as well as being higher for those who are chronically ill or poor.[22]

As evidenced above, distance plays a factor in mortality rates, but it also carries another financial burden for individuals and families. In a study with women from remote areas of Montana, Ronda Bales notes that distance is understood to be simply a reality of life, except when there is an emergency. While traveling to see a specialist or to receive a treatment is not seen as a disadvantage, for those who live outside of urban centers it takes more time away from a job, more money for gasoline to travel, and more dependency upon family members or others in the community in order to access care that is offered some distance from where one lives. And, rarely is there public transportation that assists people financially or pragmatically in getting from one place to another.[23] In Pastor Miguel's congregations, one glimpses the need to find others for transportation for cancer treatments while the mother of the young boy referred to an adolescent mental health provider would need to take time from work and would experience a loss of income if she were to try to seek the help of an adolescent psychiatrist or specialist. All of these realities have a negative impact on families, some of whom may already be experiencing financial difficulties.

Poverty, a universal issue not confined to one region or area of the world, compromises the quality of one's life. As pointed out by Mulder and Lambert, rural poverty varies most often with "family structure, marital status, and ethnicity." While their work focuses on the lives of rural women, the statistics they raise are startling to consider in general: more than half of all rural families with children younger than eighteen years of age have annual incomes below the poverty level; rural families headed by women experience greater poverty than those headed by men; 35 percent of rural female-headed families are living in poverty; nearly one-third of rural women living alone are poor (almost nine points higher than metro areas); poverty levels are highest for ethnic-minority women living in the Southeast; 26 percent of women with disabilities live in rural communities and tend to be poorer, less educated, and more dependent on government social service programs than other rural residents.[24]

Poverty in families, whether in homes headed by men or women, increases the vulnerability of children, the elderly, and those with disabilities. Children, for example, are less likely to receive preventive care, or they may be less likely to seek out mental health services. As one set of psychologists note, "Some parents in poverty, confronted with inadequate physical, mental, and financial resources, are simultaneously thwarted by the inability to provide an adequate physical environment for their children."[25] Similar realities face those who are elderly, those who depend upon Medicare or Medicaid for services, and those who are challenged physically, mentally, or emotionally. The connections between material resources, physical and mental health, and pastoral care are apparent. The lack of financial resources and poverty is an issue with which many struggle in rural areas, and it makes access to health care of all kinds more difficult.

While there are nonprofit agencies that address health-care needs in rural communities, on the whole they spend fewer financial resources to meet the needs of the poor in rural communities.[26] Rural poor remain invisible because they may live in a house off a main road that very few travel or in conditions that few witness. This often means that the church ends up trying to meet financial needs of persons who are in crisis, particularly related to health care. Again, the smaller population numbers place a greater burden upon smaller communities to try to meet health-care needs.

SPECIFIC HEALTH ISSUES

Specific health issues that need to be addressed in rural communities are no different from those in urban areas. What is distinct, however, is the higher rate in particular areas for some illnesses. A report from the South Carolina Rural Health Research Center notes that rural adults have higher rates of reported diabetes, are more likely to be obese, and less likely to follow recommendations for physical activity.[27] Overall, there is a higher incidence of chronic bronchitis, cancer, arthritis, higher death rates from cardiovascular disease, and higher rates of diabetes.[28] Death rates between 1996 and 1998 for children and young adults were highest in rural counties in all regions except the Northeast.[29] As is true in many parts of the world, children, women, persons with disabilities, and racial or ethnic groups are among the most vulnerable populations in rural areas.

Geographically, some areas of the United States have higher risks for certain kinds of illnesses. For example, while rural populations in general have higher rates of skin cancer, in rural Appalachia the death rate from various types of cancer is higher than in any other rural or urban part of the United States. Rural patients are also more likely to be diagnosed at later stages of their cancer.[30] Adolescents and adults living in rural communities are more likely to smoke than their counterparts in urban areas.[31] This, in turn, has a negative effect on cancer rates in some rural areas. In a similar way, many women located in rural farming contexts supplement income on farms, and there has been an increase in the number of automobile accidents and farm-related injuries involving women. In fact, "farm women and children suffer twice as many injuries as do other family members and 70 percent of these injuries are reported as being severe, permanent, or fatal."[32] Where people live and under what conditions has an impact on the specific health issues that are most apparent in a geographic region.

Startling, as well, are the statistics for persons who are Native American, Latino/a, or African American in the rural United States. Rural African Americans, for example, have higher incidences of problems at birth while adults suffer from elevated levels of diabetes, heart disease, and hypertension.[33] Latinos are least likely to have insurance coverage while Native Americans tend to have higher rates of diabetes and heart disease.[34] Persons who are part of the historically nondominant culture of the rural areas have more negative health issues than Caucasians.

The disparities between rural and nonrural persons related to particular health issues raise the stakes for those who lead in rural churches. While it is impossible to address every health issue, it is apparent that the wholeness of individuals, families, and communities depends upon pastoral leaders who are proactive in raising awareness about health-care needs.

MENTAL AND BEHAVIORAL HEALTH NEEDS

Mental and behavioral health issues are as prevalent in rural areas as in metropolitan communities. While the rates of incidence of mental and behavior health issues are similar between rural and nonrural areas, there are differences related to the context. Findings suggest, for example, that overall there is more alcohol abuse, methamphetamine use, and suicide in the rural West and among farmers.[35] And, the financial realities for those who live in rural communities contribute to a particularly strong "financial strain" that has an impact on mental health.

In many rural areas, the primary mental health providers are physicians[36] or clergy who may or may not have training for such work. Among women, for example, depression and stress-related disorders are more likely to be diagnosed for women in rural areas by physicians who are also central in providing medication or assistance in planning for treatment. Yet, rural women are less likely to be accurately diagnosed or referred to mental health specialists than urban women. In addition, symptoms that are often identified as depression are often "correlated with greater poverty, less education, and being unmarried."[37] In the rural United States, a larger percentage of women fall into these categories.

As noted earlier, economics and poverty have an impact in the health-care systems of rural communities. There is no doubt that where there is a greater lack of financial resources in a community, there are higher needs to respond in healthy ways to economic stress. As one set of authors note, "We know that deprived individuals live in deprived places and are less healthy than those living in affluent areas."[38] These authors go on to note that "[r]obust associations have been demonstrated between individual-level socio-economic status, mortality, and many forms of morbidity, including psychiatric. . . . Much more research has been done to understand the links between socio-economic status and the most common mental disorders (CMDs)—anxiety and depression—than with schizophrenia, where individual disability and impaired social functioning are often highly evident."[39] The mental health of women, men, and children in rural economies is dependent on the presence of services and access to them.

Those things that stand in the ways of access to mental health services are similar to those in urban settings, yet again there is a difference. With fewer mental health specialists in rural areas, finding help is often quite exhausting. Bales suggests that there are six "themes" related to rural people—self-reliance, hardiness (resiliency), conscientious consumer habits, informed risk, community support, and inadequate insurance—that work to prevent adequate care. For example, the perceived sense of self-sufficiency or self-reliance that is sometimes at work in rural communities can contribute to the desire for some families and individuals to work things out on their own.[40] In similar ways, a lack of anonymity and the awareness that others "know your business" or that the person who sees you for counseling is someone you see in the grocery store, is related to your next-door neighbor, or someone from the city and an outsider can sometimes prevent people from seeking help.

Pastors, along with other rural health-care providers, are often on the front line of interacting with people who are experiencing distress related to behavioral or mental health. The more awareness they bring to the struggles for accessing adequate support services related to providing adequate care, the more often they will find themselves in positions to advocate for the needs of their parishioners and communities. In addition, the realities of rural communities make it incumbent upon rural pastoral leaders to find strength-based ways to lead the community in identifying resources that they already have to address some of the needs for mental health in their community. Knowing who has struggled with addictions and thrived, or what family has learned how to cope with the mental illness of a son or daughter, makes it possible for pastoral leaders to draw upon the local resources available to them. There will always remain the need for more professional mental health providers in rural communities, yet pastoral leaders would do well to seek their own educational opportunities to come to deeper understandings of the dynamics related to behavioral and mental health, since they will be some of the people to whom others will turn for help.

PRACTICING CARE

Throughout this text, we have identified four themes that emerge in rural pastoral care and that are present in healing and transformative care. Attention to place, community, leadership, and diversity can help in discerning what concrete acts of care a church and its leadership might take. By returning to Pastor Miguel and his congregation it is possible to see the integration of these four themes in the larger context of pastoral care.

SHAPED BY PLACE

The case study of Pastor Miguel's church highlights how place matters in the embodiment of pastoral care. The land and geography of the Southwest, particularly those areas closer to the boundary between the United States and Mexico, are influenced deeply by the plurality of longtime residents who ranch and/or develop businesses related to the oil and gas industry, families who immigrate across the border to Texas, New Mexico, and Arizona who may or may not be documented workers, some of whom move fluidly back and forth, others of whom have come and stayed, and still others who are recent arrivals. The economic reality of this region is marked by large areas of small population centers with larger cities and communities often at quite some distance from one another. Such expanse of land in the Southwest has resulted on the one hand in a deep spirit of individualism and yet, at the same time, there is an awareness of how people are interdependent with one another at some deeper levels.

An astute pastoral care person emphasizes the healing and transformative care of the church by recognizing that communities in this part of the United States carry with them deep connections to the land in ways that can enhance spirituality. For Pastor Miguel, it is important to listen to others as they describe the various ways in which the land itself has an impact on both ranching and the businesses related to oil and gas. Here, spirituality might be tied to such things as an appreciation for the expansive sense of God's world, the importance of water in the midst of a fairly dry climate, the power of resources beneath the earth, or the beauty of canyonlands that are marked with streams that ebb and flow with the changing seasons.

Wherever the placement of the church is in this community, one can be certain that it has been a place that marks home for those who are in the midst of living and dying. There are generations of families who have drawn upon the site of this building—or others in the community that have since been given over to other uses—for their sense of belonging in the midst of a changing world. Pastor Miguel knows the importance of tending to not only the church "home," but also literally visiting the homes of those within the community. Seeing where people live and how they live can be central in knowing the most appropriate ways to reach out and offer care.

Engaging Community

The gifts and limitations of small communities are apparent in the church that Pastor Miguel serves. On the one hand, it is easy to see how people are connected to one another and how, even in the context of two different-language fellowships sharing one building, people are aware of the interdependence they have for one another. Neither fellowship could stand on its own, and even the families are interconnected in ways that are sometimes not easily noticed. The Hoppers and the stories of their family ranch and the shifting of generational claims are known to others because they are part of a "public" story. The strength of such closeness, evidenced in the fact that Pastor Miguel is aware of Jerry's illness or the needs of Raphael and his family, occurs in part because they are connected through the school system. In similar ways, the struggle of professionals who serve these small communities is also apparent in the life of Dr. Ramon. Healing and transformative pastoral care requires that we not only honor and value the closeness, but also name the limitations that arise from such "smallness" in terms of simply having fewer opportunities for friendships and relationships that extend beyond the community.

In light of what it means to be a bi-vocational pastor, it is clear that Pastor Miguel's ministry is not confined to Sunday morning, nor is he the only caregiver in the congregation. Instead, this pastor know that he cannot be present often in the middle of the day for the Hopper family or any other crisis that emerges. Hence, it is important to nurture the care that is offered by multiple others in his absence. The congregation members—both Anglo and Spanish-speaking—are the ones who offer ordinary care in the midst of life. Honoring, supporting, and nurturing that ordinary care is essential to the ministry of this church. Recognizing those in the church who live with family members because there are few options or who drive persons to medical appointments, or valuing those who can speak both languages and facilitate access to a health care that is predominantly English-speaking, and noting the vocational gift of a physician who is committed to the people in rural communities are all ways that the pastoral leader honors the ordinary care of the church.

The prophetic voice of the pastoral leader in small communities requires, as well, that he or she pay close attention to the ways in which the resources for those who live among and around them offer less access to quality care for physical illness, Alzheimer's and other chronic illnesses, and mental health resources. A healthy pastoral leader will work not only in addressing the immediate spiritual concerns of those served by the church, but will also work to proactively develop more adequate resources and seek to find ways for agencies and government entities to work together on behalf of the community.

INTERSECTING WITH LEADERSHIP

Important in Pastor Miguel's public ministry is the ability to be relational, collaborative, and patient. The leader who is aware of the power of the pastoral office and the role of the church in the community will move to engage various entities in working toward the best possibilities for everyone in the community. His ability to network with other community leaders or agencies that are beyond the local town can be important for community in gaining the listening ear of others who might be able to provide better access to quality health care. Such leadership is essential for communities where the resources are fewer and the needs are often great.

In some ways, it would be easy for Pastor Miguel to get swallowed up by the physical, emotional, and spiritual needs of those who are part of his church and community. The pastoral leader could spend all of his or her time meeting the needs of the four cases named in the beginning of this chapter. And, in some ways, this would make for good pastoral care. Yet, because pastoral care and leadership are part of one another, Pastor Miguel cannot allow the church to be satisfied with caring for one another without addressing the significant justice issues that surround them (lack of resources, inadequate care for rural communities). The church may become the place that sponsors open forums to talk about how to improve health care, provide long-term nursing care or hospice for those who need it, or offer alternative and good resources for mental health issues that emerge in every family.

Ultimately, good pastoral care leaders continue to think theologically about what is important. In light of the healing and transformative care that they hope to offer to not only individuals in their churches but also to the community itself, pastoral leaders must extend beyond the walls of their buildings and move into love and caring for those who surround them.

RESPONDING TO DIVERSITY

Perhaps one of the most significant aspects of Pastor Miguel's ministry is his ability to serve at least two diverse communities. The pastoral ability to value, care about, know, and love those who live among them and those who reside in their areas (whether they are formally a part of the church or not) cannot be overstated. In part, this means that a good pastoral presence for this community requires language skills that not all pastors bring. Similarly, in this case, it is clear that the small community cannot support or financially sustain a full-time pastor. Hence, this bi-vocational and bilingual pastor reaches out not only to offer care, but also to encourage the valuing of difference.

While Pastor Miguel cannot meet all of the physical and emotional needs of the community he serves, he is connected to the spiritual lives of those who surround him in ways that are congruent with a spirituality that is not only born out of the regional Euro-American past, but also one that carries elements of traditions from Mexico and other countries south of the border. Recognizing the importance of such traditions means finding ways to access spiritual characteristics that may not look like a traditional Protestant spirituality, even if Pastor Miguel's church is Protestant. Instead, there may be remnants of belief systems that are part of ancient indigenous Mexican culture, or aspects that reflect the syncretism of Roman Catholic culture. As a second-generation American, Pastor Miguel recognizes the power of such diversity in the healing of people's lives and in the transformation of the community.

As someone who works in two of the most significant public institutions related to small communities—the church and the school system—Pastor Miguel stands at the intersection of power and privilege, and this is something important to recognize. It would be easy for Pastor Miguel to gather knowledge about people simply because of his role as pastor and teacher. Caring about how one's power is used and learning how to draw upon power in ways that honor and respect others, yet working for change on behalf of all, is a skill that many pastoral leaders would do well to hone. The way in which Pastor Miguel moves into the community, offers care on behalf of the church, encourages the laity as caregivers, and challenges the powers of others to work to meet the needs of the community and villages that surround this church will say something about whether there is healing and transformative care at work in this church.

Notes

1. The historical functions of pastoral care have often been identified as healing, sustaining, guiding, and reconciling. Graham notes the deep connection of physical, mental health, and spiritual aliveness and suggests that "Christian modes of healing have always distinguished themselves by achieving a spiritual advance in connection with the healing process." His work goes on to note that wholeness and healing relate to the restoration of "bodily wholeness, emotional well-being, mental functioning, and spiritual aliveness." See Larry K. Graham, "Healing," in *Dictionary of Pastoral Care and Counseling*, ed. Rodney J. Hunter, H. Newton Malony, Liston O. Mills, John Patton, and Nancy J. Ramsay (Nashville: Abingdon, 2005), 497.

2. See Department of Health and Human Services, *Healthy People 2010* (October 2005), http://www.healthypeople.gov (accessed July 17, 2010).

3. Larry Gamm, Linnae Hutchison, Betty Dabney, and Alicia Dorsey, eds., *Rural Healthy People 2010: A Companion Document to Healthy People 2010*, vol. 1 (College Station: Texas A&M University System Health Science Center, 2003), 3.

4. Ibid., 5.

5. See, for example, the following resources: Committee on the Future of Rural Health Care/Board on Health Care Services/Institute of Medicine of the National Academies, *Quality Through Collaboration: The Future of Rural Health* (Washington, DC: National Academies Press, 2005); Gamm et al., eds., *Rural Healthy People 2010*; Nina Glasgow, Lois Wright Morton, and Nan E. Johnson, eds., *Critical Issues in Rural Health* (Ames, IA: Blackwell, 2004); Helen J. Lee and Charlene A. Winters, eds., *Rural Nursing: Concepts, Theory, and Practice*, 2nd ed. (New York: Springer, 2006); Nancy Lohmann and Roger A. Lohmann, eds., *Rural Social Work Practice* (New York: Columbia University Press, 2005); Hudnall B. Stamm, ed., *Rural Behavioral Health Care: An Interdisciplinary Guide* (Washington, DC: American Psychological Association, 2003); Barbara P. Yawn, Angeline Bushy, and Roy A. Yawn, eds., *Exploring Rural Medicine: Current Issues and Concepts* (Thousand Oaks, CA: Sage, 1994).

6. Glasgow, Morton, and Johnson, eds., *Critical Issues in Rural Health*, 3, 18.

7. B. Hudnall Stamm et al., "Introduction," in *Rural Behavioral Health Care*, ed. Stamm, 6.

8. Kathleen Ann Long and Clarann Weinert, "Rural Nursing: Developing the Theory Base," in *Rural Nursing: Concepts, Theory, and Practice*, ed. Lee and Winters, 9.

9. Michael D. Schulman and Doris P. Slesinger, "Health Hazards of Rural Extractive Industries and Occupations," in *Critical Issues in Rural Health*, ed. Glasgow, Morton, and Johnson, 49.

10. Ibid., 54.

11. Ibid., 54–55.

12. Wade G. Hill and Patricia Butterfield, "Environmental Risk Reduction for Rural Children," in *Rural Nursing: Concepts, Theory, and Practice*, ed. Lee and Winters, 271.

13. Larry Gamm, Graciela Castillo, Stephanie Pittman, "Access to Quality Health Services in Rural Areas—Primary Care," in *Rural Healthy People 2010*, ed. Gamm et al., 45–51. Similarly, a report from the Institute of Medicine of the National Academies, for example, has identified the need to recruit and retain persons invested in serving in health care in rural areas. As they suggest, such recruitment needs to begin with elementary-age children and continue through educational opportunities for those who serve in those areas. See *Quality Through Collaboration: The Future of Rural Health*, 78–118.

14. *Quality Through Collaboration: The Future of Rural Health,* 147–90; Norma H. Wasko, "Wired for the Future? The Impact of Information and Telecommunications Technology on Rural Social Work," in *Rural Social Work Practice,* ed. Lohmann and Lohmann, 41–72.

15. Pamela L. Mulder and Warren Lambert, "Behavior Health of Rural Women: Challenges and Stressors," in *Rural Women's Health: Mental, Behavioral, and Physical Issues,* ed. Raymond T. Coward, Lisa A. Davis, Carol H. Gold, Helen Smiciklas-Wright, Luanne E. Thorndyke, and Fred W. Vondracek (New York: Springer, 2006), 15–30.

16. *Quality Through Collaboration: The Future of Rural Health,* 1.

17. See Nina Glasgow, Nan E. Johnson, and Lois Wright Morton, "Introduction," in *Critical Issues in Rural Health,* ed. Glasgow, Morton, and Johnson, 3.

18. Robert B. Wallace, Ligia A. Grindeanu, and Dominic J. Cirillo, "Rural/Urban Contrasts in Population Morbidity Status," in *Critical Issues in Rural Health,* ed. Glasgow, Morton, and Johnson, 15–26; *Quality Through Collaboration: The Future of Rural Health;* Gamm, Castillo, and Pittman, "Access to Quality Health Services in Rural Areas," in *Rural Healthy People 2010,* ed. Gamm et al., 45–52.

19. Cortney Rawlinson and Paul Crews, "Access to Quality Health Services in Rural Areas—Emergency Medical Services," in *Rural Healthy People 2010,* ed. Gamm et al., 77.

20. *Quality Through Collaboration: The Future of Rural Health,* 39.

21. Thomas C. Ricketts III and Paige E. Heaphy, "Hospitals in Rural America," *Western Journal of Medicine* (December 2000): 418.

22. Jane Bolin and Larry Gamm, "Access to Quality Health Services in Rural Areas—Insurance," in *Rural Healthy People 2010,* ed. Gamm et al., 19–43; See also Kevin J. Bennett, Bankole Olatosi, and Janice Probst, "Health Disparities: A Rural–Urban Chartbook," HealthCare Report (South Carolina Rural Health Research Center, University of South Carolina, 2008), 16–20.

23. Ronda L. Bales, "Remote Rural Women of Childbearing and Childrearing Age," in *Rural Nursing: Concepts, Theory, and Practice,* ed. Lee and Winters, 66–78.

24. Mulder and Lambert, "Behavior Health of Rural Women," in *Rural Women's Health,* ed. Coward et al., 18.

25. Catherine Campbell, Sarah D. Richie, and David S. Hargrove, "Poverty and Rural Mental Health," in *Rural Behavioral Health Care,* ed. Stamm, 42.

26. See the work of Mark A. Hager, Amy Brimer, and Thomas H. Pollak, "The Distribution of Nonprofit Social Service Organizations along the Rural-Urban Continuum," in *Rural Social Work Practice,* ed. Lohmann and Lohmann, 73–85. The authors note that while there are comparable numbers of nonprofit social service organizations per capita across rural and urban contexts, the latter spend about two times as much per person as do rural agencies.

27. Bennett, Olatosi, and Probst, "Health Disparities: A Rural–Urban Chartbook," 16–20.

28. Wallace, Grindeanu, and Cirillo, "Rural/Urban Contrasts in Population Morbidity Status," in *Critical Issues in Rural Health,* ed. Glasgow, Morton, and Johnson, 16–17.

29. Glasgow, Morton, and Johnson, "Introduction," in *Critical Issues in Rural Health,* ed. Glasgow, Morton, and Johnson, 3.

30. Annie Gosschalk and Susan Carozza, "Cancer in Rural Areas," in *Rural Healthy People 2010,* ed. Gamm et al., 91–95.

31. *Quality Through Collaboration: The Future of Rural Health,* 38.

32. Fred W. Vondracek, Raymond T. Coward, Lisa A. Davis, Carol H. Gold, Helen Smiciklas-Wright, and Luanne E. Thorndyke, "Introduction," in *Rural Women's Health,* ed. Coward et al., 4.

33. Chuck W. Peek and Barbara A. Zsembik, "The Health of African Americans Living in Nonmetropolitan Areas," in *Critical Issues in Rural Health,* ed. Glasgow, Morton, and Johnson, 141–54.

34. Bennett, Olatosi, and Probst, "Health Disparities: A Rural–Urban Chartbook," Executive Summary.

35. Frederick O. Lorenz, K. A. S. Wickrama, and Hsiu-Chen Yeh, "Rural Mental Health: Comparing Differences and Modeling Change," in *Critical Issues in Rural Health*, ed. Glasgow, Morton, and Johnson, 75.

36. Yawn, Bushy, and Yawn, eds., *Exploring Rural Medicine*.

37. Mulder and Lambert, "Behavior Health of Rural Women," in *Rural Women's Health*, ed. Coward et al., 20–21.

38. Stephen Stansfeld, Scott Weich, Charlotte Clark, Jane Boydell, and Hugh Freeman, "Urban-Rural Differences, Socio-economic Status and Psychiatric Disorder," in *The Impact of the Environment on Psychiatric Disorder*, ed. Hugh Freeman and Stephen Stansfeld (New York: Routledge, 2008), 85.

39. Ibid., 86.

40. Ronda Bales, "Remote Rural Women of Childbearing and Childrearing Age," in *Rural Nursing: Concepts, Theory, and Practice*, ed. Charlene A. Winters and Helen J. Lee (New York: Springer, 2009), 53–65.

8

Learning from Rural Communities and Congregations

Town and country communities and congregations are distinct from other places and valuable for the whole church. This book has been an exploration in contextual pastoral theology, demonstrating the distinctive character of small rural places that calls forth distinctive practices of care within those places. Exploring context requires moving between the particular and general, which in the case of this book meant examining particular kinds of places and looking at rural places in general. It should be clear by now that all rural places are not the same; they range from the scenic wealthy retirement places in the Rocky Mountains to the persistently poor places along the Mississippi Delta. And yet there are enough similarities that certain generalizations can at least be part of the mix of seeking to understand the dynamics of any particular context. Some of the commonalities include geographic isolation, lack of anonymity, economic change or uncertainty, and growing diversity.

In each place, there are the internal local dynamics intersecting with the external global dynamics, and all of these must be taken into account in order to understand the situation at hand and to respond appropriately. This text has drawn from history, economics, sociology, psychology, anthropology, and other sources of knowledge to give depth to our reading of rural contexts. Theories developed in and for understanding larger places often need revision before they are used as a perspective on small towns and rural areas. A rich reading of the context will enable a pastoral caregiver to understand and respond more meaningfully to any situation, seeing it as a matter of both individual and social dynamics.

Our own authorial contexts have no doubt limited our perspectives on the subject matter of this book. As we described in the opening chapter, we are three different persons, all with different histories, personalities, and commitments, though there is enough similarity between us that we dared to present a single text. Our description of rural contexts is limited by our own locations; though we each have different experiences of small-town life, we are all currently located in large metropolitan areas. We are of Euro-American descent and highly educated. We are aware that this matters, and aware that we have not included a deconstruction of our own privilege in the text of this book. We look forward to the stimulating discussions that we hope the strengths and limitations of this text will inspire. In an ideal world, we would have continued to engage the rural pastors group that served as its initial percolator and out of which much wisdom emerged. We have tried to give a varied and complex picture of rural life, such as the group offered us.

In this text, we have tried not to idealize small towns but to portray the wisdom that can come from their strengths and their struggles. These themes for care arise out of the distinctive nature of town and country ministries, but their importance for pastoral care is appropriate for the whole church. The themes for healing and transformative care offered in this book arise from both the challenges and the gifts of rural churches as they seek to care for one another and their communities. Care is always shaped by place, but the how of this shaping needs attention in order to foster healing. The rural church calls the whole church to think about all of God's creation, the land and its resources, our need for home and the healing presence of God in nature. Care in the rural church points to the gift of close community and the challenge that such closeness can pose. It reminds the larger church that care is a ministry of the whole church and for the whole community. The public nature of ministry in rural communities invites every pastor and congregation to consider the intersection of social concerns with care for persons and the necessity of leadership as an aspect of care. Rural churches, like others in the United States, are experiencing growing diversity, but in small communities it is more difficult to avoid the challenges this diversity can pose for a place committed to close community. Even when the outcomes are less than hoped for, the struggles of these small churches give insight to other churches striving to care for one another across difference. These themes surely do not represent all that pastoral care is about or that is needed in order to facilitate healing and transformation toward more love and justice, nor have we fully represented their potential. They can, however, when put into practice in any community, help to bring about more love and justice in the world.

Care, when it is *pastoral*, invites theological meaning-making. Theological commitments to healing and transformation for a more just and loving world frame the theological discussions in this book. The three of us are not of one mind in the details and nuances of theological positions, but we begin with a faith commitment to love and justice, and understand such commitment as central to the practice of pastoral care. In each chapter we have tried to give direction for a theological reading of the situation and theological framework for the norms that guide care in the context of the situation. The three issues highlighted in the second part of the book—poverty, health, and violence—are not only economic, medical, sociological, or psychological concerns; they are theological concerns as well. Persons who are struggling to live life out of a Christian tradition turn to their pastors and other Christians to help them make sense of what they are facing in light of their understanding of God, Christ, and the church. Though we could not do justice to the theological issues raised in this text, engaging theological construction is crucial to the practice of care and is itself contextually grounded.

Through this text, which focuses on these aspects of care in rural communities, we hope to invite others to think about how the particulars of rural contexts can inform meaningful care in other places. We believe that rural churches can be a gift to the larger church. The pastors of the group that began this project immediately shared with us their love of rural churches and communities. They were happy serving where they were. They also immediately let us know that one of the greatest difficulties in serving as pastors of rural churches was the lack of understanding and respect the congregations received from the larger church. It is our hope that, through reading this text, others will find a passion for small-town and rural ministry and that the church as a whole will open itself to receive the holy wisdom that can be revealed in those country places.

Bibliography

Ammerman, Nancy. *Studying Congregations: A New Handbook*. Nashville: Abingdon, 1998.

Anderson, Harlene, and Diane Gehart. *Collaborative Therapy: Relationships and Conversations That Make a Difference*. New York: Routledge, 2007.

Barndt, Joseph R. *Understanding and Dismantling Racism: The Twenty-First-Century Challenge to White America*. Minneapolis: Fortress Press, 2007.

———. *Becoming an Anti-Racist Church: Journeying toward Wholeness*. Prisms. Minneapolis: Fortress Press, 2011.

Beeghley, Leonard. *Structure of Social Stratification in the United States*. Upper Saddle River, NJ: Prentice Hall, 2004.

Bennett, Kevin J., Bankole Olatosi, and Janice Probst. "Health Disparities: A Rural–Urban Chartbook." HealthCare Report, South Carolina Rural Health Research Center, University of South Carolina, 2008.

Bolin, Jane, and Larry Gamm. *Access to Quality Health Care Services in Rural Areas—Insurance*. Vol. 1 in *Rural Healthy People 2010: A Companion Document to Healthy People 2010*, 19–43. College Station: Texas A&M University System Health Science Center, School of Rural Public Health, Southwest Rural Health Research Center, 2003.

Brown, David L., and Kai A. Schafft. *Rural People and Communities in the 21st Century: Resilience and Transformation*. Cambridge, UK/Malden, MA: Polity, 2011.

Butala, Sharon. "The Myth of the Family Farm." In *Farm Communities at the Crossroads: Challenge and Resistance*, edited by Harry P. Diaz, JoAnn M. Jaffe, Robert M. Stirling, and University of Regina. Canadian Plains Research Center, 67–75. Regina, Saskatchewan: Canadian Plains Research Center, 2003.

Campbell, Catherine, Sarah D. Richie, and David S. Hargrove. "Poverty and Rural Mental Health." In *Rural Behavioral Health Care: An Interdisciplinary Guide*, edited by B. Hudnall Stamm, 41–51. Washington, DC: American Psychological Association, 2003.

Carr, Patrick J., and Maria Kefalas. *Hollowing Out the Middle: The Rural Brain Drain and What It Means for America*. Boston: Beacon, 2009.

Carroll, Jackson. *God's Potters: Pastoral Leadership and the Shaping of Congregations.* Grand Rapids: Eerdmans, 2006.

Chalquist, Craig. "Ecotherapy Research and a Psychology of Homecoming." In *Ecotherapy: Healing with Nature in Mind*, edited by Linda Buzzell and Craig Chalquist, 69–82. Berkeley, CA: Sierra Club Books, 2009.

Clinebell, Howard John. *Ecotherapy: Healing Ourselves, Healing the Earth: A Guide to Ecologically Grounded Personality Theory, Spirituality, Therapy, and Education.* Minneapolis: Fortress Press, 1996.

Cloke, Paul. "Conceptualizing Rurality." In *Handbook of Rural Studies*, edited by Paul Cloke, Terry Marsden, and Patrick Mooney, 18–28. Thousand Oaks, CA: Sage, 2007.

Committee on the Future of Rural Health Care/Board on Health Care Services/Institute of Medicine of the National Academies. *Quality through Collaboration: The Future of Rural Health.* Washington, DC: National Academies Press, 2005.

Couture, Pamela D. "Feminist, Wesleyan, Practical Theology and the Practice of Pastoral Care." In *Liberating Faith Practices*, 27. Louvain: Peeters, 1998.

Cresswell, Tim. *Place: A Short Introduction*, Short Introductions to Geography. Malden, MA: Blackwell, 2004.

Cromartie, John, and Peter Nelson. "Baby Boom Migration and Its Impact on Rural America," edited by the United States Department of Agriculture: Economic Research Service, 2009.

Cromartie, John, and Shawn Bucholtz. *Defining the "Rural" in Rural America.* Washington, DC: Economic Research Service, 2008.

DeKeseredy, Walter S., and Martin D. Schwartz. *Dangerous Exits: Escaping Abusive Relationships in Rural America*, Critical Issues in Crime and Society. New Brunswick, NJ: Rutgers University Press, 2009.

De La Torre, Miguel A. "Pastoral Care from the Latina/o Margins." In *Injustice and the Care of Souls: Taking Oppression Seriously in Pastoral Care*, edited by Sheryl A. Kujawa-Holbrook and Karen Brown Montagno, 59–72. Minneapolis: Fortress Press, 2009.

Deparment of Health and Human Services. *Healthy People 2010.* October 2005. www.healthypeople.gov (accessed July 17, 2010).

DeYmaz, Mark. *Building a Healthy Multi-Ethnic Church: Mandate, Committment, and Practices of a Diverse Congregation.* San Francisco: Jossey-Bass, 2007.

Dillon, Michele, and Sarah Savage. *Values and Religion in Rural America: Attitudes toward Abortion and Same-Sex Relations.* Durham, NH: University of New Hampshire, Carsey Institute, Fall 2006.

Donnermeyer, Joseph. "Crime in Rural Communities: The Impact, the Causes, the Prevention." In *International Conference on Rural Crime*. University of New England, Armidale, New South Wales, Australia, 2006.

Donnermeyer, Joseph F., and Ken Tunnell. "In Our Own Backyard: Methamphetamine Manufacturing, Trafficking and Abuse in Rural America," 2. Columbia, MO: Rural Sociological Society, 2007.

Dressler, W. W. "Review of Worlds Apart: Why Rural Poverty Persists in Rural America." *Journal of Political Ecology: Case Studies in History and Society* 8 (2001): http://jpe.library.arizona.edu/volume_8/501Dressler.html.

Duncan, Cynthia M. *Worlds Apart: Why Rural Poverty Persists in Rural America.* New Haven: Yale University Press, 1999.

Fitzgerald, Amy J., Linda Kalof, and Thomas Dietz. "Slaughterhouses and Increased Crime Rates: An Empirical Analysis of the Spillover from 'the Jungle' into the Surrounding Community." *Organization and Environment* 22, no. 2 (2009): 158–84.

Flora, Cornelia Butler, and Jan L. Flora. *Rural Communities: Legacy and Change.* 4th ed. Boulder, CO: Westview, 2012.

Freire, Paulo. *Pedagogy of the Oppressed.* 30th anniversary ed. New York: Continuum, 2000.

Friedman, E. *Generation to Generation: Family Process in Church and Synagogue.* New York: Guilford, 2011.

Gamm, Larry, Graciela Castillo, and Stephanie Pittman. *Access to Quality Health Services in Rural Areas—Primary Care.* Vol. 1 in *Rural Healthy People 2010: A Companion Document to Healthy People 2010,* edited by Larry Gamm, Linnae Hutchison, Betty Dabney, and Alicia Dorsey, 45–75. College Station: Texas A&M University System Health Science Center, School of Rural Public Health, Southwest Rural Health Research Center, 2003.

Gamm, Larry, Linnae Hutchison, Betty Dabney, and Alicia Dorsey. *Rural Healthy People 2010: A Companion Document to Healthy People 2010.* Vol. 1. College Station: Texas A&M University System Health Science Center, 2003.

Gilbert, Dennis. *The American Class Structure in an Age of Growing Inequality.* Beverly, MA: Wadsworth, 2002.

Glasgow, Nina, Nan E. Johnson, and Lois Wright Morton. "Introduction." In *Critical Issues in Rural Health,* edited by Nina Glasgow, Nan E. Johnson, and Lois Wright Morton, 3–11. Ames, IA: Blackwell, 2004.

Glasgow, Nina, Lois Wright Morton, and Nan E. Johnson. *Critical Issues in Rural Health.* Ames, IA: Blackwell, 2004.

Gosschalk, Annie, and Susan Carozza. *Cancer in Rural Areas.* Vol. 1 in *Rural Healthy People 2010: A Companion Document to Healthy People 2010*, edited by Larry Gamm, Linnae Hutchison, Betty Dabney, and Alicia Dorsey, 91–107. College Station: Texas A&M University Health Science Center, 2003.

Graham, Larry. *Care of Persons, Care of Worlds: A Psychosystems Approach to Pastoral Care and Counseling.* Nashville: Abingdon, 1992.

———. "Healing." In *Dictionary of Pastoral Care and Counseling*, edited by Rodney J. Hunter, H. Newton Malony, Liston O. Mills, John Patton, and Nancy J. Ramsay, 497–501. Nashville: Abingdon, 2005.

Greider, Kathleen. "Soul Care Amid Religious Plurality." In *Women out of Order: Risking Change and Creating Care in a Multicultural World*, edited by Jeanne Stevenson Moessner and Teresa E. Snorton, 314–30. Minneapolis: Fortress Press, 2009.

Gunderson, Gary. *Deeply Woven Roots: Improving the Quality of Life in Your Community.* Minneapolis: Fortress Press, 1997.

Haddon, Arlene, Marilyn Merritt-Gray, and Judith Wuest. "Private Matters and Public Knowledge in Rural Communities: The Paradox." In *Understanding Abuse, Partnering for Change*, edited by Mary Lou Stirling, Catherine Ann Cameron, Nancy Nason-Clark, and Baukje Miedema, 249–66. Toronto: University of Toronto Press, 2009.

Halfacree, Keith. "Rural Space: Constructing a Three-Fold Architecture." In *Handbook of Rural Studies*, edited by Paul Cloke, Terry Marsden, and Patrick Mooney, 44–62. Thousand Oaks, CA: Sage, 2007.

Harris, Rosalind P., and Dreamal Worthen. "African Americans in Rural America." In *Challenges for Rural America in the Twenty-First Century*, 32–42. University Park: Pennsylvania State University Press, 2003.

Heifetz, Ronald A., Alexander Grashow, and Marty Linsky. *The Practice of Adaptive Leadership: Tools and Tactics for Changing Your Organization and the World.* Boston: Harvard Business Press, 2009.

Hill, Wade G., and Patricia Butterfield. "Environmental Risk Reduction for Rural Children." In *Rural Nursing: Concepts, Theory, and Practice*, edited by Helen J. Lee and Charlene A. Winters, 270–81. New York: Springer, 2006.

hooks, bell. *Belonging: A Culture of Place.* New York: Routledge, 2008.

Hopewell, J. *Congregation: Stories and Structures.* Philadelphia: Fortress Press, 1987.

Howley, Aimee. "The Poor Little Rich District: The Effects of Suburbanization on a Rural School and Community." *Journal of Research in Rural Education* 20, no. 9 (2005): 1–14.

Howell, James C., and Arlen Egley. "Gangs in Small Towns and Rural Counties." Office of Juvenile Justice and Delinquency Prevention, *NYGC Bulletin,* June 2005.

Hummon, David Mark. *Commonplaces: Community Ideology and Identity in American Culture,* Suny Series in the Sociology of Culture. Albany: State University of New York Press, 1990.

Inge, John. "Explorations in Practical, Pastoral, and Empirical Theology." In *A Christian Theology of Place.* Aldershot, UK/Burlington, VT: Ashgate, 2003.

Jung, L. Shannon. *Hunger and Happiness: Feeding the Hungry, Nourishing Our Souls.* Minneapolis: Augsburg Books, 2009.

———. *Rural Ministry: The Shape of the Renewal to Come.* Nashville: Abingdon, 1998.

Kaylen, Maria T., and William A. Pridemore. "A Reassessment of the Association between Social Disorganization and Youth Violence in Rural Areas." *Social Science Quarterly* 92, no. 4 (2011): 978–1001.

Kujawa-Holbrook, Sheryl A. *A House of Prayer for All Peoples: Congregations Building Multiracial Community.* Bethesda, MD: Alban Institute, 2002.

Lane, Belden C. *Landscapes of the Sacred: Geography and Narrative in American Spirituality.* Expanded ed. Baltimore: Johns Hopkins University Press, 2002.

Lanier, Christina, and Michael O. Maume. "Intimate Partner Violence and Social Isolation across the Rural/Urban Divide." *Violence Against Women* 15, no. 11 (2009): 1311–30.

Lartey, Emmanuel. *In Living Color: An Intercultural Approach to Pastoral Care and Counseling.* London: Jessica Kingsley Press, 2003.

———. *Pastoral Theology in an Intercultural World.* Peterborough England: Epworth, 2006.

Law, Eric H. F. *The Wolf Shall Dwell with the Lamb: A Spirituality for Leadership in a Multicultural Community.* St. Louis: Chalice, 1993.

———. *Inclusion: Making Room for Grace.* St. Louis: Chalice, 2000.

Lischer, Richard. *Open Secrets: A Memoir of Faith and Discovery.* New York: Broadway Books, 2002.

Lee, Helen J., and Charlene A. Winters. *Rural Nursing: Concepts, Theory, and Practice.* 2nd ed. New York: Springer, 2006.

Lohmann, Nancy, and Roger A. Lohmann. *Rural Social Work Practice.* New York: Columbia University Press, 2005.

Long, Kathleen Ann, and Clarann Weinert. "Rural Nursing: Developing the Theory Base." In *Rural Nursing: Concepts, Theory, and Practice*, edited by Helen J. Lee and Charlene A. Winters, 3–16. New York: Springer, 2006.

Marshall, Joretta L. "Collaborative Generativity: The What, Who, and How of Supervision in a Modern/Postmodern Context." *Reflective Practice: Formation and Supervision in Ministry* 31 (2011): 151–65.

Martin, Philip. *Importing Poverty? Immigration and the Changing Face of Rural America*. New Haven: Yale University Press, 2009.

Mattingly, Marybeth J., and Wendy A. Walsh. *Rural Families with a Child Abuse Report Are More Likely Headed by a Single Parent and Endure Economic and Family Stress*. Carsey Institute, University of New Hampshire, 2010.

McFague, Sallie. *The Body of God: An Ecological Theology*. Minneapolis: Fortress Press, 1993.

Millard, Ann V., and Jorge Chapa. *Apple Pie and Enchiladas: Latino Newcomers in the Rural Midwest*. Austin: University of Texas Press, 2004.

Miller-McLemore, Bonnie. "Are There Limits to Multicultural Inclusion? Difficult Questions for Feminist Pastoral Theology." In *Women out of Order: Risking Change and Creating Care in a Multicultural World*, edited by Jeanne Stevenson Moessner and Teresa E. Snorton, 314–30. Minneapolis: Fortress Press, 2009.

Mulder, Pamela L., and Warren Lambert. "Behavior Health of Rural Women: Challenges and Stressors." In *Rural Women's Health: Mental, Behavioral, and Physical Issues*, edited by Raymond T. Coward, Lisa A. Davis, Carol H. Gold, Helen Smiciklas-Wright, Luanne E. Thorndyke, and Fred W. Vondracek, 15–30. New York: Springer, 2006.

Neuger, Christie Cozad. *Counseling Women: A Narrative, Pastoral Approach*. Minneapolis: Fortress Press, 2001.

Nicholas, Doris. "The Health of Rural Minorities." In *Rural Social Work Practice*, edited by Nancy Lohmann and Roger A. Lohmann, 211–31. New York: Columbia University Press, 2005.

Norris-Baker, Carolyn, and Rick J. Scheidt. "On Community as Home: Places That Endure in Rural Kansas." In *Home and Identity in Late Life International Perspectives*, edited by Graham D. Rowles and Habib Chaudhury, 279–96. New York: Springer, 2005.

Patton, John. *Pastoral Care in Context: An Introduction to Pastoral Care*. 1st ed. Louisville: Westminster John Knox, 1993.

Poling-Goldenne, David, and L. Shannon Jung, *Discovering Hope: Building Vitality in Rural Congregations*. Minneapolis, Augsburg Fortress, 2001.

Ponzetti, James J., Jr. "Growing Old in Rural Communities: A Visual Methodology for Stuidying Place Attachment." *Journal of Rural Community Psychology*, E6 (2003).

Probst, Janice C., Michael E. Samuels, Kristen P. Jespersen, Karin Willert, R. Suzanne Swann, and Joshua A. McDuffie. *Minorities in Rural America: An Overview of Population Characteristics.* Columbia: South Carolina Rural Health Research Center, 2002.

Pruitt, Lisa R., and Janet L. Wallace. "Judging Parents, Judging Place: Poverty, Rurality and Termination of Parental Rights." *Missouri Law Review* 77 (2011): 95–147.

Race and Ethnicity in Rural America. Housing Assistance Council, April 2012.

Ramsay, Nancy. "Where Race and Gender Collide." In *Women out of Order: Risking Change and Creating Care in a Multicultural World*, edited by Jeanne Stevenson Moessner and Teresa E. Snorton, 331–48. Minneapolis: Fortress Press, 2009.

Rawlinson, Cortney, and Paul Crews. *Access to Quality Health Services in Rural Areas—Emergency Medical Services.* Vol. 1 in *Rural Healthy People 2010: A Companion Document to Healthy People 2010*, 77–89. College Station: Texas A&M University System Health Science Center, School of Rural Public Health, Southwest Rural Health Research Center, 2003.

Ricketts, Thomas C. III, and Paige E. Heaphy. "Hospitals in Rural America." *Western Journal of Medicine* 173, no. 6 (December 2000): 418–22.

Rowles, Graham D., and Habib Chaudhury, eds. *Home and Identity in Late Life International Perspectives.* New York: Springer, 2005.

Salamon, Sonya. *Newcomers to Old Towns: Suburbanization of the Heartland.* Chicago: University of Chicago Press, 2003.

Schulman, Michael D., and Doris P. Slesinger. "Health Hazards of Rural Extractive Industries and Occupations." In *Critical Issues in Rural Health*, edited by Nina Glasgow, Lois Wright Morton, and Nan E. Johnson, 49–60. Ames, IA: Blackwell, 2004.

Shandy, Dianna J., and Katherine Fennelly. "A Comparison of the Integration Experiences of Two African Immigrant Populations in a Rural Community." *Journal of Religion & Spirituality in Social Work* 25, no. 1 (2006): 23–45.

Sisk, Ronald D. *The Competent Pastor: Skills and Self-Knowledge for Serving Well.* Herndon, VA: The Alban Institute, 2005.

Snow, Luther. *The Power of Asset Mapping: How Your Congregation Can Act on Its Gifts.* Herndon, VA: The Alban Institute, 2004.

Snyder, Larry. *Think and Act Anew: How Poverty in America Affects Us All And What you Can Do About It.* Maryknoll, NY: Orbis, 2010.

South Carolina Rural Health Research Center. http://rhr.sph.sc.edu/index.php (accessed July 12, 2010).

Stamm, B. Hudnall, ed. *Rural Behavioral Health Care: An Interdisciplinary Guide.* Washington, DC: American Psychological Association, 2003.

Stansfeld, Stephen, Scott Weich, Charlotte Clark, Jane Boydell, and Hugh Freeman. "Urban-Rural Differences, Socio-Economic Status and Psychiatric Disorder." In *The Impact of the Environment on Psychiatric Disorder*, by Hugh Freeman and Stephen Stansfeld, 80–126. New York: Routledge, 2008.

"Statement on the Doctrine of Discovery and Its Enduring Impact on Indigenous Peoples." Bossey, Switzerland: Word Council of Churches, 2012.

Stetzer, Ed, and Warren Bird. *Viral Churches: Helping Church Planters Become Movement Makers.* San Francisco: Jossey-Bass, 2010.

Strange, Marty. *Family Farming: A New Economic Vision.* New ed. Lincoln: University of Nebraska Press; Institute for Food and Development Policy, 2008.

Tanner, Kathryn. *Economy of Grace.* Minneapolis: Fortress Press, 2005.

Taylor, Stephanie. *Narratives of Identity and Place.* New York: Routledge, 2010.

Thompson, William E., and Joseph V. Hickey. *Society in Focus: An Introduction to Sociology.* Boston: Pearson, Allyn and Bacon, 2005.

Tinker, George E. *Spirit and Resistance: Political Theology and American Indian Liberation.* Minneapolis: Fortress Press, 2004.

"The Distribution of Nonprofit Social Service Organizations along the Rural-Urban Continuum." In *Rural Social Work Practice*, edited by Nancy Lohmann and Roger A. Lohmann, 73–85. New York: Columbia University Press, 2005.

Volf, Miroslav. *Exclusion and Embrace: A Theological Exploration of Identity, Otherness, and Reconciliation.* Nashville: Abingdon, 1996.

Wallace, Robert B., Ligia A. Grindeanu, and Dominic J. Cirillo. "Rural/Urban Contrasts in Population Morbidity Status." In *Critical Issues in Rurual Health*, edited by Nina E. Glasgow, Lois Wright Morton, and Nan E. Johnson, 15–26. Ames, IA: Blackwell, 2004.

Wasko, Norma H. "Wired for the Future? The Impact of Information and Telecommunications Technology on Rural Social Work." In *Rural Social Work Practice*, edited by Nancy Lohmann and Roger A. Lohmann, 41–72. New York: Columbia University Press, 2005.

Way, Peggy. *Created by God: Pastoral Care for All God's People*. St. Louis: Chalice, 2005.

Weisheit, Ralph A., David N. Falcone, and L. Edward Wells. *Crime and Policing in Rural and Small-Town America*. 3rd ed. Long Grove, IL: Waveland, 2006.

Weisheit, Ralph A., and L. Edward Wells. "Youth Gangs in Rural America." *NIJ Journal* 251 (2004): 1–5.

White, M. *Maps of Narrative Practice*. New York: W. W. Norton, 2007.

Wimberly, Edward P. "The Bible as Pastor: An African American Perspective." *Journal of Pastoral Theology* 16, no. 1 (2006): 63–80.

Yawn, Barbara P., Angeline Bushy, and Roy A. Yawn. *Exploring Rural Medicine: Current Issues and Concepts*. Thousand Oaks, CA: Sage, 1994.

Index